Financial Times Pitman Publishing books

We work with leading authors to develop the strongest ideas in business and finance, bringing cutting-edge thinking and best practice to a global market.

We craft high quality books which help readers to understand and apply their content, whether studying or at work.

To find out more about Financial Times Pitman Publishing books, visit our website:

www.ftmanagement.com

£22.99

D0299020

This b
last da

THE
HUMAN RESOURCE FUNCTION

The Dynamics of Change and Development

Dr Laura Hall

and

Professor Derek Torrington

Manchester School of Management
UMIST

FINANCIAL TIMES
PITMAN PUBLISHING

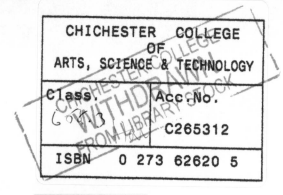
FINANCIAL TIMES
MANAGEMENT
LONDON · SAN FRANCISCO
KUALA LUMPUR · JOHANNESBURG

*Financial Times Management delivers the knowledge,
skills and understanding that enable students,
managers and organisations to achieve their ambitiuons,
whatever their needs, wherever they are.*

London Office:
128 Long Acre, London WC2E 9AN
Tel: +44 (0)171 447 2000
Fax: +44 (0)171 240 5771
Website: www.ftmanagement.com

A Division of Financial Times Professional Limited

First published in Great Britain in 1998

ISBN 0 273 62620 5

British Library Cataloguing in Publication Data
A CIP catalogue record for this book can be obtained from the British Library.

10 9 8 7 6 5 4 3 2 1

Typeset by M Rules
Printed and bound in Great Britain by Bell and Bain Ltd, Glasgow

The Publishers' policy is to use paper manufactured from sustainable forests.

Contents

Preface

The publication of books on the content of personnel and human resource management has increased exponentially to keep pace with developments in activities and techniques in managing human resources in organisations. However, there has been much less attention to the developments in the specialist personnel/HR role and related processes. While some articles and books have focused on single aspects of the changing specialist role, such as devolution of personnel activities to line managers, we found no source which provided a comprehensive analysis of the whole range of changes relevant to the specialist's role in today's organisations. It was this apparent lack which encouraged us to write this book – we felt it was important to provide an overview of the nature and implications of such themes as the decentralisation of personnel specialists, the devolution of personnel activities, the outsourcing of such activities, the nature of strategic involvement and the pressures for the function to market itself internally.

This book is based on recently conducted research – via both questionnaires and interviews – and from this we have been able to indicate current trends and, more importantly, to explore the complexity of the above themes and discuss what they mean for both personnel/HR specialists and other managers. The aspects that we have researched have, to varying degrees, always been part of the framework through which organisations use and interrelate with their personnel/HR specialists, but there is some evidence to suggest that organisations are now more likely to consider explicitly the impact of the specialist role, structure and processes, and consciously manipulate them. In particular, Hendry and Pettigrew (1992) have identified the part that such dimensions play in the way that human resources are managed within the organisation. By starting to put some flesh on these bones, we hope that this book will encourage more research and debate on what is clearly an important perspective on the management of human resources.

We would like to thank, in particular, the ESRC who financed the research on which this book is based and the IPD who provided practical support. We would also like to thank all those IPD students and personnel/human resource managers and directors who completed our lengthy questionnaire, and especially those who agreed to be interviewed. In addition, our thanks go to Catherine Allen, our Research Assistant, whose enthusiasm was unlimited, and to Sue Haffner who carried the secretarial load unflinchingly. We would also like to thank our dissertation students who stimulated the development of our ideas, and in particular Brendan Farrell for the time he has spent discussing the text of the chapter on devolution of operational personnel activities with one of the authors. Thanks also go to our families who provided constant support while we were engrossed in writing this book.

Manchester   *Laura Hall*
February 1998   *Derek Torrington*

1

Introduction

The focus of this book

The personnel function of management is of major social and economic importance in the life of the nation, as well as being a key contributor to the success of the individual business within which it is located. The 1996 annual report of the Institute of Personnel and Development quotes Sir John Harvey-Jones as saying:

> The single most important factor for the success of a business is the capability and performance of the people within it.
>
> (IPD, 1996, p. 6)

At the same time some of the most pressing social and economic concerns of the day are employment, training, careers, earnings, pensions, equality of opportunity, the impact of working practices on personal well-being, and the safety of the workplace. All of these are part of the work of personnel specialists, so the way the personnel function is developing is of concern to all members of society, not only the half million people who earn their living under the personnel label.

There is undoubtedly considerable change taking place in personnel management, but what exactly is going on? Are there minor changes of emphasis or major changes in direction? Are personnel managers losing or gaining influence? Are they motivated exclusively in the service of narrow, short-term management interests, or by broader considerations? Are they effective?

As yet there has only been a limited amount of research to determine the extent and nature of these changes on the ground. Similarly, there has only been a limited amount of research and discussion exploring what these changes mean or may mean for personnel specialists and their development. It was this lack which encouraged us to write this book. However, before we launch into these areas in detail there is a need to explain our perspective and locate it within previous work done on the role of the specialist personnel/HR function.

This book focuses on the processes and mechanisms by which specialist personnel/HR professionals are involved in managing human resources in the business. Our aim is to present an analysis of differing aspects of these processes which are currently being debated by academics and practitioners, and we include in our definition of 'process' such characteristics as the specified and enacted role of specialists, their location in the organisation, their relationship with the line, and the allocation of personnel activities between specialists within the business and specialists outside. We are not here concerned with the activities of personnel professionals, that is with the substantive content of their work and contribution, but with the factors which enable and/or constrain the nature of the contribution that they make. However, we do of course, need to refer to activities broadly as a context for the role which we are discussing. The book offers a rare insight into the perspective of personnel specialists since the previous major work in the area by Watson (1977) and is based on recent research (most of which was supported by the ESRC) with senior personnel practitioners set against an analysis of the relevant current literature. It is not intended to offer a prescription of what is considered to be best practice, but rather to analyse the issues and debate their potential consequences.

Our attention to the process reflects its importance in relation to the achievement of the task. The literature on the importance of process is extensive (for example, in terms of strategy, Mintzberg, 1987), but Dyer (1984) argues that much of the work on human resource strategy has been about content rather than process. Hendry and Pettigrew (1992) make a significant contribution to the process debate. In their model of strategic change and human resource management, the HRM context, which they specify as role, definition, organisation and outputs, is identified as having a direct influence on the HRM content in terms of HR flows, work systems, reward systems and employee relations. They comment that 'while changes in human resource practice can be conceived as a response to business strategy, the scope of the HRM function to respond effectively is therefore limited by its role and resourcing' (p. 139). In other words the way that the HR function is defined, structured, organised and staffed has an impact on the way that people are managed in the organisation. Hendry and Pettigrew's model also makes explicit the factors which impact on the role and organisation of personnel professionals. For example, they identify organisational culture and structure, business environment and performance as having an influence. Lundenberg (1985) also identifies past performance and consequent expectations of the function as key.

Much of the literature relating to the central process aspects of the HRM function and specialist practitioners, such as role and structure, have been neatly summarised in the form of typologies. Legge's (1978) groundbreaking analysis of the contingent nature of personnel management led her to identify two broad personnel roles – the conformist innovator and the deviant innovator based on the approach to solving organisational problems. Tyson and Fell (1986) adopt a form of contingency approach in their analysis of the personnel role in the organisation using the construction industry as a metaphor, and identifying the three role descriptions in 1986 of architect, contracts manager and clerk of works. They stress that each role develops in relation to the organisational context, and neither is any 'better' than the others. In more recent years Storey (1992) has produced a four-fold typology of the personnel role (changemakers, advisers, regulators and handmaidens) based on two criteria – extent of intervention and extent of involvement in strategic as opposed to operational matters. Guest (1990) identifies four approaches to the management of human resources – traditional/conservative; radical/conservative; pluralist/innovative and unitarist/innovative. Monks (1992) develops a four-fold classification based on the adaption of the types identified above, and Torrington and Hall (1998) identify seven types based on a historical analysis of developments within the function. Typologies of the personnel role are well-trodden ground.

While a range of criteria have been used to characterise the roles in each of these typologies, there has been little exploration of these dimensions in their own right – except perhaps for strategic involvement – and no exploration of how different dimensions fit (or fail to fit) with each other. There has been little attention given to dimensions relating to the way that the specialist personnnel role is organised. Similarly, there has been little work on the implications of these characteristics for the selection and development of personnel specialists, and for the way that human resources are managed in the organisation. It is this gap that we will address.

A brief introduction to the source and characteristics of our data

The research on which this volume is primarily based was funded by the ESRC and collected in 1994/5. It is based on the analysis of 214 completed questionnaires mainly representing establishments in England (85 per cent), but with some representation from Scotland and Wales. The questionnaire aimed to chart developments in the professional personnel function, particularly over the last 10 years and included both aspects of role and activity. The results in respect of activity, which are not dealt with here, are published elsewhere. We asked respondents to answer our questions in relation to practice within the establishment rather than in relation to the overall corporate organisation of which the establishment was a part (70 per cent of establishments were part of a larger organisation). Thirty-two per cent of the establishments employed less than 200 staff; 38 per cent employed between 200 and 999 staff; and 30 per cent employed 1000 or more staff. We requested that the questionnaire be completed in conjunction with the most senior person responsible for human resources in the establishment, so we are reflecting the perspective of the personnel function (in 96 per cent of cases) rather than the perspective of senior, general or first line managers. We contacted our sample through tutors of human resources and personnel courses at centres of higher education, and hence we were tapping into establishments which had already demonstrated some commitment to human resources by supporting a part-time student on a course of professional personnel education and training. In addition to the questionnaire, we carried out 30 interviews (90 per cent of which were in establishments that completed the questionnaire). We aimed to interview the most senior member of the personnel function, and we achieved this in 60 per cent of cases. In other cases the second most senior person was interviewed, except for three establishments where we interviewed two general managers and one operations manager, as these were identified as the most senior person on-site responsible for HR matters. Due to the nature of our sample we cannot claim that it is representative of organisations generally, but rather of those organisations that sponsor the professional development of personnel/HR specialists. We could argue that this financial commitment demonstrates that these organisations are generally more committed to enhancing human resource management than others.

As our sample was not large we have restricted ourselves to basic statistics and have avoided claiming any statistical relationships and inferences. We have included further details of our sample in Appendix 1, but we provide below a brief introduction to the key characteristics of the personnel functions which we surveyed. (By way of providing a context to our findings on the specialist role we have also enclosed a brief summary of our findings on content in Appendix 2, and a copy of the questionnaire that we used and the interview schedule are shown in Appendices 3 and 4.)

Of the 214 establishments which responded to this questionnaire 89 per cent (n = 188) did have a specialist personnel/HR department, and of those providing a department title 70 per cent (n = 132) included the word 'personnel' compared with 24 per cent (n = 45) which included the words 'human resources'. The remainder used alternative titles such as 'staff office' or 'staff planning unit'. This heavy emphasis on labelling the function as personnel rather than human resources confirms other research (for example, Guest and Hoque, 1993, in their analysis of the Workplace Industrial Relations in Transition Survey). However, some interviewees expressed a desire to move from 'personnel' to 'human resources', and one American-owned organisation had forced the UK business to change even though this was not their preference. The signs are that there will continue to be a move towards 'human resources', even though this trend may be very gradual. This is why we have chosen to title this book *'The Human Resource Function'* – *The Dynamics of*

Change and Development – however, in the text we refer to the *personnel* function and the *HR* function interchangeably, without any specific connotation, unless otherwise specified, as this reflects the reality of organisational life at present.

Information from the interviews revealed that on some occasions the function would be termed 'personnel', but that the director or head of the function would have a 'human resource' title. However, when we analysed the title of the person responsible for the function together with the existence of board membership we found that having a 'human resource' title did not mean that the individual was more or less likely to be a board member.

Irrespective of their title, 63 per cent (n = 101) of those responding had a place on the board at the establishment level, with the majority having a decision-making role. This compares very favourably with the 21 per cent which we found in a similar survey 12 years ago (Mackay and Torrington, 1986), and is similar to results reported by Brewster and Smith (1990), at corporate level. However, other surveys have found lower percentages, for example, Millward *et al.* (1992) quote a figure of 40 per cent from the third Workplace Industrial Relations Survey. Some of the differences here may well result from the way in which we contacted our respondents and also the way in which we worded our questions. However, the comparison with our previous survey, where organisations were contacted in exactly the same manner, suggests that in spite of these caveats real change has taken place.

The numbers employed within the specialist departments ranged from 1 to 264, with the majority, 63 per cent (n = 114), employing 10 or less. A total of 2919 personnel staff were covered by the survey, and of these 809 (or 28 per cent of the total) had professional personnel qualifications. The percentages within each establishment are perhaps more telling – in 7 per cent of cases (n = 12) there were no professionally qualified staff in the personnel department, and in 12 per cent of cases all staff were qualified. In 43 per cent of cases (n = 78) half or more of the staff were professionally qualified. The overall ratio of all personnel department staff to employees was 1 to 90; however, this ratio needs to be interpreted in the light of the organisational context. We only asked about the establishment itself, and depending on the level of decentralisation of the personnel functions we have surveyed, the figures for the whole organisation may result in a different ratio.

In addition to this data, we draw upon results from other recent research carried out by masters students, some of whom we have worked with closely. This research from other sources will be specified as such when dealt with in the text. Where no other source is given the data reported is from our own research.

How the book is organised

The following two chapters provide background to the transitions in the personnel role – Chapter 2 concentrates on the changing nature of employment and the scope and implications that this has for the personnel role; Chapter 3 provides an overview of the implications that these changes have for the management of the employment relationship.

In Chapters 4 through to 10 we discuss current and emerging issues in the organisation of the professional role, and in each chapter we compare our research results, in different ways, with a review of the key literature in the area and discuss the implications of these changes. Chapter 4 focuses on the devolution of operational personnel activities to the line, differentiating this from decentralisation by the move from specialist to non-specialist responsibility. Almost all establishments we visited were actively pursuing devolution, but despite the apparent enthusiasm for this by personnel specialists the progress made was generally very slow. Both line managers and personnel specialists held back from devolution for a number of reasons. Devolution of personnel and training budgets was a contentious issue, with most central departments holding on to the reins. Chapter 5 concentrates on the decentralisation of personnel specialists, and in particular decentralisation within the business unit to departmental level. We found a modest level of physical decentralisation of specialists, and a more favoured option was 'virtual' decentralisation where specialists retained a central location but worked specifically for one or a small group of departments – this was sometimes tied in with the operation of formal internal markets. In Chapter 6 we turn to the strategic involvement of personnel specialists – our respondents reported an increasing level of enthusiasm for, and involvement in, HR strategy, albeit that the strategy was piecemeal. The opportunity for strategic involvement was often driven by the needs of the business and depended less on formal status than on the personality, competencies and reputation of the specialist. Chapter 7 deals with the outsourcing of personnel activities and identifies training and legal work as the areas most likely to be outsourced. Chapter 8 focuses on the internal marketing of the personnel function and highlights the difference between outsourcing of HR activities when they are commissioned and managed by the HR function and outsourcing of personnel activities when they are commissioned and managed by line departments. We also discuss the conflicts between the service provider role of HR, where the line manager is the customer, and strategic involvement, where the HR specialist works in partnership with the line. In Chapter 9 we explore a range of personnel/HR roles and styles of working relationship and relate them to the different ways in which the specialist function is organised. Chapter 10 reviews the history of the development of professional qualifications for the personnel function and we discuss the implications of our findings and the range of different roles and styles for on-the-job development of the personnel specialist. Finally, in Chapter 11, we summarise our findings and, by pulling the threads together, attempt an understanding of what is happening in the function and anticipate some of the implications of this.

References

Dyer, L. (1984) 'Studying human resource strategy – an approach and an agenda', *Industrial Relations*, 23, 156–69.

Guest, D. (1990) 'Human resource management and the American dream', *Journal of Management Studies*, 27(4).

Guest, D. and Hoque, K. (1993) 'The mystery of the missing human resource manager', *Personnel Management*, June.

Hendry, C. and Pettigrew, A. (1992) 'Patterns of strategic change in the development of human resource management', *British Journal of Management*, 3, 137–56.

IPD (1996) *IPD Annual Report 1996*, London: Institute of Personnel and Development.

Legge, K. (1978) *Power Innovation and Problem Solving in Personnel Management*, London: McGraw-Hill.

Lundenberg, C. C. (1985) 'Towards a contextual model of human resource strategy: lessons from the Reynolds Corporation', *Human Resource Management Journal*, 4(1), 91–112.

Mackay, L. and Torrington, D. (1986) *The Changing Nature of Personnel Management*, London: IPM.

Millward, N., Stevens, M., Smart, D. and Hawes, W. R. (1992) *Workplace Industrial Relations in Transition: The ED/ESRC/PSI/ACAS Surveys*, Aldershot: Dartmouth ED/ESRC/PSI/ACAS.

Mintzberg, H. (1987) 'Crafting strategy', *Harvard Business Review*, July–August.

Monks, K. (1992) 'Models of personnel management: a means of understanding the diversity of personnel practices', *Human Resource Management Journal*, 3(2).

Storey, J. (1992) *Developments in Human Resource Management*, Oxford: Blackwell.

Torrington, D. and Hall, L. (1998) *Human Resource Management*, Hemel Hempstead: Prentice-Hall.

Tyson, S. and Fell, A. (1986) *Evaluating the Personnel Function*, London: Hutchinson.

Watson, T. (1977) *The Personnel Managers*, London: Routledge and Kegan Paul.

2

Personnel management and the changing nature of employment

A historical perspective

The history of personnel management can be traced back to a specific milestone, Edward Cadbury's appointment of Mary Wood to be the first welfare officer in 1896. The nature of employment at that time can be summed up by the following extract from a letter to his employees from the first Lord Leverhulme. He had introduced the unbelievable initiative of profit sharing and the first share-out amounted to £8 per employee, but:

> £8 is an amount of money which is soon spent, and it will not do you much good if you send it down your throats in the form of bottles of whiskey, bags of sweets, or fat geese for Christmas. On the other hand, if you leave this money with me, I shall use it to provide for you everything which makes life pleasant – nice houses, comfortable homes, and healthy recreation. Besides I am disposed to allow profit sharing under no other form.
>
> (Wilson, 1954, p. 146)

Writing nearly a century later a contemporary guru states:

> Transnational corporations are blazing a path across national boundaries, transforming and disrupting the lives of billions of people in their search for global markets. The casualties . . . are beginning to mount as millions of workers are riffed to make room for more efficient and profitable machine surrogates. Unemployment is rising and tempers are flaring in country after country caught up in the corporate crossfire to improve production performance at all costs.
>
> (Rifkin, 1995, p. 287)

Those two extracts define the change taking place in our experience of employment as well as the change that has been induced in the personnel function as a result of adjusting to the consequent social upheaval.

Lord Leverhulme was the archetypal benevolent despot of the late Victorian age. Hugely wealthy as a result of his soap business he spent large sums of money on providing for his employees, but providing what he thought they needed, regardless of what they might actually want. He and his contemporaries Edward Cadbury and Joseph Rowntree enjoyed wealth, privilege and the power of unchallenged ownership of prosperous businesses. They were also devout Christian non-conformists with a clear Protestant belief in the need to do good to one's less fortunate fellow humans. Their view of employment, however, and the practices which they promulgated were based on an uncompromising commitment to maintaining a clear class structure. This conviction was as unshaken and unchallenged for them as it had been a century before for the anti-slavery campaigner William Wilberforce. He sought the abolition of slavery, but could see nothing inappropriate in the social divisions of his own land:

> The more lowly path of the poor is allotted to them by the hand of God. It is for them faithfully to accept its inconveniences and loyally discharge its obligations.

The way in which people were employed, and any changes in those arrangements, depended entirely on the preferences of the individuals who employed them, and the employers were working against a background of security, prosperity and absolute confidence in both their ability to do the right thing and the continuing opportunity to make decisions unilaterally.

At the close of the twentieth century Rifkin describes an experience of employment, dominated not by individual entrepreneurs but by anonymous corporations. Our destinies determined not by the goodwill or ill will of powerful men, but by the remorseless, grim logic of market forces and discounted cash flow. All this against a background not of security and confidence, but of acute anxiety and uncertainty. Charles Handy spells out the employment implications:

> The employee society is on the wane. New models are needed, new role players who will make the new ways less frightening. Political society will also have to make changes: resolving once and for all that children grow up with something to sell to the world . . . and that the helpless and the failures of this new order do not suffer too much, or bring too much suffering.'
>
> (Handy, 1995, p. 31)

Handy's reference to 'the employee society' reminds us of the irony that we now regret the passing of a form of life which our early nineteenth-century predecessors resisted: the factory system. Regular employment was virtually unknown and the idea of spending all one's working time in a specific place outside the home was unpalatable to most people, even though the alternative of a very hard, indigent life in agriculture was so gruelling. The early factory owners resorted to harsh discipline and long hours as a crude method of converting men, women and children to this radically new way of working:

> The new virtues that the workers were persuaded to adopt were those requisite for a

material civilisation: regularity, punctuality, obedience, thrift, providence, sobriety and industry.

(Chapman and Chambers, 1970)

In the north of England the town of Macclesfield became a centre for silk manufacture at the beginning of the eighteenth century. The work was carried out by individuals or small family units working in garrets producing buttons to order for merchandisers and being paid by the piece, as and when there was business to be done. They were all home workers.

The nearby village of Styal developed slightly later around a mill that represented a different mode of working. Instead of work being put out to people, people were brought in to the work, which was in a factory. There was an apprentice house, where foundlings were housed and both cared for and exploited during their teen years. Begun in 1783, the firm employed 2000 people by 1834. This was the beginning of a trend that was to continue uninterrupted until very recently.

At school we learn that the worst iniquities of the factory system were brought to an end by Lord Shaftesbury's legislation of 1847, although 'working in a factory' has remained a way of earning one's living that most people try to avoid. Many of the principles of factory work, however, became the epitome of 'the good job' that most people seek. The work is provided and organised by someone else, at a specified location. There is a predictable order to the working day, working week and working year; you receive a predictable, regular amount of money for the work you do and the main responsibility for your livelihood is with someone else. In that sense an office is a factory, so is a hospital, a school, a bank, a legal firm, a travel company or an advertising agency. The norm has become to work in a factory, except that we have a new name for it: the organisation.

The organisation has become the focus for economic activity and it has also become the vehicle for our working lives. We became employees, the organisation took over the responsibility for our jobs and our livelihood, our training and our security in old age. Welfare officers, like Mary Wood, were appointed and later turned into personnel officers. Trade unions were developed to look after us. We devised elaborate structures of authority and lines of responsibility to provide a social structure in which we felt secure at the same time we grumbled about its rigidity and impersonality.

Rifkin, Handy and many others tell us that the employment form that has been developed over two centuries is not that on which we can rely in the future. Perhaps we shall be like the home workers of eighteenth-century Macclesfield, except that we shall not be home workers, but teleworkers. The principle remains the same, but the technology has changed, from the loom to the computer. To some this conjures up an idyllic vision of independence and autonomy, working at one's own pace, picking one's own projects and drinking one's own coffee, just when you feel like it. It may be like that for some, but not for many. A survey of 197 teleworking translators in a number of European countries found a situation in many ways similar to that of the Macclesfield silk workers, with the teleworkers feeling their autonomy strictly limited by employers' deadlines, and their sense of security undermined by their need to keep going.

> Periods without work were times of hardship, and anxiety for the source of the next job. Many teleworkers feel obliged to keep working instead of taking breaks with their families, running up exceptionally long hours.
>
> (Bolger, 1996, p. 9)

After the factory had been invented, the later Victorian benevolent autocrats engaged people like Mary Wood as acolytes of their benevolence. The practice of personnel management has followed changing patterns of employment and, as a new millennium is about to dawn, contemporary personnel specialists – perhaps – stand ready to be Handy's 'new role players to make the new ways less frightening'.

Evolution of the personnel function

The remainder of this chapter develops the key themes in the century of personnel management, showing the changes from Mary Wood to the present day, and we shall see not a process of one set of practices replacing another, but a process of personnel practice becoming steadily more diverse and demanding, still incorporating what Mary Wood did at the same time as grappling with the daunting challenge of the future. The evolution is best understood by seeing how the core activities expanded due to the addition of different roles.

The welfare officer

Before personnel emerged as a specialist management activity, there were those in the nineteenth century who tried to intervene in industrial affairs to support the position of the severely underprivileged factory worker. Social reformers like Lord Shaftesbury and Robert Owen produced some easing of this hardship, mainly by standing outside the organisation and the workplace, offering criticism of employer behaviour within and inducing some changes. This was also the time when the novels of Charles Dickens, especially *Hard Times*, began to expose factory conditions for the observation of his readers. Friedrich Engels was a prosperous young German businessman, who came to help with the management of the family business in Manchester. He reacted both to the conditions in the company's factory and to the grim circumstances in which his employees lived, by developing his ideas on social reform. He formed a lifelong association with Karl Marx, with whom he wrote *The Condition of the Working Class in England*. This combination led, of course, to the development of communism that spread rapidly to all parts of the world.

Although these people remained personally detached from the factory system which they criticised, it was their influence and agitation that led to welfare officers being appointed, and provided the first frame of reference for those early appointees.

The welfare officers saw their role as being to provide benefits to the deserving and unfortunate employees. The motivation was the Christian charity of the employer, who was prepared to provide these comforts, partly because the employees deserved them, but mainly because he was disposed to provide them. The perspective was completely class-based: the well-meaning middle class enabling the prosperous owners to *dispense* what they were inclined to dispense (remember Lord Leverhulme's comment, quoted at the beginning of this chapter, '. . . I am disposed to allow profit sharing under no other form.') There was no consideration of *employment rights*, only paternalist disposition. Writing *Pygmalion* in 1912, George Bernard Shaw gave Eliza Doolittle's father the penetrating observation:

> I'm one of the undeserving poor: that's what I am. Think of what it means to a man. It means that he's up against middle class morality all the time. What is middle class morality? Just an excuse for never giving me anything.

The Quaker families of Cadbury and Rowntree, and the Lever Brothers all set up progressive schemes of unemployment benefit, sick pay and subsidised housing for their employees at the end of the nineteenth century and the beginning of the twentieth. Cadbury-Schweppes and Unilever remain among the most efficient and profitable businesses in the United Kingdom a hundred years after the foundation of the Bournville village and Port Sunlight.

A contemporary development was the growth of organised resistance to employers' employment practices through the trade union movement, which was gradually establishing itself as a viable force and winning legal rights. The Institute of Welfare Officers was established in 1913 at a meeting in the Rowntree factory in York and the early history of personnel management is only understood if one sees the approach to the management of employment during this period having a twin-track, or alternative, orientation. Trade unionists were usually suspicious of welfare officers or hostile to them, because of their close affinity with the employers. The motivation behind union membership was the inadequacy or unacceptability of employer benevolence where it existed.

Trade unionism and the welfare movement both drew strength from legislation. For unions it was the Taff Vale decision, the Trade Disputes Act of 1906 and the Trade Union Act of 1913. For welfare officers there was the support of the various Factories Acts, the 1901 Factory and Workshop Act and the setting up of Whitley Councils in 1917.

The welfare tradition remains a central feature in contemporary personnel management, although it has lost its social class orientation. There is constant comment on the provision of facilities like childcare and health screening, as well as the occasional discussion about business ethics (for example, Pocock, 1989). The extent to which contemporary working practices for professional and executive employees make unreasonable demands of time and inconvenience is receiving increasing attention, as is the need for employees of all types to balance work and domestic responsibilities:

> Care-friendly employment practices will be the phenomenon of the future. Only by addressing the needs of employees caring for children, dependants with disabilities and the elderly, will employers be able to attract and retain the non-traditional sectors of the workforce which are forecast to form the workforce of the 1990s.
>
> (Worman, 1990)

Another inheritance from this early stage is the sense of dependence on a more powerful figure. Our research showed a widespread reliance of personnel managers on the support of the Chief Executive to be able to carry through their programmes. In one case it was referred to as 'the HR mindset', but the message was almost universally the same: personnel depends on a powerful patron to be effective.

The staff manager

The nature of employment took on an extra dimension when the simple hierarchy of the factory evolved into the complex hierarchy of bureaucracy. Employing organisations were getting bigger and specialisation was emerging in the management levels as well as on the shopfloor. Gradually a cadre of employees grew that carried the generic label of 'staff', as opposed to 'works'. This group were socially a cut above the factory workers, working shorter hours, with longer holidays and earning salaries rather than wages.

Welfare officers had been concerned exclusively with improving physical working conditions. As their responsibilities expanded they also had to acquire expertise on what can be generally called staffing, with great concern about role specification, careful selection, training and placement. The staff manager was learning to operate within a bureaucracy, serving organisational rather than paternalist–employer objectives, but was still committed to a basically humanitarian role.

The religious imperative behind the welfare movement was modified by a willingness to look to social science for support. Much of the scientific management philosophy of F. W. Taylor was absorbed into personnel practice. Taylor's idea was that work should be made more efficient by analysis of what was required and the careful selection and training of the worker, who would then be supported by the management in a spirit of positive co-operation.

The Frenchman Henri Fayol considered not the worker but the management process, and his analytical framework for management is sometimes known as scientific administration, as his approach had much in common with Taylor's.

The bureaucracy theme in the development of personnel thinking was also influenced by the human relations school of thought, which was in many ways a reaction against scientific management, or a reaction against the way in which scientific management was being applied. Taylor found that his managerial philosophy was seldom fully appreciated, and scientific management became identified with over-specialisation of work and very tight systems of payment.

The human relations approach appealed immediately to those who were concerned about industrial conflict and the apparent dehumanising potential of scientific management. The main advocate was Elton Mayo and the central idea was to emphasise informal social relationships and employee morale as contributors to organisational efficiency.

There is a clear understanding that welfare and efficiency go hand in hand: one cannot have the one without also having the other. Tony Watson makes the point that the interest in welfare had become integrated into management itself and that the identification of welfare with efficiency was propounded by Cadbury as early as 1912:

> The supreme principle has been the belief that business efficiency and the welfare of employees are but different sides of the same problem. Character is an economic asset; and business efficiency depends not merely on the physical conditions of employees, but on their general attitude and feeling to the employer. The test of any scheme of factory organisation is the extent to which it creates and fosters the atmosphere and spirit of co-operation and goodwill, without in any sense lessening the loyalty of the worker to his own class and its organisations.
>
> (Cadbury, 1912, p. 17)

Working within a bureaucracy, and in collaboration with social scientists, led to the development of the core technology of personnel work that is still central. Job analysis was initially used as an aid to selection, but is now used also in training, job evaluation, career development and performance appraisal. The use of tests to assess intelligence, personality and vocational aptitude remains widespread, and systematic approaches to selection interviewing have been developed to cover a variety of face-to-face situations.

In 1934 a Staff Management Association was established alongside the Institute of Labour Management, which had evolved from the Institute of Welfare Officers. Although a relatively small body, it maintained a separate existence for over 30 years.

The industrial relations officer

Welfare officers and staff managers worked on the basis of there being one source of authority and influence in the business. The proprietor or senior managers decided what to do, and that was that. In the period after the Second World War two related factors brought about major change. There was relatively full employment, so that labour was a scarce resource, and trade unions extended their membership. Employers had to change firm, traditional unitarism to accommodate what Allan Flanders, the leading industrial relations analyst of the 1960s, was to call 'the challenge from below'.

In 1926 the General Strike produced a situation close to class war and the loss of 160 000 000 working days during the year at a time when there were just over 5 000 000 members of trade unions. By 1946 the number of union members had reached nearly 9 000 000 and membership growth was to continue to outstrip the increase in size of the working population until the majority of employees were union members. Now the complex of personnel work was further enlarged by adding the activity of negotiation. Effective representation of employee interests was now of two sorts. The trade union official was the accredited representative of the employees, while the personnel officer was on 'the other side'. Anthony and Crichton reported the results of a 1957 study:

> It was particularly concerned with the problems of the roles and relationships of the personnel officer to the rest of management and to the employees who might seek his counsel. How could he manage to be seen as unbiased by these employees whilst at other times acting as management's agent and representing their viewpoint? And how could he be identified with the management group whilst reminding them of the workers' views? Should he seek concessions on employees' behalf? The study group argued that his role was that of 'remembrancer' so that workpeople's views would be taken into consideration in making policies (but not their representative).
>
> (Anthony and Crichton, 1969, pp. 200–1)

Trade union assertiveness brought a shift towards bargaining by the employer on at least some matters. There was a growth of joint consultation and the establishment of joint production committees and suggestion schemes. Nationalised industries were set up, with a statutory duty placed on employers to negotiate with unions representing employees. The government encouraged the appointment of personnel officers and set up courses for them to be trained at universities. A personnel management advisory service was set up at the Ministry of Labour, and this still survives in ACAS. When ACAS was founded in 1974, it was initially to deal with conciliation and arbitration only: CAS. Then the value of the pre-existing advisory work was recognised, so we now have the Advisory, Conciliation and Arbitration Service.

There is a temptation to think that negotiating with trade unions is a thing of the past, and there can be no doubt that the situation has changed dramatically. Fifty-five per cent of the working population were union members in 1979, but only 33 per cent were members in 1995. Industrial action is reduced, collective bargaining has less coverage and scope, and many personnel specialists have never had any dealing with trade unions. However:

> Trade unions are recognised by employers in about half of all workplaces employing 25 people or more, and over ten million people work in unionised establishments. Although collective bargaining is less central to employee relations in the mid-1990s, it is still the mechanism by which pay is determined for about half the workforce.
>
> (Marchington and Wilkinson, 1996, p. 224)

The industrial relations officer has joined the welfare officer and the staff manager: the roles are growing.

Management development advisor

In academia, personnel management was never recognised as a respectable subject. There were professors of occupational psychology, or industrial relations and labour economics, but there has never been a professor of personnel management in a British university, although chairs in human resource management have become commonplace in the 1990s. The influence of academia on management practice is always difficult to judge, but it is probably greater in the broad area of personnel and human resource management than in other aspects. By the late 1960s there was a new field of academic work that gained respectability: organisation behaviour and its associates of organisational analysis and organisation development.

People began to be appointed in large businesses to advise on the effectiveness of the organisation as a whole. There was an attempt to understand the interaction between organisational structures and the people who make up the organisation.

The significance of this development was that it marked a change of focus among personnel specialists, away from dealing with the rank-and-file employee on behalf of the management towards dealing with the management and integration of managerial activity.

Although now buried in history, the most notable early example of this approach was the Glacier Metal Project, conceived by Professor Elliott Jaques of Brunel University and Wilfred Brown, Chairman and Managing Director of the Glacier Metal Company. They identified three social systems: executive, representative and legislative, and stressed the concepts of structure and role, so as to reduce the significance of personality factors in organisation (Brown, 1971).

This type of approach to management is very strong currently in programmes of organisation and management development, as companies subcontract much of their routine work to peripheral employees, and concentrate on developing and retaining an elite core of people with specialist expertise on whom the business depends for its future.

The human resource planner

The role of human resource or manpower planner required the personnel specialist to count and to cost. A development of the general management anxiety to quantify decisions has been a move towards regarding people as manpower or human resources. It is not to do with individuals but aggregates, not people but categories.

Developed before there was such widespread concern about sexist terminology, it was known as manpower planning:

> ... manpower planning comprises the activities of forecasting the future demand for labour and the supply of labour, comparing the two profiles, and making action plans to reconcile them.

> (Storey and Sisson, 1993, p. 110)

Although originally based on an assumption of organisational expansion, manpower planning was reshaped during organisational contraction to ensure the closest possible fit between the number of people and skills required and what is available. It has also evolved into human resource planning, which is not just a change of label, but the introduction of broader considerations than just number crunching. It brings us very close to human resource management.

The human resource manager

The latest and most wide-ranging role is undoubtedly that of the human resource manager, an idea that took the personnel world by storm in the 1980s and which may be the most significant change in emphasis in the last 50 years. Huge amounts of hot air and pages of print have been devoted to defining human resource management (HRM) and the ways in which it differs, or does not differ, from personnel management. Much of this discussion is of a strictly academic nature, similar to arguments about how many angels can balance on the head of a pin. Also there is little disagreement that human resource management is an activity of all managers, rather than just the personnel specialists, who are the subject of this book.

Human resource management arrived in the UK in the mid-1980s as a fully formed set of values and prescriptions that had been formulated at Harvard Business School. In the United States personnel management had never achieved the degree of recognition that it had in Britain, even though British personnel practitioners spend so much time deploring their lack of influence. The first formulation to receive any widespread exposure on this side of the Atlantic was that of Fombrun, Tichy and Devanna (1984) who set out the proposition that HRM had four generic functions: selection, appraisal, development and reward. At first sight this sounded like elementary personnel management, but they added the comment that all of these were directed at performance. Although obvious, it was this emphasis that gave the concept an edge; there was a different spin on the ball.

There is always an interest in pursuing new ideas and HRM rapidly became the smart thing to do and to talk about. For some while personnel specialists had maintained their place in the organisational pecking order because of their consensus negotiator role. The perceived power of trade unions was a bogey with which to frighten their managerial colleagues. Coupled with the growing complexity of employment law, it enabled the personnel people to say '. . . just leave it to us'. By the early 1980s it became apparent that there really was a change. The position of unions was altering, the raised level of unemployment had the effect of reducing staff turnover and thus reducing the amount of activity in recruitment and selection, and personnel people had good reason to develop their paranoia about being misunderstood, unloved and not listened to.

Another feature was the impact of the change in industrial relations practice in academia and on research. This has been significant in the area of people management since personnel specialists first looked to social science for ideas in the inter-war period. By the 1980s universities had departments of organisational behaviour, occupational psychology, labour economics and industrial relations. Quite quickly the industrial relations academics found that their research money was drying up and students were beginning to desert their classes. Looking for a new area of expertise, they latched on to HRM. It seemed so much more progressive than traditional personnel that academics readily consigned personnel management to the managerial backwaters.

Practitioners and academics together heralded HRM as being strategic and having a long-term outlook (Storey, 1989), contrasting it with personnel which they condemned as 'merely operational' (Gennard and Kelly, 1994). Because of an enhanced use of planning, HRM was described as proactive, whereas personnel was reactive and downstream (Schuler, 1989; Miller, 1987). HRM added value, while personnel was welfare-oriented (Storey, 1989). HRM would be integrated with the rest of the business, personnel was simply picking up the pieces (Guest, 1987). HR managers would be architects, whereas personnel practitioners were administrators and clerks.

The extraordinary litany of disparagement included almost every criticism of personnel managers that had been made in the previous hundred years, and taking very little account of any evidence other than opinion. The overall message was always the same: everything to do with HRM was good, and anything associated with personnel was bad.

Finally tiring of this debate, academics moved on in the early 1990s to look for evidence of the HRM phenomenon. The three main research projects with this aim have been Storey's case studies of 15 organisations (1992), the Workplace and Industrial Relations Survey (Millward *et al.*, 1992) and the Warwick Company Level Industrial Relations Survey (Marginson *et al.*, 1993). The conclusions drawn from these surveys are nearly all pessimistic. Few organisations are living up to the ideal. Personnel managers are less effective than they should be (Guest, 1990), they are not as strategic as they should be (Storey, 1989), and they are only implementing strategies which have been formulated in other functions (Storey, 1989). They are not 'architects' but 'clerks and contract managers' (Sisson, 1995). In general, 'the picture is hardly flattering' and is 'extremely disappointing' (Guest, 1991; Sisson, 1995).

Sisson concludes that personnel managers are 'working against the grain' (Sisson, 1995). If this is true, then arguably it is a grain that academics have created for them. Our evidence suggests that the theory of HRM presents a false and unobtainable image for personnel practitioners to aspire to. Furthermore, it is doubtful that the type of role described is the most useful in contributing to business success and individual well-being in employment.

Representation on the board

It is widely held that any function or set of interests gains influence in a business if it has the head of the function on the management board. Although this does not automatically confer influence, it does confer status and it does demonstrate an overall commitment to the significance of that function. Research has indicated that companies with a main board personnel director are more likely to take personnel matters into account in strategic business decisions (Marginson *et al.*, 1993). Certainly, if personnel expertise and the human resource perspective is not represented when these decisions are made, it is possible that decisions will be flawed, and the personnel people will spend a lot of time picking up the pieces from the fall-out, as Keith Sisson has suggested.

Survey evidence of board-level representation is sketchy and conflicting. The Warwick CLIRS (1992) survey reported that personnel had only limited involvement in strategic business decisions (Marginson *et al.*, 1993). The latest WIRS survey indicates that specialist representation has remained restricted to a minority of companies – about thirty to forty per cent being a fairly constant figure (Millward *et al.*, 1992) – but the same survey reveals that personnel had board representation in some form, if not necessarily by specialist representation, in around two-thirds of companies, which could indicate that HR issues are *so* integrated into the business that they do not need specialist representation. In contrast, the recent Price Waterhouse Cranfield Survey found direct personnel representation on the boards of over two-thirds of British companies employing over 200 employees (Brewster and Smith, 1990). Our own research showed 63 per cent of respondents reporting the presence of a main board director representing the personnel function. This is a three-fold increase on the 21 per cent reported in our similar survey of 1983/4.

Table 2.1 shows the proportion of companies in our sample which had an HR/personnel presence on the board at both establishment level and national level, where applicable. One striking feature is that only 20 per cent report no representation at all at the establishment level board, a figure which was even lower for boards at the national level. To put this another way, *over eighty per cent* of the sample had personnel representation in some form on both boards. This may be because we did not confine our question simply to specialist personnel representation and because our analysis included the variety of roles which the professional might play on the board rather than just formal attendance. But it seems clear that personnel has a substantial presence at board level, even if those present are not always full board members.

Table 2.1 Representation of the most senior personnel person on the board

Nature of role	No. of responses	% of responses
Yes, a decision-making role	85	53
Yes, a place on the board, but not as a decision-maker	16	10
No place on the board	58	37
Total	159*	100

* The figures are responses to the question, 'Does the most senior personnel manager have a decision-making place on the board where you work? Please circle category.' Fifty-five responses were excluded as there was no board at establishment level.

Further light was shed on this issue during the interview stage of our work. One important point which came out of the interviews was that not having a formal board presence did not necessarily impede personnel's influence. In a number of businesses where there was no personnel presence on the board the head of the function found other more informal ways to exert influence. If they had no formal place they often attended board meetings on an ad hoc basis, or were brought into meetings when any new initiative had an impact on the human side of the business.

One HR Director of a Training and Enterprise Council was not a member of the board but attended about a third of all meetings on a regular basis, claiming that as he could not effect a structural change he had 'a political way of dealing with it'. Interestingly, the formal personnel voice on the board was through the strategic director, which overtly demonstrates the company's commitment to human resource issues.

Conversely, having personnel representation on the board did not necessarily increase personnel's influence. In some cases when there was a direct voice on the board the function did not have much of a say in the decisions but dealt mainly with the implications, implementation and flow-down of the strategic initiatives. For example, the human resource director of a large building society sat on the board, but the department still very much dealt with the 'back end' of the planning process. Another interesting example was that of a publisher where the 'Company and HR Director' formally voiced personnel issues at board level, but it was the personnel manager who had much of the real influence.

Generally, therefore, formal positioning on the board, or the lack of it, did not seem to make much difference to the extent of personnel's influence. They often found ways round it by informal networking, political interplay and old-fashioned expertise and hard work, which in some cases may have been more successful than if they had formal board status. Interestingly though, most non-board members did seem to aspire to this status and were either fighting for it or expressing discontent that they did not have it.

Numbers are not enough. We also need to consider the quality of the representation. There are undoubtedly still some 'Old Joe' problems. The following is a comment by the managing director of a company that had recently taken over another:

> When we merged the two companies I obviously wanted my own team, so most of the pre-existing board took up the same roles in the new business. I clearly also needed to keep one or two of the directors from the company we had bought. There was a very good operations guy, who was glad to take on that function in the merged business and a marketing man, who was very shrewd and experienced. We made him Director for Personnel and General Affairs, so that he can now fill in for any of the others who are away for a spell.

The idea clearly was that someone who was shrewd and experienced would be adequately equipped to run personnel matters – or any other jobs that happened to come along. More research needs to be carried out in this field to enable us to understand the role which a personnel director might play at board level (Gennard and Kelly, 1994). Having a presence on the board may have a symbolic significance, but too many Old Joes could mean *mis*representation in practice.

Professor Karen Legge has been one of the shrewdest commentators on personnel management for the last 30 years and she avers that the key differences in emphasis are, first, that HRM concentrates more on the development of the management team than on the affairs of non-managers. Second, it is an activity owned by all managers, not just the personnel specialists, and third, that it emphasises organisational culture as the central activity for senior management.

> These three differences in emphasis all point to HRM, in theory, being essentially a more central strategic management task than personnel management in that it is

experienced by managers, as the most valued company resource to be managed, it concerns them in the achievement of business goals and it expresses senior management's preferred organisational values. From this perspective it is not surprising that Fowler (1987, p. 3) identifies the real difference . . . as 'not what it is, but who is saying it. In a nutshell HRM represents the discovery of personnel management by chief executives'.

(Legge, 1995, pp. 75–6)

We argue that the emphasis on developing the management team has been a part of personnel management since the emergence of the management development adviser 30 years ago, although the relative abandonment of everyone else is a much more recent phenomenon. Furthermore, our research suggests that this may be much more in the rhetoric than the reality. If chief executives have only just discovered personnel management, we wonder what it was that Wilfred Brown discovered in the 1960s, or Edward Cadbury before him. We have found very few personnel specialists who agree that they are concerned with the management team, but not with the rank and file.

If we concentrate on the development of the personnel function, which is the purpose of this book, we can see how the work of the personnel specialists is again extended by this role enlargement.

Figure 2.1 shows the six roles that make up the contemporary composite of the personnel function.

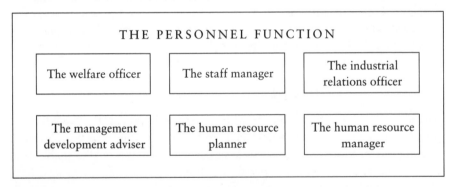

Fig. 2.1 The composite of the contemporary personnel function

Deviant or conformist innovation

The extent to which personnel specialists are identified with central management interests presents a nice question about how can they be most effective, by being right on the inside or by being a little bit independent. Twenty years ago Karen Legge identified two alternative methods of personnel people seeking power in organisations (Legge, 1978, pp. 67–94). *Conformist innovation* was where personnel specialists identified their activities closely with the objective of organisational success, cost benefit and conforming to the success criteria of managerial colleagues, who usually have greater power. In contrast, *deviant innovators* identify their activities with a set of norms or values that are distinct from, but not necessarily in conflict with, the norms of organisational success: social values rather than cost benefit, in a similar way to the company doctor, for example, whose power derives from an independent, professional stance for dealing with managerial clients.

The comparison with the company doctor is apt. If the company doctor simply tells managerial colleagues what they want to hear and pursues the objectives of organisational success whilst disregarding the norms of the medical profession, then that doctor is not only compromised, but becomes useless as a result.

Total quality management has been one of the more effective approaches to improving business performance and research has demonstrated how critical the personnel people can be in making it a success (Wilkinson, 1995). Very often it is their very 'neutrality' or slight detachment from central management that enables them to ensure the effectiveness of management initiatives.

Total commitment to conformist innovation can mean a loss of distinctive identity, unless there is some expert, 'deviant' contribution, no matter how wide and general the management responsibility. After all, no management team would value the contribution of marketing specialists who did not vigorously interpret and represent the customer interest.

The great preoccupation with strategy has emphasised the values of conformist innovation. From our research we have been led to question the wisdom in concentrating too much on strategy at the expense of operational matters (Torrington and Hall, 1996).

The end of the factory?

The century since the appointment of Mary Wood has seen a great enrichment of the personnel role and function, which has enlarged as organisations have grown and patterns of employment have changed. The continuing constant element has been the organisational boundary: the factory. The welfare officer had concerns with off-duty activity, but was predominantly concerned with what happened inside the factory gates. The staff manager was concerned almost entirely with managing the interface between the individual and the bureaucratic structure. The industrial relations officer monitored the national scene in order to cope more effectively with the employee relations inside the business. The management development adviser and the human resource planner similarly concentrated on running the organisation.

We are now beginning to lose the certainty of the factory, the organisation as an entity. Employment has developed as an activity that we undertake in a place to which we go on a regular basis and where we interact with systems of communication, political infighting, hierarchies for career advancement and all the rest. Personnel management has developed to fit and manage that type of experience. If the organisational boundary is ceasing to be the arena for our employment experience, then it really is a different ball game.

References

Anthony, P. and Crichton, A. (1969) *Industrial Relations and the Personnel Specialists*, London: Batsford.

Bolger, A., 'Families hit by teleworking', *Financial Times*, 28 October 1996.

Brewster, C. and Smith, C. (1990) 'Corporate strategy: a no-go area for personnel', *Personnel Management*, 22(7).

Brown, W. (1971) *Organisation*, London: Heinemann.

Cadbury, E. (1912) *Experiments in Industrial Organisation*, London: Longmans, quoted in Watson, T. (1977) *The Personnel Managers*, London: Routledge and Kegan Paul, 42.

Chapman, S. D. and Chambers, J. D. (1970) *The Beginnings of Industrial Britain*, quoted in Quarry Bank Mill Trust, (1986) *Mill Life at Styal*, Altrincham, Cheshire: Willow Publishing.

Fombrun, C. Tichy, N. M. and Devanna, M. A. (1984) *Strategic Human Resource Management*, Sussex: John Wiley.

Gennard, J. and Kelly, J. (1994) 'Human resource management: the views of personnel directors', *Human Resource Management Journal*, 5(1).

Guest, D. (1987) 'Human resource management and industrial relations', *Journal of Management Studies*, 24(5), 377–97.

Guest, D. (1990) 'Human resource management and the American dream', *Journal of Management Studies*, 27(4), 377–97.

Guest, D. (1991) 'Personnel management: the end of orthodoxy', *British Journal of Industrial Relations*, 29(2), 149–76.

Legge, K. (1995) *Human Resource Management: Rhetorics and Realities*, London: Macmillan.

Marchington, M. P. and Wilkinson, A. J. (1996) *Core Personnel and Development*, London: IPD.

Marginson, P., Armstrong, P., Edwards, P. and Purcell, J. (1993) *The Control of Industrial Relations in Large Companies*, Warwick: Industrial Relations Research Unit.

Miller, P. (1987) 'Strategic industrial relations and human resource management', *Journal of Management Studies*, 24(4), 347–61.

Millward, N., Stevens, M., Smart, D. and Hawes, W. R. (1992) *Workplace Industrial Relations in Transition: the ED/ESRC/PSI/ACAS Surveys*, Aldershot: Dartmouth ED/ESRC/PSI/ACAS.

Pocock, P. (1989) 'Is business ethics a contradiction in terms?', *Personnel Management*, 21(11).

Rifkin, J. R. (1995) *The End of Work*, New York: Archer Putnam.

Schuler, R. S. (1989) 'Repositioning the human resource function', *Academy of Management Executive*, 4(3), 49–60.

Sisson, K. (1995) 'Human resource management and the personnel function', in J. Storey (ed.) *Human Resource Management: a Critical Text*, London: Routledge.

Storey, J. (1989) *New Perspectives on Human Resource Management*, London: Routledge and Kegan Paul.

Storey, J. (1992) *Developments in the Management of Human Resources*, Oxford: Blackwell.

Storey, J. and Sisson, K. (1993) *Managing Human Resources and Industrial Relations*, Milton Keynes: Open University Press.

Torrington, D. P. and Hall, L. A. (1996) 'Chasing the rainbow: how seeking status through strategy misses the point for the personnel function', *Employee Relations*, 18(6), 79–96.

Wilson, C. (1954) *The History of Unilever*, London: George Allen & Unwin.

Worman, D. (1990) 'The forgotten carers', *Personnel Management*, 22(1).

Managing the changes in employment

The reality of change in the nature of employment is obvious. What needs further analysis is the way in which the form of the changes alters the practice of personnel management. One of the core activities for personnel specialists – both now and 50 years ago – is training and development, but changing patterns of employment mean that the practice is now much different. In the 1940s and 1950s, most training was for young people and the emphasis was on preparing them for semi-permanent positions in a single organisation. That involved an approach and the use of methods that are no longer appropriate for a time when skill needs change so rapidly and employment horizons are shorter.

In this chapter we are going to examine three of the main change factors – culture, labour markets and contracts – before concluding with a consideration of the ways in which all of these are managed.

Changing cultures of organisation

The dwindling of hierarchy

The simple fact that the use of the word 'culture' about an organisation is now commonplace indicates a major cultural change in itself. Harold Leavitt was an internationally renowned analyst of organisations. In 1973 he published, with two colleagues, a bestselling text *The Organizational World*, in which references to culture are very hard to find, because the notion had not been conceived. Organisations had structures, and these structures could be likened to human systems in constant interaction with their environment, but the notion of culture was missing, even though it had long been a salient feature of organisation.

In the Second World War RAF squadrons of fighter aircraft and their personnel were relatively informal in the way they behaved, with a creative approach to such things as uniform. In contrast, the Coldstream Guards regarded tight, formal discipline and strict adherence to the minute, detailed requirements of uniform as essential. Both groups were among the most effective military units in the world. They were both bound by the same King's Regulations and both on the same side in the same war. Both had very high morale and a high rate of applications to join, yet the way in which they behaved, the way in which they worked was very different.

To a great extent these differences were due to the nature of their work. Fighter pilots were on their own when they killed their opponents and relied on individual flair and courage. The guards operated as integrated units, where the requirement – both to win the battle and to stay alive – came from an acceptance of the fact that you instantly obeyed orders without question.

Contemporary organisations are similar in having varying norms of behaviour. Formally dressed people, who quietly get on with their jobs, typically make up the majority of the staff of accountancy firms. Advertising agencies employ people tending to greater variety of dress and spend a great deal of time in creative tension, including turbulent working relationships. In a university a group of physicists will generally behave in a completely different way from a group of social scientists.

This type of variation is what management students have been trying to capture in recent years by developing the concept of culture, the 'soft', energising and intangible aspect of organisations that makes them function in such a variety of ways.

Before the interest in culture, the notion of structure was widely used and understood as the basis of many personnel activities. One of the favourite pursuits of the personnel function was succession planning. Figure 3.1. illustrates the approach, with a clear hierarchy describing a stable situation that will be sustained, even if people have minds of their own:

> However carefully developed, succession plans can never be perfect. Supplies often become short through promising managers leaving the company because of various attractions elsewhere. A sudden company reorganisation could throw the whole scheme out and create an excess of budding senior managers. It is, nevertheless, imperative to have succession plans in order to sort out the mess afterwards.
>
> (Thomas, 1973, p. 24)

Somehow or other the comfortable security and certainty of the plan would be restored after the mess had been cleared up.

Another creation of organisation structure is the notion of the hierarchical procedure to deal with problems; referring matters up the chain of command for resolution at a higher level. The main manifestation in the personnel area is grievance and discipline. Again there is the emphasis on order and clarity:

> to ensure that those with effective authority within the two parties can be reached in an orderly way and also to provide for a review of decisions by a new level of authority at each succeeding stage.
>
> (Thomson and Murray, 1976, p. 129)

27

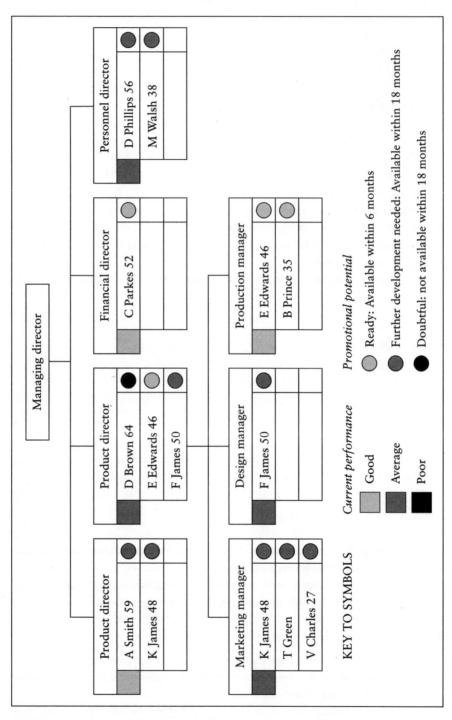

Fig. 3.1 Managerial replacement organisation chart

Similar thinking justified collective bargaining generally, especially when it reached its 1970s apogee of productivity bargaining:

> Prior to productivity bargaining, decisions were made in terms of precedent, customary practice and the dictates of stewards and foremen. Such a control system could be characterised as haphazard and personal. By contrast, under productivity bargaining the control system becomes much more deliberate, rational and professional.
>
> (McKersie and Hunter, 1973, p. 287)

Organisational culture is an alternative way of describing the same thing as structure, but concept and the language are different, our approach and resultant methods are different as well. Consider some of the contrasts:

- Structure is firm; culture is soft.
- Structure is clear; culture is intangible.
- Structure is about systems to which people have to adapt; culture is about people who have norms and values in common.
- Structure is about the distribution of authority; culture is about how people work together.

Through the 1980s, in particular, there was great interest in organisational culture as the key to improved organisational effectiveness (for example, Deal and Kennedy, 1982; Handy, 1985) by improving on the limited explanations and methods that the earlier pre-occupation with organisational structure provided. Organisation charts may help to clarify reporting relations and subtleties of seniority, but the culture or ethos of the business is equally, or more, important in determining the effectiveness of the business. Making sense of organisational culture depends as heavily on language as does wine connoisseurship, because it is always an attempt to grasp at something that is intangible. In describing structures it is possible to draw the set of hierarchical relationships that constitute and produce an organisation chart. In describing cultures one is left with metaphors.

This is not to suggest that culture has now taken over from structure as the sole form of company organisation. They are as interdependent as lungs and oxygen in providing the business with life and purpose. Personnel activities are profoundly affected and the work of personnel specialists is either redundant or needs to be thought through and practised in a different way.

The culture of performance

Although effective working was always an objective of personnel work, the central focus was always to administer the contract of *employment*. There were positions to be filled and jobs to be done, but the idea of influencing, or even being able to influence, the way jobs were done was not prominent. The prominent position of trade unions emphasised collectivism rather than individualism. Shortly before he left office in 1979, Prime Minister James Callaghan summed up that attitude by saying, 'Nothing should divide man from man.' Personnel managers negotiated agreements with their union counterparts that dealt largely with 'concessions' by one side or the other. Both employers and unions were anxious to maintain a 'united front', so that the ground-breaking productivity agreements at Fawley could only proceed by 'breaking ranks':

> The first and most famous of productivity agreements signed in 1960 at the non-federated refinery of Esso at Fawley, near Southampton, was viewed with little enthusiasm by employers' associations . . . Even where withdrawal from an association was not a necessary pre-condition of a productivity agreement, the proposals of a particular company may demand an agreement so different from those prevailing in the rest of industry as to render continued membership of the association a serious embarrassment.'
>
> (Clegg, 1970, p. 151)

The tendency to use military terminology emphasised the idea that improvements in productivity could only be made by collective movement: individuals did not exist. This was also manifest in the so-called incentive pay schemes that were widespread. There was no place for Stakhanovite workers outstripping the efforts of their colleagues by outstanding individual achievement. Whatever was formally agreed, it was clearly understood that there would be output norms to which all would conform.

Although most working people still have contracts of employment, they are increasingly employed on what is effectively a contract for *performance*. There is an expectation of performance by individuals, as well as by teams and businesses. This has produced much activity in the area of performance-related pay, profit-related pay, performance assessment, objective setting, on-target earnings, and the general, intangible of commitment. The talking up of commitment has the positive features of enthusiasm, seeing the results of your own efforts, empowerment, getting positive feedback from the satisfied customer and so forth. For some people, however, there can be meaningless game-playing and unproductive anxiety. For most people it involves working harder. The idea of a mid-day break of an hour for lunch has been much reduced, to be superseded by sandwiches at the desk, and there are some quite laughable exercises to be seen in trying not to be too early out of the car park in the evening.

The language of performance culture understandably stresses the positive, although sometimes to unrealistic excess:

1 Organizations are no longer described by what they produce or do; they have mission statements instead.
2 Mission statements are meant to 'cascade down' the organization and are the means of individual 'empowerment'.

3 This empowerment in turn leads to great teams who run hot, who play passionately (even chaotically), towards the corporate mission, united in their common vision.

4 Organizations are no longer run by managers but by heroes who are insanely great in what they do. They turn threats into opportunities . . .

(Wilson, 1993, pp. 79–80)

All of this is very good fun, even if it flies in the face of the experience of many who find their managers to be villains who are insanely bad at what they do. However, it enables managers to escape from the tedious routine of 'getting things out by Friday' into a nice, fluffy world of academic discussion and redefinition of terms. Also, the first rule of propaganda is that if you tell people something often enough, they will eventually believe it.

Apart from the window-dressing of mission statements, the most familiar cultural developments in performance have been to increase customer orientation. Before that there was a widespread notion that managers ran the business and then sales representatives sold the product to customers. Management was concerned principally with the internal dynamics of the organisation and technological innovation was either to make production more efficient or because it was interesting: the customer was somewhere else, and the marketing people were a different breed, wearing sharp suits and driving company cars that they did not deserve.

In the 1950s one of the authors worked in a manufacturing company, where each of the supervisors worked hard to accumulate a 'backlog'. When there was a large number of unfilled orders, they felt that they had controlled the uncertainty of input sufficiently to 'set out their stalls' to keep production running smoothly, calling forward orders for completion that fitted in with their need for a steady flow rather than the date of the order or the urgency of the customer's requirements.

The change to a customer orientation has been one of the main challenges of the manufacturing sector in particular, and this is a cultural change, getting people to look at things differently.

How one changes or develops culture to focus on performance is illuminated by an American study of 200 companies by John Kotter and James Heskett. Their conclusions were (a) that corporate culture has a significant impact on the long-term economic performance of a business, (b) that it is likely to be even more significant in the future as a determinant of success or failure, (c) that corporate cultures inhibiting financial performance develop easily, even in organisations that are full of intelligent and reasonable people, and (d) that corporate cultures can be altered to improve performance, even though they are

31

very difficult to change (Kotter and Heskett, 1992, p. 89). They also identified two levels of culture: shared values and group behaviour norms, the first being much harder to change than the second.

It has long been recognised that attitudes are harder to change than behaviour: actually trying a free sample of a new detergent is much more likely to make you believe it is better than lengthy explanation of its virtues. In developing corporate culture we have to start with trying to change norms of behaviour; over time those changed behaviours may lead to a change in the more deeply-held beliefs of shared norms. Customer care is a good example. Company trainers may go to great lengths to explain the value of customers and the allegiance, but it is often quicker simply to tell staff what to say and how to handle queries or complaints. That can produce the cringe-making robotic behaviour of some telesales people ('Hello, is that Mr Smith? This is XYZ Ltd, Mandy speaking. We make widgets and I would like to take just a few minutes of your time to tell you something about our latest line'), but in face-to-face situations it can produce a friendly reaction from the customer. When the behaviour pays off, then the attitudes and beliefs gradually shift.

Personnel managers have many of their activities geared in to the concept of the organisation as entity rather than process; administering the state of employment, rather than the process of performance; looking inwards to the organisation, rather than outwards to the customer.

The culture of insecurity

Close to the emphasis on performance and commitment is the experience of insecurity. The chronic insecurity of the urban worker before the development of trade unions was a motivation towards establishing security of employment as a take-for-granted value throughout the western world from the middle of the twentieth century. In management circles it had become an expectation even earlier than that ('as long as you keep your nose clean, they'll never throw you out'). One of the problems of the personnel function establishing credibility, was its frequent use as a dumping ground for the Old Joes referred to in the last chapter. If someone had been over-promoted, or had lost their nerve, or was no longer able to keep up, then a posting to personnel was often the remedy; dismissal was unthinkable.

The frequent reductions in hierarchical levels during the 1980s produced redundancies among middle managers that were enough to change that sense of security and to bring in the idea that security of employment may be comfortable for individuals, but could be harmful for businesses. At first it was a one-off shake-out, then it was a strategy that would only continue 'during the recession', but now it is increasingly regarded as a way to maintain the vitality and competitiveness of a business, as people regularly 'move on', until there is nowhere left for them to move on to. Outplacement has become a major consultancy activity and fixed-term contracts have become common.

Charles Handy has used the apt concept of the mercenary to describe the situation:

> . . . we are on hire to the best bidder for as long as we are useful to that bidder and then we hope we will be useful to another bidder. We are mercenaries, all of us, and organisations too. You can see why that might make sense in terms of short-term efficiency but . . . it does not build continuity, any sense of pride or any sense of commitment.

> (Handy, 1997, p. 35)

This sense of insecurity may have become a self-fulfilling prophecy, as the sense seems to have been greater than the substance. Many of the reductions have been made 'painlessly' by the process of retiring people early. A normal male expectation of retirement in the 1980s was to work until the age of 65. It is now the minority who continue until that age, and very large numbers have finished working in their 50s, even their early 50s. Half of all men over 60 are now economically inactive. The proportion of economically inactive men in the age group 45 – 59 is 13.6 per cent, compared with 5.8 per cent of those between 25 and 44. The situation for women is directly opposite, as Table 3.2 demonstrates, with an increase in both age groups, despite the fact that women at the moment can retire on full pension at 60.

Table 3.1 Percentages of economically active men and women in two age groups, 1986/1996

	45–59 men	*45–59 women*	*60+ men*	*60+ women*
1986	88.8	64.0	53.8	19.1
1996	86.4	70.4	50.4	26.6

Source: Central Statistical Office, 1996, p. 84.

The rhetoric surrounding this situation is especially strong in considering careers, which are not what they were. We are now more likely to progress in a variety of roles and situations rather than remaining with one. We are likely to make one or more career transitions, changing to a different career area in the same or a different organisation. Opportunities for moving *up* a career ladder are decreasing as such ladders do not remain in place for very long. Lateral moves and career development through job expansion may be more realistic and attractive alternatives.

Constant organisation change and reshaping makes career planning over the longer term an exercise in fortune telling and in any case there is clear evidence that individuals have not in the past planned their careers to any great extent. The sense of insecurity, however, makes it logical that people take greater responsibility for their own career development, taking account of personal and family needs, including children's education, partner's career, and quality of life. Career development needs to be viewed in the context of the life and development of the whole person and not just the person as employee.

The last two paragraphs are part of the current rhetoric, and make perfect sense, but current practice may not always be like that. Bowden (1996) studied career development for bio-scientists in eight different companies and found traditional systems and traditional values still firmly established in all of them.

If a career is the property of the individual then clearly the responsibility for managing this rests with that person, who should identify career goals, adopt strategies to support them and devise plans to achieve the goal.

There is, however, a considerable amount of research indicating that many people fail to plan. Pringle and Gold (1989) found a lack of career planning in their sample of 50 'achieving' men and women managers. Only around a quarter of people had plans for the future and many identified luck, opportunity or being in the right place at the right time as the reason they had achieved promotions. Harlan and Weiss (1982) found both men and women drifting into positions created through coincidences.

The issue for the personnel manager is how to develop the personnel role in the career area, when many people will be looking beyond the boundary of the present business. Career management that enables people to leave even though the business wishes to keep them is putting the outplacement boot on the other foot.

Demographic factors and the labour market

In 1971, 900 000 babies were born in the United Kingdom; in 1977 there were fewer than 700 000 and the annual birth rate has since failed to reach 800 000. Another way of putting that is to say that the number of 18-year-olds in 1995 was 22 per cent less than six years earlier and has risen only slightly since. Personnel managers knew this phenomenon in the late 1980s as the demographic time bomb. Fewer school-leavers entering the workforce, more being siphoned off into higher education; what would we do?

The time bomb famously failed to explode, partly because of a reduced demand for labour, partly because more women returned to work more quickly after child-bearing and partly because the 18-year-old became a less attractive prospect for employers, who were less inclined to invest time and effort in their training.

Although the time bomb failed to explode when expected, maybe it had a slower-burning fuse than we realised. By the year 2000 there will be about 2.3

million more people aged between 25 and 64 in the labour force than there were in 1995, and about 1.3 million fewer aged under 25. The result is a growing workforce of which an increasing proportion is older.)

Due to the decline in population growth, employers will have to rely more on increasing the readiness of individuals to work. Current civilian activity rates (the proportion of the population in or seeking work) are expected to continue their trend of recent years, which means that while male activity rates decline, female rates will continue to increase. So marked are these effects that almost all of the expected increase in labour supply to the year 2000 is among women, who will then comprise 44 per cent of the labour force. The ability of employers to attract female recruits may well depend on provision of facilities such as crèches, training for returners and career breaks.)

(Demand for labour in manual and unskilled jobs is expected to continue to contract during the 1990s. The growth in demand for labour will therefore be concentrated among the higher skilled occupations, and in particular among professional, scientific and technical occupations.)

University graduates are the main source of supply for these higher skilled occupations, but there is a particular need for two specific types: the technologist, required by the electronic, electrical engineering and computing sectors, and the high flyer, increasingly sought to meet the long-term needs of senior management. Many employers are attempting to solve their problems by broadening the entry requirements, so that now nearly half the vacancies currently advertised are open to all graduates.

Contracts

Part-time working

Although the emphasis of the contract under which we are employed has changed towards that of a contract for performance, the overall, formal title is still the contract of employment.

It has been conventional to think of employment as full-time employment, but gradually a range of alternative forms is emerging. Full-time employment has been in steady decline for some time and the fall in the numbers of people registered as unemployed has been attributable mainly to the increasing number of part-time jobs available.

By 1994 the proportion of jobs in Britain that were part time was 28 per cent and rising, having almost doubled since reaching 15 per cent in 1971. This proportion seems to be greater than that in most other EU countries (*Labour Force Survey*, 1993, p. 119), although there is some difficulty of definition. What is part-time? At the moment the British method of calculation classifies anything less than the normal weekly hours at the place of work to be part time, so a part-timer could be working six hours a week or 35.

It is not long ago that part-time working was generally regarded by employers as a favour granted to the employee, as it was administratively inconvenient and, because of National Insurance costs, relatively expensive. That view has now changed as part-time working has been seen as one of the ways to increase flexibility in the workforce. The change is allied to the increased proportion of women in the workforce: ninety per cent of the recent rise in part-time working has been female. This has coincided with campaigns to enhance the employment opportunities of women, with the Equal Opportunities Commission advocating the development of job sharing. Part-time still, however, lacks the status of full-time employment and it is now more often described as a problem to be overcome rather than an opportunity for flexibility. A proportion of part-time posts gives the management flexibility in staffing the operation and employment opportunity for those who do not seek full-time work. Too many part-time posts destabilise the staffing of the operation through increasing the training costs, requiring close supervision and costly administration while deploying people who have little understanding of the business. At the same time people who are seeking full-time work are denied the opportunity.

Marks & Spencer has long been the standard-setter for part-time working, with 40 years' experience of pursuing it as a positive policy. They now feel that some stores are using too many part timers and have reduced their part-time workforce from eighty per cent to seventy per cent (*The Times*, 14 June 1994, p. 29).

Shift working

Shift working is a practice with which personnel officers are much more familiar. Recently, however, there has been an extension of shift-working patterns and an increase in the number of people working shifts.

> Four million employees in Great Britain work shifts, according to the most recent Labour Force survey. Over a million employees regularly work a two-shift system, around three quarters of a million three-shift or 'continental' patterns and over 300,000 are regular nightshift workers.
>
> (CSO, 1996, p. 32)

In addition to these well-established patterns, which were gradually involving more people, there has also been the considerable growth in shifts at weekends to deal with extended opening hours.

It is striking that a quarter of all those in employment worked on Saturdays only and one in ten on both Saturdays and Sundays. Furthermore this was in the spring, not the frantic run-up to Christmas. The need to stagger working hours grows greater rather than less.

Table 3.2 People usually engaged in weekend working Spring 1993

	Total number	*Percentage of all in employment*
Saturdays only	6 054 000	23.9
Both Saturdays and Sundays	2 543 000	10.0
Sundays only	2 990 000	11.8

Source: Central Statistical Office, 1994, p. 60.

Annual hours

The use of annual hours' contracts has proved to be an effective method of enhancing workforce flexibility. This is most common where there are seasonal fluctuations in demand, or where there is a need for people to work long shifts. The principle of each annual hours' agreement is that the period of time within which full-time employees must work their contractual hours is defined over a whole year, rather than a day, a week or a month; for example, an average 38-hour week becomes 1748 annual hours, assuming five weeks for holiday entitlement and statutory days. Individual employees then negotiate with the employer when they will work their hours, so gaining a greater degree of autonomy and control over their personal lives. In our research we found just over one respondent in ten reporting some form of annualised hours' arrangement working in their business.

The move to annual hours is a significant step for a business to take and should not be undertaken without careful consideration and planning. The benefits to employees is that they contract to provide the employer with a specified number of hours' work per year and then enjoy considerable latitude in deciding when to work those hours, subject to employer needs and priorities. The tangible savings for the business include all those things that are not only measurable but are capable of being measured before the scheme is put in. Other savings such as reduced absenteeism are measurable only after the scheme has been running and therefore cannot be counted as part of the cost justification. A less tangible consideration for both parties is the degree of distance that is introduced between employer and employee, who becomes less a part of the business and more like a sub-contractor. Another problem can be the carrying forward of assumptions from the previous working regime to the new. One agreement is being superseded by another and, as every industrial relations practitioner knows, anything that happened before which is not specifically excluded from a new agreement then becomes a precedent. In October 1996 such a situation had to be resolved by the Court of Appeal:

> In the Court of Appeal's view it was in the nature of such an agreement that it had to be clear and concise in order to be readily understood by all who were concerned with its operation . . . If any topic were left uncovered by the agreement, the natural

inference, in the Court's opinion, was . . . that the topic had been purposefully left out of the agreement on the basis that it was considered too controversial or too complicated to justify any variation of the main terms of the agreement to take account of it.'

(IDS, 1996, p. 3)

Zero hours

The least attractive form of part-time working for most people is where the employee is not guaranteed any hours' work at all, but may be called in if there is a need. This has long been the practice in some areas of employment, such as agency nurses and members of the acting profession, but it has recently been used to some extent in other areas, such as retailing, to deal with emergencies or unforeseen circumstances.

Temporary contracts

Although no contract is permanent, most are semi-permanent in the sense that the intention by both parties is that it should continue indefinitely and it will only be terminated if something goes wrong. It is widely recognised that more people are being employed currently on temporary contracts, either with an explicit termination date or with an understanding that the job is for a limited time without a date being pre-determined. Our research gave some interesting indications about the prevalence of this practice. First, we asked about the proportion of all those employed by the respondent organisations that had temporary contracts. Table 3.3 shows a modest proportion.

Table 3.3 Employees with temporary contracts

	Manual	Non-manual	Managers
Percentage of employees in this category who have temporary contracts	10%	6%	2%

The implication here seems clearly that the numbers of individual people with temporary contracts is small. Another approach is to see the number of establishments having at least one person on a temporary contract.

Table 3.4 Establishments having employees with temporary contracts

	Manual	Non-manual	Managers
Percentage of establishments having at least one employee on a temporary contract	71%	64%	26%

If one asks the question taking a longer retrospective view, and including the possibility of sub-contracting, a different picture emerges in Table 3.5.

Table 3.5 Establishments using temporary staff in previous year

	Manual	Non-manual	Managers
Establishments which have used temporary staff as an alternative to appointing a permanent employee in the previous year	76%	79%	22%
Establishments which have used sub-contracting as an alternative to appointing a permanent employee in the previous year	45%	26%	12%

This suggests that the practice of temporary contracts is much more widespread than the number of individual people affected, and the majority of businesses are likely to use temporary appointments at some time.

That brings us to the question of why employers choose this method. Some of the reasons are obvious. Retail stores need more staff immediately before Christmas than in February and icecream manufacturers need more people in July than November, so both types of business have seasonal fluctuations. Nowadays, however, there is the additional factor of flexibility in the face of uncertainty. Will the new line sell? Will there be sustained business after we have completed this particular contract?

There are a number of ways in which managers find the temporary employee to be an asset. In the early days of the government-funded Youth Training Scheme or YTS, it was referred to as the 'free trial offer'. A manager was able to try out a prospective new employee without any commitment and could decide after a few weeks or months whether the person was appointable or not. This remains a common view, so that the early months are almost a form of probation. Increasingly graduate recruitment by smaller employers operates on this basis.

Research by Geary in the Republic of Ireland found that the use of temporary contracts gave management a greater degree of control over labour. The temporary employee worked under the constant, unspoken threat of dismissal and felt the need to behave with total compliance to avoid this. Managers were uncomfortable about the working relationship, feeling that it was divisive and unfair, but maintained that the main reason for employing temporary staff was their motivation. They put a lot of effort into their work in the hope of being made permanent and were seldom absent. Their presence also improved control over permanent staff:

> Very often when temporary workers felt obliged to do overtime, for instance, so did their permanent counterparts. A shop steward who had worked in the plant for eight years told me of the frustration by many permanent employees, 'People complain to me about the level of overtime. But what can you do when you have 20 temps and 5 permanent people on a line? Temps feel obliged to come in at the weekend and so do permanent people as a result.'

(Geary, 1992, p. 56)

Unpublished research by Curtis (1996) in the West Midlands largely supports Geary's conclusions, but adds the fear by managers of having to go through the trauma of redundancies. Having had to make large proportions of the workforce redundant in previous years, they were anxious to avoid a repetition of that at all costs.

There was also a strong tendency for managers to regard temporary workers quite differently from permanent workers, often not regarding them as employees at all; 'people who are not here'. This is reflected in the relatively low level of benefits available to temporary staff, such as sick pay, holiday pay and the general raft of workers' rights to which they have no statutory entitlement.

Teleworkers

Incomes Data Services report a definition of teleworking based on a survey by Huws (1996) that puts it in two categories:

> The first is the individualised form of teleworking which involves work completed away from the employer's premises, such as home-based teleworking or multi-locational working. The second category is a collective form of teleworking, which covers work completed on non-domestic premises and managed by the employer or third party. This includes call centres and tele-cottages.
>
> (IDS, 1996, p. 2)

The number of people engaged in distance working or teleworking is difficult to estimate, as there are so many people who have always worked in this way, such as sales representatives, and by no means all fall into the stereotype category of someone sitting at a remote computer terminal. The total number is certainly small, but it is also growing, despite some of the drawbacks mentioned in the last chapter. The main advantage, for both the employer and the employee, is the flexibility it provides, but the employer also benefits from reduced office accommodation costs and an increase in productivity.

The scale of tele-cottaging is easier to assess, as there is a Tele-Cottage and Tele-Centre Association, which reports 90 tele-cottages in 1994, and 154 in 1996. A typical centre provides computer and telecommunications equipment for use by its members. The staple activity is usually training in IT skills, but commercial usage by members is also an important feature.

Managing the changes

Managing the changes in approach and method that have been described requires sophisticated understanding by personnel specialists, but it also involves doing some things differently and doing some different things.

Making culture work

As the sense of organisational entity wanes, so the significance of structure and hierarchy wanes also. The relative insecurity and detachment of people doing the work of the business means that the power of these assumptions declines.

The underlying thinking of much personnel work is based on hierarchy – 'Who do you report to . . .? Do you understand the grievance procedure . . .? Do you see where you fit in . . .? Do you feel settled . . .? Do you understand how you might achieve promotion . . .?' Questions like these are implicit in much personnel work. Although they remain relevant and important, they are no longer universally valid and we believe that one of the keys to making contemporary organisations effective is to develop a parallel set of assumptions, without the hierarchical assumption.

If we think of working relationships as *transactions*, this produces a choice, as the working relationship can either be set in a marketplace, where one buys services from another, or it can be set in a hierarchy, where one obtains work from another. The latter is the conventional situation we have had for the last century and the former is more akin to what we had before the emergence of large-scale organisations and what a growing proportion of the workforce experience today.

That simple but profound change of emphasis in thinking about organisation also changes the emphasis of what personnel people do. Fundamental to its operation is the core/periphery type split in the workforce. The core contains all those activities which will be carried out by 'permanent' employees, while the periphery contains activities that will be undertaken by temporary staff, teleworkers, put out to tender by contractors or moved elsewhere in the supply chain. The crucial decisions relate to which activities should be in which area. The core should contain those skills, which are specialised to the business, rare or secret. Logically all the other activities are put in the periphery, but what if there is an unexpected shortage of people to provide peripheral skills? Also, where does the logical balance lie in ensuring the necessary degree of social cohesion among all the people doing the work of the business?

The approach to the core employees is to give them a strong sense of identification with the business and its success, through developing a robust corporate culture, with shared values and reinforced, consistent behaviours. Those on the periphery will need to identify with the culture and respond to its imperatives. That will involve relentless communication and effort to militate against the natural tendency for core people to ignore or exclude those on the periphery.

Personnel expertise is going to be needed at both the strategic and operational level. The key strategic decisions will deal with labour market considerations and ensuring an effective culture. The personnel people will need up-to-date knowledge of the various labour markets with which the business is concerned and a profound understanding of the culture of the business, so that they can ensure the core/periphery balance that will deliver the right standards of quality, productivity and commitment. Although this type of thing has always been present in personnel thinking, it now requires a sharper edge and more thorough analysis. At the operational level personnel specialists will deploy expertise in both transaction and contract negotiation. The traditional focus on recruiting and selecting employees will need to broaden and vary to include deals with teleworkers, suppliers of services, part-time employees and sub-contractors.

Making communication work

Personnel managers have always been concerned with communication, but this is usually limited to communicating with those inside the organisational boundary. Other communication is undertaken by PR and marketing people. If, however, we are losing the sense of organisation as entity and re-discovering organisation as process, then the approach to communication changes. The Roman god Janus was always depicted as facing two ways at once, and the personnel manager must do the same, looking outward as well as inward. The business is part of a *supply chain* and employees, whether core or peripheral, are not insulated from suppliers and customers, but dependent on them and need constant information and explanation about them. They need not to see where they are on the organisation chart, but where they fit in the process.

Teleworkers need to know the pattern of regular links and contacts to be followed. Those newly recruited need the same induction information as regular employees, but as they are working independently with less supervision they will need additional material.

The relentless communication that is needed partly compensates for the declining sense of community that a business has. Some commentators (for example, Devanna and Tichy, 1990) describe the boundary-less organisation. This is taking the concept of the core and periphery workforce rather further, particularly in reference to the supply chain, and loosens many familiar constraints:

> A boundaryless organization eliminates barriers that separate functions (e.g., marketing versus manufacturing), domestic and foreign operations, different levels of work (managerial versus hourly), and between the organization and its customers and suppliers. Boundaryless organizations ensure that the specifications and requirements of the suppliers, producers, and consumers are all well integrated to achieve objectives.
>
> (Milkovich and Boudreau, 1994, p. 123)

Although some needless limitations are taken away, cohesion can also be lost without enhanced communication.

Personnel people will also need to sharpen and broaden their traditional skills in face-to-face interaction, in order to conduct a more diverse range of interviews effectively.

A more subtle aspect of communication will be the need to explain things by the use of metaphors. Charles Handy has become the most widely-read British management guru, not only because of his brilliant insights, but also because of the way in which he has communicated complex explanations by vivid metaphors. Hundreds of MBA students and others have found understanding by such concepts as the spider's web, the Greek temple, the shamrock and the empty raincoat. In a time of rapid change and uncertainty, the personnel specialist needs to disseminate understanding by increasing use of explanatory metaphor.

Staffing the business

The technology of personnel work is most well-developed in the area of finding the people and fitting them to their jobs. We have job analysis, role analysis, job descriptions, job outlines, personnel specifications, training needs analysis and so forth. This is no longer sufficient in the days of core and periphery.

If people are going to be engaged under a variety of different contracts, the conventional sources of supply may be insufficient. Press advertising remains the main medium used by businesses, but there needs to be greater use of agencies and networks. Sub-contractors whose businesses have been set up as a result of company hive-offs or buy-outs are a potential source of services, and professors in well-known departments are increasingly being asked for suggestions and recommendations about ex-students or others who may be available. Information regarding the relevant public and private agencies and consultants may well be something which more personnel managers need to acquire.

The ways of connecting with suppliers of skills, whether they be individuals or agencies, are also becoming differently balanced. Most personnel selection processes assume that the employer is in charge and the applicant dances to the specified tune, by filling in the right form and going through whichever form of selection obstacle course the company specifies. Once we start thinking of transactions as the basis of working relationships, and the work being done by someone off-site, then the method can change, with a greater concern with prior achievements, objectives, target times and costs. Job specification is important in all selection processes but is critical in most forms of geographically and contractually distant working, particularly in sub-contracted work. It is important to set out clearly defined parameters of action, criteria for decision-making and issues which need to be referred back. Person specifications are also crucial since in much distance working there is less scope for employees to be trained or socialised on-the-job. In addition, 'small business' skills are likely to be needed by teleworkers, networkers, consultants and sub-contractors.

All members of the business, whether permanent, temporary, on-site or off will need to develop self-reliance and independence. They can no longer rely on a single employer 'to look after them'. As Kanter has observed, we all need to focus less on employment and more on our employability. Each business will find ways of developing that independence among their people, partly as a way of meeting social obligations and the reasonable expectations of individuals who devote some part of the energies and enthusiasm to their business, but also because the boundary-less organisation works best when people are self-reliant rather than awaiting orders.

Pay and performance

In using consultants, sub-contractors or teleworkers, managers must be able to specify job targets and requirements accurately and to clarify and agree these with the employees or sub-contractors concerned. The personnel manager is the broker of these agreements. Where a fee rather than a salary is paid, the onus is on the manager to ensure the work has been completed satisfactorily. Others may be paid on the basis of time, and it is for the supervisor to ensure the right level and quality of output for that payment. Here we see the risks of sub-contracting too much. It is essential always to retain sufficient expertise in the business in order to manage the expert input coming from outside the business, a matter we return to in Chapter 7.

It is difficult to relate pay levels of peripheral staff to internal systems and one great advantage of extending the variety of peripheral workers is the ability to move outside those constraints, which may no longer be appropriate. It is necessary, however, to guard against the possibility of discriminating against them because of their relative vulnerability.

References

Bowden, V. (1995) *Managing to Make a Difference* (unpublished PhD thesis), Manchester School of Management, UMIST.

Central Statistical Office (1994) *Social Trends*, 24, London: HMSO.

Central Statistical Office (1996) *Social Trends*, 26, London: HMSO.

Clegg, H. A. (1970) *The System of Industrial Relations in Great Britain*, Oxford: Blackwell.

Curtis, S. (1996) *Differences in Conditions of Employment Between Temporary and Permanent Shopfloor Workers in Three Manufacturing Companies*, unpublished MSc. dissertation, UMIST.

Deal, T. E. and Kennedy, A. A. (1982) *Corporate Cultures: the Rites and Rituals of Corporate Life*, Reading, MA: Addison-Wesley.

Geary, J. F. (1992) 'Employment flexibility and human resource management: the case of three electronics plants', *Work, Employment and Society*, 4(2), 157–88.

Handy, C. B. (1985) and (1993) *Understanding Organizations* (3rd and 4th edns), Harmondsworth: Penguin.

Handy, C. B. (1997) 'What's it all for: re-inventing capitalism for the next decade', *Royal Society of Arts Journal*, CXLIV, (5475), 33–40.

Harlan, A. and Weiss, C. L. (1982) 'Sex differences in factors affecting managerial career advancement', in P. Wallace (ed.) *Women in the Workforce*, Boston, MA: Auburn House.

Huws, U. (1996) *Teleworking: An Overview of the Research*, London: HMSO.

Incomes Data Services (1996a) *Teleworking*, IDS Study 616, London: Incomes Data Services Ltd.

Incomes Data Services, (1996b) *Brief 579*, December, London: Incomes Data Services Ltd.

Kotter, J. P. and Heskett, J. L. (1992) *Corporate Culture and Performance*, New York: Free Press.

Leavitt, H. J., Dill, W. R. and Eyring, H. B. (1973) *The Organizational World*, New York: Harcourt, Brace Jovanovich.

McKersie, R. B. and Hunter, L. C. (1973) *Pay, Productivity and Collective Bargaining*, London: Macmillan.

Milkovich, G. T. and Boudreau, J. W. (1994) *Human Resource Management*, Burr Ridge, Illinois: Richard D. Irwin.

Office des Publications Officielles des Communautés Européenes (1993) *Labour Force Survey*, Luxembourg.

Pringle, J. K. and Gold, U. O. (1989) 'How useful is career planning for today's managers?', *Journal of Management Development*, 8(3), 21–6.

Thomas, G. (1973) 'Planning managerial manpower needs', in D. P. Torrington and D. F. Sutton (eds) *Handbook of Management Development*, Epping, Essex: Gower Press.

Thomson, A. W. J. and Murray, V. V. (1976) *Grievance Procedures*, London: Saxon House.

Wilson, D. C. (1993) *A Strategy of Change*, London: Routledge.

4

Devolution of personnel activities

Introduction

There has always been a debate about the division of personnel activities between line managers and personnel specialists (*see*, for example, Northcott, 1945), and the emergence of HRM has given a high profile to this issue. In our current research we found that devolution of more personnel activities was an identified priority for most of our interviewees. They saw this as central to both the viability and effectiveness of personnel work. However, in our previous research in 1984 we also found a strong emphasis on devolving personnel activities to the line (Mackay and Torrington, 1986). This begs the question as to what progress had been made in the intervening period, and the degree to which things had changed in reality. Related to this there is the question of the extent to which personnel specialists ever did carry out some of these activities. Other issues we will explore in this chapter are the attitudes of personnel specialists to devolution, the reaction of line managers and the implementation of devolution.

Definitions and issues

The word 'devolution' has been used in different ways in relation to the personnel function, and in related literature the term has often been confused with decentralisation of personnel activities.

> Devolution of responsibilities from central personnel departments to local level was one of the 'hot' personnel topics of the late 1980s and early 1990s. Our survey of devolution of duties to line management and unit/site personnel staff in 30 organisations provides a snapshot of the extent of devolution and its consequences.
>
> (IRS, 1994, p. 6)

In this particular work, as with others, no differentiation is made between, on one hand, the reallocation of personnel activities from specialists to line managers, and, on the other, the reallocation of activities to other specialists at different levels and/or locations in the organisation. Other writers use the terms 'devolution' and 'decentralisation' as if they were broadly synonymous. Kinnie (1990) provides a useful distinction when he argues that a 'decentralisation of structures is not necessarily associated with a devolution of genuine discretion' (p. 30). Decentralisation then could be used to apply to changes in departmental *structure*, and devolution to changes in the allocation of *authority*. In our work we make a clear distinction. Decentralisation is to do with where personnel specialists are located. Are they centralised in the organisation, so as to provide a strong concentration of skill, expertise and influential advice and services; or are they decentralised by being spread around the business, working very closely with line managers and identifying themselves with individual departments? In contrast, devolution is to do with line managers, as the personnel function transfers some of its responsibilities and activities out of the personnel function altogether so that line managers have a fuller responsibility and scope to do their jobs. As the impact of each of these two approaches to reallocating the work of the personnel department may well be quite different it is important to consider them separately, and hence we will use the term devolution to refer, *only*, to the reallocation of personnel activities to line managers.

Furthermore there is little, if any, distinction in the literature between the devolution of personnel *activities* and the devolution of the associated personnel *budget*. Returning to Kinnie's point about authority – it could be argued that devolving authority necessarily involves devolving decision-making capacity in financial terms. There is an argument, that if associated budgets are not devolved, then it is responsibility that is being devolved, not authority. In Chapter 5 we will consider decentralisation as a separate issue, although, as we found in our research, some establishments will be pursuing both. Figure 4.1 shows how the issues of devolution of activities, devolution of budgets and decentralisation were related in our interview sample.

A further point of clarification is also needed at this point. We are concerned in this chapter with operational issues only, rather than strategy, and again the literature reveals a lack of clarification between the two. For example, Oswick and Grant (1996) with reference to the public sector describe changes in the personnel role. While they provide evidence of devolution to line managers, and other changes, such as a move from specialist to generalist personnel roles, they are not specifically concerned with differentiating between changes at a strategic and an operational level. The literature specifically concerned with line management involvement in operational personnel activities (the most notable exceptions being Hutchinson and Wood, 1995) is very sparse compared with that dealing with both levels together and particularly with that relating purely to strategic activities. Research is gradually increasing in this area, but to date there has been very little emphasis on the processes by which operational tasks have been transferred. Our reasoning behind separating out

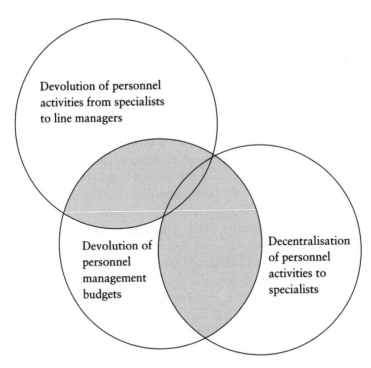

Fig. 4.1 The relationship between devolution of personnel activities, devolution of personnel budgets and decentralisation in our interview sample

strategic and operational activities (as far as this is possible) is that each of these has very different implications for line managers, personnel specialists and the personnel function.

The devolution of personnel activities is often discussed as a generality without any exploration of exactly what is being devolved. One area of exploration needs to be a review of the areas (as in, for example, recruitment, selection, discipline and so on) of activities which are being devolved to the line and the areas which are less often released. As we have already mentioned, the second is concerned with the devolution of associated budgets, and a third aspect is the extent to which the relevant skills and knowledge have been 'devolved' to line managers. In other words, are the capacity and resources to carry out these activities also relocated? We will address each of these issues in this chapter.

The adoption of the term 'devolution' is in itself interesting. While its meaning of delegation of power to another may correspond well with the process of decentralisation – there are at least two hidden meanings when devolution is applied to the line manager. One is that it implies that the power was naturally owned by the party that passed it on (i.e. the personnel function). Yet on the surface there appears to be general agreement that these tasks *should* be owned by the line, or as Armstrong (1989), in reference to a Peat Marwick Report (1984), puts it '. . . the responsibility for personnel has been "returned to the line"' (p. 165). This suggests some inherent contradictions on who really has legitimate authority for these tasks. The second is that it implies a passing down to a 'lower level' rather than merely a redistribution to equals, or indeed those more senior in the hierarchy. This ties in with the emphasis in the limited existing literature on operational issues, that most of the work is related to devolution to supervisor and first line manager level (*see*, for example, Lowe, 1992), rather than more senior levels. While it might be argued that it is these lower levels which have a greater people management responsibility in terms of numbers, this does not necessarily make these levels more important in terms of an ongoing change. Kanter (1989), for example, has identified the importance of senior manager role models in the management of change, and Schein (1991), in relation to implementing TQM, identifies one of the blocks to change as the failure of upper and middle managers to commit themselves to it. In particular, a report by the Cabinet Office (1993) identified lack of support from top management as one of the main barriers to the devolution of responsibilities in relation to human resource development, as they were unclear about what the implications were for them. Indeed, if we accept that devolution to the line is a part of the HRM 'ideal' (*see*, for example, Tyson, 1995; Krulis-Randa, 1990; Kilpatrick *et al.*, 1992) and that, as Storey (1995a) emphasises 'the panoply of HRM technology is seen in its fullest form in the management of managers' (p. 7), we should be very much interested in the devolution of operational personnel tasks to line managers at a senior level.

So we have a further contradiction in the use of the term 'devolution'. We will return to these issues in the interpretation of our research results. The remainder of this chapter focuses on different aspects of our findings in the following order: the extent of devolution; areas of devolution; devolution of budgets; personnel manager attitudes; line manager attitudes; and implementation.

The extent of devolution

The most common role that our questionnaire respondents played in relation to operational personnel tasks was to make decisions in conjunction with line managers, as detailed in Table 4.1. In 11 of the 13 areas we listed, this joint approach attracted more responses than the alternatives. For example, out of a choice of four possible roles, 60 per cent (n = 104) of our respondents identified that this role represented their own activities in relation to discipline and grievance. For training the figure was 55 per cent (n = 94) and for employee relations and involvement it was 54 per cent (n = 94). In only two areas was the

Table 4.1 Answers to the question, 'Which of the following most closely describes the nature of the personnel function's involvement on a day-to-day basis in each of the following areas listed?'

	Makes decisions alone	Makes decisions in conjunction with the line	Provides advice and information/ consultancy	No involvement on a day-to- day basis	Not applicable to this establishment
Recruitment and selection	11% (n = 20)	22% (n = 110)	17% (n = 30)	7% (n = 12)	3% (n = 5)
Job evaluation	13% (n = 19)	41% (n = 59)	25% (n = 36)	7% (n = 10)	14% (n = 21)
Redundancy and dismissal	6% (n = 11)	52% (n = 93)	25% (n = 45)	11% (n = 20)	6% (n = 10)
Appraisals	7% (n = 12)	27% (n = 44)	42% (n = 69)	12% (n = 19)	12% (n = 19)
Quality initiatives	5% (n = 5)	25% (n = 41)	31% (n = 50)	12% (n = 19)	28% (n = 45)
Training	6% (n = 11)	55% (n = 94)	25% (n = 43)	5% (n = 9)	9% (n = 15)
Career planning	5% (n = 8)	43% (n = 72)	28% (n = 46)	4% (n = 7)	20% (n = 33)
Communications	9% (n = 16)	48% (n = 85)	26% (n = 46)	10% (n = 18)	7% (n = 12)
Employee relations/ involvement	16% (n = 28)	54% (n = 94)	23% (n = 40)	5% (n = 8)	3% (n = 5)
Health and safety	12% (n = 20)	34% (n = 55)	26% (n = 42)	12% (n = 20)	16% (n = 27)
Discipline and grievance	10% (n = 17)	60% (n = 104)	24% (n = 42)	4% (n = 7)	2% (n = 3)
Payment administration	28% (n = 49)	28% (n = 48)	17% (n = 29)	10% (n = 18)	17% (n = 29)
Fringe benefits	21% (n = 31)	29% (n = 43)	22% (n = 33)	11% (n = 16)	16% (n = 24)

Row total +100% (+ or – due to rounding).

consultancy/adviser/information provider role the most common, although in every other area (bar one) it was the second most commonly identified role. Much smaller numbers (typically around 10 per cent) indicated that, as personnel professionals, they made operational personnel decisions alone.

This data, then, suggests that while it is least common for personnel professionals to make operational decisions independently, it is most common for them to share joint decision making with the line. The much-vaunted consultancy/adviser role (*see*, for example, Keenoy, 1990; Kilpatrick *et al.*, 1992; Towers Perrin, undated) is not the most common, but is strongly in contention. These figures, of course, only give us a snapshot, at one point in time, of how decisions are distributed between personnel and the line, and do not tell us the extent to which any change has taken place in each of the establishments represented in the sample. The interviews shed more light on the extent of change. Twenty-six of our 30 interview respondents stated that they had a deliberate policy to devolve personnel decisions to the line, and stated that they were actively trying to achieve this. For example, 'there is a deliberate policy to push personnel issues to the line' (from an HR manager in electronics). There was also a clear view, from 12 of the 26 establishments currently devolving, that the personnel function should be an advisory and consultancy role rather than a 'doer' role. For example, 'internally our role is adviser, to provide support and guidance' (from a personnel operations manager in local government). Some gave examples of activities they had previously carried out, and which line managers had now adopted:

> We try to pass down as much as we can to line managers, so that they are looking after the day to day . . . It's not a case of, 'Well I have to discipline someone so I get personnel' – it doesn't work like that anymore. We are very much advisory to them if they need help, and run courses on how to discipline people – but we won't do it for them.
>
> (Personnel and training manager, hospitality)

The initial picture from the interviews is much more positive about the extent of devolution than the questionnaire results suggest, and some personnel managers were able to give clear examples of how things had changed:

> What has happened over the last five years is helping supervisors to deal with what has been traditionally termed as IR issues at the source of the problem. Things like 'I haven't been getting my share of the overtime'. Those things used to come to Personnel and we used to have to arbitrate, investigate. It happens much less now . . . we often say every supervisor, every manager, should be their own personnel person.
>
> (Company personnel manager, food)

However, despite some changes, there appeared to be a distinct difference between espoused intention and the reality of what had been achieved. Many of the comments about devolution were couched in terms of 'trying to', 'beginning to', 'should be' or 'will do' rather than 'are doing' and 'have done'. For example:

> We're trying to push managers to take more and more responsibility for staff unless its difficult – but personnel still seem heavily involved and influential in decisions.
>
> (Head of personnel, retail)

and:

> It's been a sort of tennis really – it has been a deliberate policy to do it (devolution), but a lot of it has bounced straight back, and that's not being critical – it's giving an airing to the context in which we are working.
>
> (Director of HR and corporate affairs, health)

This director spoke of a 'genuine desire, but real practical problems' in achieving devolution. This suggests continued effort but little in the way of actual change. Indeed, one establishment in central government stated that they were not attempting to devolve as they had tried to do this and failed. One explanation for this may relate to the attitudes behind the process. Our interviewees frequently used phrases such as 'pushing down' personnel activities to the line. This sounds more like dumping tasks on those with lower status rather than sharing tasks with equals, and certainly contains no suggestion that these line managers will be empowered. We will return to this point when we consider the attitudes of personnel professionals in more detail.

It is useful at this stage to make some comparisons with our results in 1984. Of the 30 interviews completed at that time it is interesting that exactly the same proportion 87 per cent (n = 26) stated that they were in the process of devolving (n = 16) or had devolved 33 per cent (n = 10) some personnel activities to the line. It is also interesting that the relationship of the interview data with the questionnaire data was similar in that the interviews provide a more positive view of the extent of devolution. For example, the most common area to have been devolved was changes in work organisation 23 per cent (n = 80), training 18 per cent (n = 63) and employee relations 16 per cent (n = 55). The full details are shown in Table 4.2. Either, very selective areas only, have been devolved, or the process is in its early stages – or both. The interviews certainly provide support for the view that the process is in its early stages. The question is – if devolution was in its early stages in 1984, why does it still appear to be in its early stages in 1995? Is devolution nothing new, but an ongoing saga of trying to persuade the line to take on more operational personnel responsibilities? (if indeed the push is coming from the personnel function) and why has there been so little success? Is it destined never to be successful? Or alternatively, is it an incremental process which has no finite end (unless a personnel department no longer exists) and involves the gradual moving of boundaries in one direction or another? The idea of an ongoing, long-term incremental

Table 4.2 Results from our research in 1984. Answers to the question, 'Over the last three years, has line management taken over more of the former role of the personnel function? And, if so, in which of the following areas?'

Areas of personnel management	Yes (%)	n	No (%)	n
Manpower planning	13	44	1	3
Training	18	63	1	4
Appraisal	16	55	1	3
Payment administration	3	11	1	4
Employee relations	16	55	1	3
Redundancy and dismissal	9	30	1	4
Changes in work organisation	23	80	1	3
Recruitment and selection	16	55	1	4
Organisation and management development	10	36	1	3
Job evaluation	6	22	1	3
Fringe benefits	4	13	1	4
Discipline/grievance	15	52	1	4
Health, safety and welfare	13	47	1	4
New technology	14	50	1	3

Multi response Base = 350.
(Adapted from Mackay and Torrington, 1986, p. 164.)

approach can be supported in two ways by our current research data. First, from the interviews where a gradual process of 'handholding' and 'support' was explained:

> . . . the lid is off – they are talking about 'can I sack this guy or what can I do?' in an open forum whereas before they were never encouraged to talk about those issues. It was just 'I've got a problem – here you are Personnel – tell me what to do. But now the focus is going back to them.
>
> (Divisional personnel adviser, insurance)

and:

> Our service is an advisory service rather than a 'do it' service. The responsibility is theirs to actually manage the people . . . so the ownership is with them, and I see us as there to help them solve their problems. It's taken a while to get *that* far.
>
> (HR manager, electronics)

Second, the emphasis on joint decision making in the questionnaire could be explained as a stage in progressing from personnel taking a lead in operational decision making and problem solving to the line taking the lead and personnel acting as an adviser, to be consulted when needed.

Devolution in different areas

We have drawn a broad picture of the extent of devolution, and before progressing to discuss the devolution of budgets and attitudes to devolution we will review some more detailed comparisons of the extent to which different areas of personnel activity have been devolved. As shown in Table 4.1, the areas where the greatest number of personnel managers continue to make operational personnel decisions *alone* are payment administration, fringe benefits and employee relations/involvement. If columns one and two are combined (direct involvement in decision making) and are compared with the sum of columns three and four (indirect, or no, involvement) a slightly different picture emerges. Direct involvement in recruitment and selection decision making is greater than in any other area 72 per cent (n = 130) and is over three times greater than indirect or no involvement. Employee relations and involvement is a close second 70 per cent (n = 122) almost equalled by discipline and grievance 70 per cent (n = 121). In both these areas direct involvement is over twice as common as indirect or no involvement. Training 61 per cent (n = 105) is similarly placed, although the comparison is not so pronounced with redundancy and dismissal 58 per cent (n = 104).

What explanations can we find for this pattern, and how does it compare with the pattern we found in 1984? We asked a different question in 1984 than we did in 1994, as shown in Table 4.2, so we cannot make direct comparisons, but we can still look at the data together. The areas where the line had least often taken over the former role of the personnel function were payment administration 3 per cent (n = 11), fringe benefits 4 per cent (n = 13) and job evaluation 6 per cent (n = 22). At the other end where the line had most often taken over the former personnel role were changes in work organisation 23 per cent (n = 80), training 18 per cent (n = 63), very closely followed by appraisal, employee relations' recruitment, selection, discipline and grievance (in that order).

The most consistent message that comes from both sets of data is that the personnel function is very likely to retain direct influence in operational reward issues. The emphasis on devolving training, employee relations, recruitment, selection, discipline and grievance in 1984 does not appear to translate into greater devolution in these areas in 1994. Indeed, these are (primarily) the areas where the personnel function seems to retain most decision-making control. There are three possible explanations for this. One is that the emphasis on devolving these areas was greater than it is now, that there is currently less push to devolve these areas, and that indeed there may have been some reining back. However, the interview information we have (albeit limited) on the devolution of different areas would not support this conclusion. A second explanation is that much effort has been made over the years to devolve these areas but that practical and attitudinal barriers to this have resulted in little progress being made – we cannot specifically corroborate or refute this possibility, but we do have further questionnaire data which offers some support. We broke down personnel and line activities into more detail in the employee relations area and Table 4.3 indicates that personnel involvement increases in accordance with the potential gravity of the activity – thus less involvement in verbal warnings and greater involvement in dismissals. This suggests a perceived *practical* need for involvement to ensure compliance with legislation. In Table 4.4 we also provide more detail on involvement in recruitment and selection activities. One key message that can be drawn from this table is that personnel involvement varies with the nature of the specific task. Interestingly, using comparisons for non-manual workers, the personnel function interviewed job candidates in 69 per cent (n = 146) of our establishments, but were only involved in the selection decision in 29 per cent (n = 62) of establishments, and only involved in deciding whether there is a vacancy to be filled in 23 per cent (n = 49) of establishments. It is hard to find a *convincing* practical explanation for this, although an *attitudinal* one could be suggested which is exemplified by an interview comment from the retail HR manager of a building society: 'Eighteen months ago we put recruitment out to the line – something we'd jealously hung on to in HR'. In other words, personnel professionals *like* interviewing and don't want to give it up. The fact that these areas were perceived as the most important areas of personnel contribution to the business, both in 1984 and 1994, can also be interpreted as giving some weight to this view. The third, perhaps most likely explanation, is that these were areas that were more heavily controlled by the personnel function to start with. In other words we cannot assume that the base levels of personnel vs. line involvement are the same for each area, therefore we cannot assume that no progress has been made. Indeed, if we consider how personnel managers allocated their time in 1984 it is these areas that are given priority. We thus have some support for the third explanation and cannot refute the second, so the reality may well be a combination of these. Our discussion of comparisons between different activity areas has led us to the attitudes of personnel specialists to devolution, which we will explore further when we have reviewed the devolution of associated budgets.

Table 4.3 In what way is the personnel function involved in any of the following forms of disciplinary action?

	Acting independently of line management	Acting in collaboration with line management	Provides advice and information to line management	Acting in response to line managers' requests	Not involved	Total respondents
Counselling	14% (n = 28)	38% (n = 74)	33% (n = 63)	8% (n = 16)	7% (n = 13)	n = 194
Verbal warnings	1% (n = 1)	33% (n = 65)	52% (n = 103)	5% (n = 10)	10% (n = 20)	199 cases
Written warnings	1% (n = 1)	48% (n = 96)	45% (n = 89)	3% (n = 5)	4% (n = 8)	n = 199
Financial penalties	4% (n = 7)	49% (n = 83)	20% (n = 33)	5% (n = 9)	22% (n = 38)	n = 170
Suspension	2% (n = 4)	60% (n = 116)	24% (n = 46)	4% (n = 8)	10% (n = 20)	n = 194
Transfer demotion	1% (n = 2)	60% (n = 116)	24% (n = 46)	5% (n = 10)	9% (n = 18)	n = 192
Dismissals	3% (n = 5)	64% (n = 127)	27% (n = 54)	4% (n = 7)	3% (n = 5)	n = 198

Table 4.4 A comparison of the personnel role in different aspects of recruitment and selection

Aspect I: Answers to the question, 'Who makes the decision to recruit for the various categories of jobs? In other words who decides if there is to be a vacancy that is to be filled?'

Who is involved in the decision?	Manual	Non-manual	Managers
Immediate manager	42% (n = 62)	38% (n = 70)	29% (n = 54)
Level of authority above immediate manager	47% (n = 70)	56% (n = 104)	63% (n = 118)
Personnel	23% (n = 34)	25% (n = 47)	30% (n = 55)
Other	5% (n = 7)	6% (n = 11)	8% (n = 14)

Only for those establishments having a personnel function
186 of the 188 establishments with a personnel function answered each box (Manual – 148)

Aspect II: Answers to the question, 'Who generally interviews candidates for the different categories of jobs?'

Who is involved in interviewing?	Manual	Non-manual	Managers
Immediate manager	82% (n = 121)	79% (n = 147)	66% (n = 124)
Level of authority above immediate manager	25% (n = 37)	42% (n = 79)	66% (n = 123)
Personnel	55% (n = 82)	75% (n = 140)	77% (n = 143)
Assessment centre process	3% (n = 5)	6% (n = 12)	22% (n = 41)
Other	1% (n = 2)	1% (n = 2)	5% (n = 9)

187 respondents answered this question (Manual – 148)

Aspect III: Answers to the question, 'Who generally makes the final selection decision for the different categories of job?'

Who is involved in making the decision?	Manual	Non-manual	Managers
Immediate manager	62% (n = 91)	53% (n = 99)	32% (n = 59)
Level of authority above immediate manager	17% (n = 25)	24% (n = 44)	47% (n = 87)
Personnel	22% (n = 32)	32% (n = 59)	28% (n = 52)
Panel	17% (n = 25)	29% (n = 53)	39% (n = 73)
Other	0	0	2% (n = 3)

186 establishments responded to this question (Manual – 147)

Devolution of associated budgets

This was not an area about which we enquired in the questionnaire, but after a number of interviews the allocation of personnel budgets emerged as a key issue. We have analysed the interview information which we had collected in this area, and one of our conclusions has to be that further, more detailed research is required to understand, more fully, the impact of budget allocation. We began our analysis in this area by trying to determine whether personnel budgets were devolved, or not, in each interview establishment, and quickly found that this was not a question which could be answered in a yes/no fashion. First, we needed a view on what constituted 'personnel budgets', and as shown in Figure 4.2, this varied quite widely. Most establishments at which we discussed budgets distinguished between 'personnel' and 'training' budgets, and often treated the two quite differently with the training budget more often being devolved. Second, there was a difference in the nature of the budgets being devolved – whether the budgets were associated with outside spend (e.g. advertising costs, cost of an external training course) or whether they included internal costs (e.g. personnel staff time, or specific events such as training courses which are a representation of this). At one extreme the personnel function has no budget whatsoever, and although this only applied on one of our interview establishments, three others were close. In these cases it was recognised that line departments could buy their personnel services externally, although this had never yet happened. At the other extreme the personnel department holds all funds relating to personnel and training on behalf of line managers. A third dimension was whether, given the first scenario above, line departments paid the personnel department for personnel services specifically requested and contracted; or whether they were required to pay a general sum related to the size of the line department and sometimes specific costs which had been incurred on their behalf. A fourth dimension was whether the line department held the staffing budget for their own department, and hence the extent of flexibility they had in making staffing choices.

The above characteristics emerged from our research interviews and require much more attention than we have been able to give them, in terms of the way that each impacts on the autonomy and authority of line managers in making personnel decisions. Even in terms of the characteristics we have identified there was an array of different arrangements and combinations. What we can do with our interview data is to broadly group the way personnel budgets were allocated in terms of whether they were heavily devolved; strongly retained by the personnel function; or presented a very mixed picture. Of the 22 establishments where we discussed budgets we found that eight were heavily devolved (six of the eight being public sector); ten were strongly retained by the personnel function (seven of the ten being public sector); and four which presented a

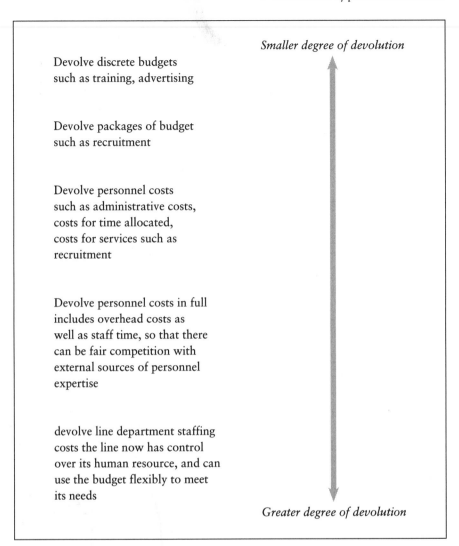

Fig. 4.2 Defining personnel budgets: a continuum

mix (all private sector). It was noticeable that those establishments who had demonstrated a greater degree of devolution of personnel activities all had either heavily devolved or mixed budgeting arrangements.

The devolution of budgets was sometimes seen as a pressure for the personnel function to work more closely with the line – for example, ensuring that they understand the line's priorities when they formed and resourced training plans. Another impact was the identification of the need to market the personnel function and its services. We will look at both these implications later in the book, particularly in Chapter 8 on internal marketing and the HR function.

However, even when budgets were devolved there were indications from three establishments of mechanisms that the personnel function used to retain control of personnel activities. Two respondents spoke of offering set 'packages' of personnel services to line managers which forced them to buy some things they didn't want in order to get the things that they did want to buy. As one explained:

> . . . they do actually value our service quite highly, which we need them to do of course, because otherwise in theory they could buy it outside . . .

and when asked whether there was anything to stop them doing that:

> No, but we do point out to them that they would lose the payroll service at the same time, and do they really not want their employees to get paid on the nth of the month in advance, because nobody else will offer the same capabilities. I seem to recall one business thought about it, and very fast changed their minds when they realised what it implied, because it's a bundled service.

> (HR adviser, services)

Attitudes of personnel specialists to devolution

It is always difficult in organisations to identify from where a particular idea originated, and there is some research to suggest that devolution is being imposed on the personnel function from senior levels in the organisation (*see*, for example, Wilkinson *et al.*, 1994). In other words are personnel activities being *given* away or *taken* away? Although we did not ask directly about where the pressure for devolution was coming from, our interviewees (with a few exceptions) spoke of the transfer of activities in very positive terms and appeared enthusiastic. No one suggested outright that they did not agree with the idea, and some spoke of advantages in terms of the release of time for more appropriate activities such as strategic involvement. There was no direct mention from our interviewees in 1995 (as there was in 1984) that the objective of the personnel department 'should be to eliminate itself' (group personnel director, mechanical engineering) (Mackay and Torrington, 1986, p. 165). However, there was a view from one personnel manager who agreed that this was a possibility, and from some that the size of the function should be smaller, and run at minimum cost. Others refuted the idea that the personnel function would be 'doing itself out of a job'. Predominant views centred around the refocusing of the personnel role – principally into the strategic arena, although consultancy and monitoring roles were mentioned. Indeed, there were indications that the operational role was being rejected in order that the personnel function could be more heavily involved in what was perceived as higher status strategic activity. The word 'push' was often used in explaining efforts to devolve – such as 'a deliberate policy to push personnel issues to the line' (HR manager, electronics).

The word 'delegate' was also used, perhaps indicating something sufficiently unimportant that it could be passed on to others. Similarly one personnel manager reported that:

> We try to *pass down* as much as we can to the line managers, so they are looking after the day to day.
>
> (Personnel and training manager, hospitality)

and:

> There is definitely an intention to move it (operational personnel tasks) *down the line* as far as possible.
>
> (Personnel adviser, central government)

The operational–strategic trade-off is highlighted in the following comments made by a regional personnel advisor, communications, when asked if devolution made the personnel function redundant:

> No, because then I think we can concentrate on the important things like strategic issues.

and:

> Want to get into a position where my role is purely supportive and don't have to be involved in the detailed man management stuff – what we should be doing is (strategy stuff basically).
>
> (HR manager, electronics)

who later went on to say:

> We're moving from a department which does things to a department which influences, a driving force, to be involved in the actual business issues rather than a welfare function.

and one personnel manager, TEC, spoke of:

> Desperately trying to remove the administrative side and desperately trying to concentrate on strategic things.

There were other interviewees who identified devolution as a mechanism to rid the personnel department of its administrative image. While the attitudes of interviewees appeared positive, only eight interviewees (out of 16 with whom we discussed rationale for devolution) expressed it as a better way to manage, but only one talked of a more strategic philosophy behind it. In five cases interviewees identified devolution as a pragmatic response to changing circumstances – for example a reduced personnel function, or geographical changes. This practical response to a reduced personnel function is illustrated by the following quote from a HR manager in a second electronics company:

> The way that we see ourselves is that we are consultants to the line manager, because

we are not going to have the administration capacity or the staffing levels to solve everybody's problems – so the line managers will *have* to do it – what we will be able to do is to advise and consult on a lot of issues.

So, on the surface, devolution did not appear to be perceived by our interviewees as a direct threat (although the views of the staff working for them may see things completely differently). They either viewed it as an opportunity, or identified it as a pragmatic response to changing circumstances and were 'making the best of it'. If we look under the surface and, whatever the impetus for devolution, ask the question, 'are personnel managers letting go or holding on?' there is evidence to suggest that personnel managers have a schizophrenic attitude to devolution – being prepared to give some things away and not others. First, this schizophrenic attitude comes across in the interview comment (previously quoted on p. 55) where the HR Manager, having explained a deliberate policy to devolve, talks about jealously holding on to recruitment. It is understandable that personnel specialists who have developed and enjoy using a specific skill, such as interviewing, are sometimes less than happy to give this up to replace it with exercising another skill – consultancy and facilitation – with which they may be less experienced and confident.

Second, personnel managers seemed very keen to rid themselves of administrative chores and of some operational activities, but were much less keen to divest themselves of the associated budgets. In other words they were happy to hand over the responsibility for personnel activities, but not the authority, in that they wanted to retain control. This was not expressed directly, but is an interpretation of relevant comments. We have already discussed the wide variety of arrangements which are used in budget distribution, but in broad terms our interviewees who remained heavily centralised provided us with reasons why they *could not* devolve the budgets. These were most often expressed in terms of being too small to divide and more especially that it was not cost effective to allow managers to spend their budgets separately (say for recruitment advertising) when better discounts could be obtained if the services were purchased centrally by the personnel function. However, other establishments had found practical ways around these problems, and one personnel manager (TEC), having moved to a devolved system of budgeting, identified the old system as a 'real policing thing'. In one establishment where the personnel function held the personnel and training budgets, and the departments were backcharged for these services, the head of personnel (retail) stated that this system enabled the personnel officers to check out the departments plans, and, another personnel operations manager (local government) stated that as the personnel function held the budgets it enabled them to 'look at the bids for training and measure it against the department's need, strategy, or whatever'. One regional stores personnel manager (retail) asserted that she would not favour devolved budgets, as presently the personnel and training budget which she held was the largest and this 'gives me great power'. In Figure 4.3 we identify four different models of devolution which result from varied combinations of devolving activities and devolving authority.

One more subtle approach to these dilemmas was giving things away on the surface, but underneath retaining control. In an establishment where personnel and training budgets had been devolved to the line the HR manager commented:

> They think they've got control, but we can use our expertise as well. Enables us to be in quite a powerful position.

> (Head of personnel, retail)

This concept of *appearing* to give operational personnel away to the line, as opposed to *really* giving it away, is reminiscent of Lowe's (1992) comments in relation to a group of first line supervisors who were supposed to be taking on a personnel role. He argued that devolution could not happen in practice as the

Model 1   Line driven

	Authority	Responsibility
Line	✓	
Personnel		✓

Model 2   Personnel driven

	Authority	Responsibility
Line		✓
Personnel	✓	

Model 3   Consultancy model (or absence model)

	Authority	Responsibility
Line	✓	✓
Personnel		

Model 4   Abdication model

	Authority	Responsibility
Line		
Personnel	✓	✓

Fig. 4.3 Modelling operational activities

line managers in question were unprepared, in terms of background, training and experiences to take on these responsibilities.

Attitudes of line managers to devolution

As we did not speak directly with line managers in our research, the information we have on line manager attitudes is mediated by the perspective of the personnel managers whom we interviewed. Line managers were sometimes described as reacting in either of two ways – either feeling liberated by having control over personnel activities, or feeling dumped on, for example:

> Some managers feel liberated because they don't have to come running to personnel to get everything done.
>
> (Personnel manager, TEC)

Alternatively, some line managers felt that personnel was not their job and that they had not developed the skills to carry out the activities which had been passed over to them. In explaining why one establishment was not pursuing the devolution route the personnel manager explained:

> No, mainly because of a reluctance on the part of line managers to take those responsibilities on, also I think because of an awareness of the fact that they may not have been provided with the capacity, ability . . .
>
> (Personnel manager, central government)

and similarly:

> Yes, a few of them are apprehensive because of the counselling/coaching skills which are at the forefront now in a lot of what goes on. Those who don't have it or have an inclination to have it – they were selected on their technical merit rather than their people orientation.
>
> (Divisional personnel adviser, insurance)

> Some accept it more readily than others . . . some have grasped the responsibility and responded to it positively – they welcome our guidance but don't want us to interfere anymore. But some still say 'Oh that's personnel's job'.
>
> (HR manager, electronics)

A lack of enthusiasm on behalf of many line managers was portrayed:

> We're trying to push managers to take more and more responsibility for staff.
>
> (Head of personnel, retail)

and:

> We keep trying to move it (devolution) but we do meet some resistance – 'why aren't you doing that for me? – I've got a problem, why can't you sort it out for me?'.
>
> (Personnel adviser, central government)

Guest (1987) makes a critical point when he talks of the 'attitudes and behaviours' of line managers and the need for them to recognise the importance of the human resource and the need for them to 'engage in practices which reflect this understanding is crucial'. So in other words it is insufficient for line managers to accept that a greater range of people management activities are their responsibility. The attitudes they have to this, reflected in the way that they carry it out, are critical. Line manager attitudes seemed to be one of the reasons why, in some cases, operational activities had been devolved, but the personnel function was still heavily involved, for example:

> . . . so it ends up that personnel do the chasing – e.g. job descriptions – managers don't do it, they don't see the value.
>
> (HR manager, electronics)

One manager spoke of 'trying to get the line to own issues and sort them out' (Retail stores personnel manager).

So how representative is this picture of many line managers being unwilling or unable to take on devolved personnel responsibilities? Would all line managers have the same view? Similar conclusions were drawn by Hutchinson and Wood (1995), who included both line managers and personnel managers in their study of 27 different organisations, and Lowe (1992), who used a case study approach involving supervisors, production managers and personnel managers. There is little work purely on the perspective of line managers, with Holden and Roberts, (1996), for example, being one of the few exceptions.

Their work, however, looks very broadly at changes in the middle manager role, while including in that some aspects of devolution. They found that although many managers mentioned the positive aspects of devolution, there was an air of scepticism towards these changes as 'being dumped on' and 'cost-cutting'. They felt pressure from managing these issues within very tight budgets and a recognition that when the pressure is on 'luxuries' like HRM are the things that get lost.

One Masters research study which specifically focused on line managers' responses to devolution was carried out by Leach (1995) whose case study covered three quite different directorates in a local government organisation which had consciously pursued a policy of devolution of HRM. She found that although there were some line managers who were either unaware that they should be taking on more personnel responsibilities, or who felt that this did not impact on their job, the majority of line managers welcomed the involvement and control that the transfer of these responsibilities gave them. The benefits of devolution were identified by most, who felt that they had more ownership of personnel matters and were able to achieve speedier decisions – although the take-up of personnel responsibilities varied widely. Many of the line managers interviewed did not feel that they were competent in some personnel activities, particularly counselling, and although there were appropriate courses available in the organisation the managers argued that they had not had time to attend. One senior manager who was interviewed felt that not all managers would be able to achieve the required competence in personnel activities, as they had been chosen on technical merit rather than on any other criteria.

The line managers did not generally feel empowered by the changes, because they felt constrained by other characteristics of the way that the organisation functioned. Each directorate adopted personnel practices relevant to the culture of that directorate and personnel decisions in all directorates generally appeared to be governed by the constraints of short-term financial outcomes. Some managers were concerned that devolution gave the potential for inconsistency and inequality in the way that employees were treated.

Budgets had been devolved in this organisation in a bid to improve the financial standing of the organisation, among other things. Indeed, two-thirds of the managers interviewed felt that the devolution of budgets had been one of the biggest factors in encouraging them to take on more responsibility for their staff. Leach (1995) states that:

> Many felt that taking on more responsibility for their employees was almost a side effect of having devolved budgets . . . The devolution of budgets was also seen to be the most significant change in their role in recent years. Managers immediately identified with this change in their role, but when asked how their role had changed in managing human resources they could not easily identify such a significant change. (p. 85)

The relationship perceived by line managers between devolution of budgets and devolution of personnel activities mirrors the conclusions from our own research.

Implementation

The way in which devolution is implemented appears to have an impact on its success, and we found that speed of implementation, training and coaching support, practical support tools, and organisation culture were all important variables. The speed of change appeared to be a critical issue, for example:

> It (devolution) was rapidly established but we had line managers who weren't equipped to deal with it – so we backtracked – so now we have much more of a consensus co-operative approach rather than just handing it over to them.
>
> (Personnel manager, central government)

and:

> In the past personnel would do everything – line management wouldn't even be involved in selecting staff, except external candidates, and then personnel would put

forward a favoured candidate. We're moving more towards enabling managers to do selection and recruitment, but it's very much a handholding exercise. We are going slowly in some areas.

(Divisional personnel adviser, insurance)

There's a mixed response – some are cautious about taking on new responsibilities, but some are very keen. It's being done on a gradual basis – there's inevitable caution about taking on something new. More of a management culture is developing in divisions which will embrace this. Budgets are devolved alongside and they will be accountable.

(Personnel manager, police)

and:

There used to be a personnel department that delivered things, that actually do things for them and sort out problems – so there's still a bit of a *dependency culture*.

Those personnel departments which had attempted to manage the change slowly and provide considerable support had made greater progress towards devolution. The support often came in the form of 'toolkits', frameworks, guidelines and telephone 'helplines'. But whatever had been provided there was sometimes a recognition that more could have been done:

There was a lot more we could have done in hindsight in terms of frameworks, toolkits etc.

(Head of retail HR, financial services)

While many personnel managers talked about the need to provide training to support managers in taking on their new role, the concept of coaching and 'handholding' was less common. However, this seemed to be associated with those establishments which had made greater progress towards devolution:

It works (devolution) to a greater or lesser extent depending on the receptivity of people. What you've got to do is coach people to do it – but then it's part of their responsibility, part of the enhancement of their own role that they should be responsible for carrying it through . . . it's quite a culture change

(Regional stores personnel adviser, retail)

In looking back over the previous quotes it is interesting to see how often the word 'culture' appears. For the purposes of this book we are defining organisational culture as 'the pattern of basic assumptions that a given group has invented, discovered or developed, in learning to cope with its problems of external adaption and internal integration (Schein, 1984), or put more superficially, 'the way we do things around here'. We found that organisational culture was important in two respects. First, that those establishments where there had previously been a strong 'people management' culture had generally made more progress in devolving personnel tasks. Second, the recognition by many interviewees that devolution was, in fact, a major culture change. Yet, bar two clear exceptions, it was not treated or introduced as such. The question is 'why'? One reason may be found in Leach's work, where the same situation pertains. She found that line managers had found their own rationale for devolution, and had fitted this in with their view of the world so it appeared to have benefits for them. As a consequence different line managers had a different understanding of why devolution had been introduced, yet on the whole they were favourable to devolution because they had put their own interpretation on it. Leach argues that this may be a better way forward than to impose a rationale that some line managers may reject. However, this lack of clarity also brings problems.

Leach reports that not only were there very different interpretations of the perceived purpose of devolution, but also that the personnel duties which had been handed over to line managers had never been made explicit, and it was left to managers' own interpretations of what they thought was appropriate for them to take on. We found the same picture, as demonstrated by the following:

> I think you've got to have some sort of contract with the line as to where responsibility lies and what we're finding – we haven't formulated this at all.
>
> (HR director, pharmaceuticals)

This lack of clarity is bound to be a barrier to devolution, and indeed was also recognised as such by Hutchinson and Wood. It could be argued that internal marketing has a role to play here.

Conclusions

Our main findings in the area of devolution of operational personnel activities are that personnel managers appeared, on the surface, to be generally enthusiastic about this transfer of activities. They often saw it as an opportunity to swap operational tasks for perceived higher value strategic involvement, and indeed, there is some evidence, which we present in Chapter 6, to demonstrate that they had achieved a greater involvement than previously in the strategic area. This can be construed as a deliberate attempt to reposition personnel specialists and the personnel function within the organisation. If this perspective is accepted, the trend towards devolution does not necessarily reflect the actual value of operational personnel activities to the organisation, but rather the perceived value to the personnel function. Strategic activities rather than administrative, operational activities and employee support services may be viewed as heightening the visibility, status and centrality of the personnel function. We are not suggesting the personnel specialists can choose their activities at will, as there is much evidence both in the literature and within our current research to suggest that the personnel function does what it is *allowed* to do.

However, the current environment provides the opportunity for a shift, as we explore in Chapter 6.

In contrast to a general enthusiasm for devolution, some concerns were expressed. There were indications that the 'letting go' of some operational activities was difficult, not necessarily for the more senior specialists who we interviewed, but for those professionals lower down the hierarchy. It is often argued that in a change situation that it is easier to take on new tasks and responsibilities rather than let go of the old ones. If personnel specialists have enjoyed recruitment interviewing, hands on training, employee counselling and so on, it may be threatening to be told that this is no longer of value and that their role is to be reconstructed as an internal consultant and facilitator. From doing familiar tasks with confidence, personnel specialists may be faced with a new role for which they may have had little preparation, and about which they may feel very uncertain. Not many of these middle range staff are likely to feel excited by the pull of strategic involvement, as such involvement for them, would probably be very limited. Those who have been in the personnel function for a longer period, who completed their professional qualification some time ago, or who have worked their way up the hierarchy from administrative positions are most vulnerable when faced with these changes. Continuous professional development may have a role to play here.

Other concerns centre around the loss of skills. Although professional qualifications are a sound basis on which to operate, there is an argument that if these skills are not practised with some regularity (particularly those involved with changing legislation), they will deteriorate. Perhaps more fundamentally, there are concerns, almost unspoken, about loss of control and power. This was particularly related to letting go of personnel and training budgets, and it appeared that barriers were erected to this aspect of devolution, under the guise of impracticality, as a protective measure.

This leads us to question the genuine desire of personnel specialists to devolve operational activities. Although our interviewees *appeared* enthusiastic about the proposition, there were underlying concerns which occasionally broke the surface. We could argue that our interviewees were putting a brave face on a change which was forced upon them by a shrinking personnel function and by pressure from the top of the organisation due to the march towards 'decentralising' responsibility and accountability. This perspective could be supported by the fact that very few of our interviewees made any attempt to justify devolution in terms of an underpinning philosophy, although a significant minority did see it as a 'better way to manage'. However, it could be argued that the senior managers who we spoke to were genuinely enthusiastic about devolution, because this change in the nature of the function would only enhance their own status, and indeed actively managing a shrinking personnel function could well be career enhancing. If we follow the second scenario, the apparent schizophrenic attitudes to devolution may well reflect the desire to rid their departments of mundane operational tasks, but retain the associated budgets in order to retain power and control. In other words, give away the day-to-day responsibility, but retain the authority.

In spite of the deliberate intent to devolve in the establishment, we found that progress was mixed, and generally limited – those establishments where greater progress had been made tended to have introduced devolution more slowly and provided significant support to managers in the form of guidelines, training course, toolkits, helplines and coaching. Alternatively, or in addition, they also tended to be establishments where there had previously been a culture of 'people management'.

We now turn to the perspective of the line manager – the other side of the devolution equation. Line managers also presented a mixed response to devolution – most seeing potential benefits, but, at the same time, expressing concerns that they had not developed the required skills, and had not been given time to do this. A few felt liberated, but most felt dumped on – perhaps understandable given the degree of work intensification to which managers are subject. However, if line managers have a degree of control over personnel budgets this appears to induce them to view devolution in a more favourable light. It could therefore be argued that they have an instrumental approach to devolution.

Given the above findings it appears that devolution will be an uphill struggle in most organisations, unless devolution of tasks is accompanied by budgetary devolution. If managers do gain such controls, one concern is that human resources will be managed in line with short-term priorities (for example, meeting annual budget targets), rather than a long-term strategic vision. This point has been well made by Armstrong (1991). The implication of this is that managers will be guided by business operational needs in their HR decisions rather than by any long-term HR strategy. As a consequence, different departments will follow different practices, meeting their particular needs (*see*, for example, Leach, 1995) and thus inconsistency reigns, and makes the organisation open to legal challenge. Personnel specialists may support devolution as it allows them greater opportunities to be involved in the *development* of HR strategy. Given this, it is paradoxical that devolution also has the consequence that the *implementation* of that HR strategy is made, almost, impossible.

Given this potential dilemma personnel specialists may search for alternative ways forward. One way forward is for the personnel function to produce manuals and procedures to be followed by the line to ensure consistency, and then monitor activity closely. We did find some evidence of this approach, as elsewhere (*see*, for example, IRS, 1997). This however smacks of the old 'policeman role' which the function seems desperate to avoid, and also backs line managers into a corner, from which the only escape is probably deception, and keeping the personnel function at arm's length.

A more positive way forward takes us back to Guest's (1987) comments about the importance of line manager attitudes and behaviours which reflect an understanding of HRM, and perhaps this is where effort should be concentrated. A greater degree of direct training is obviously one option, although this may be problematic for already overbusy line managers, and not necessarily a successful method of attitude change. Perhaps a more successful approach lies in increasing the ownership that line managers have of the organisation's HR strategy. This implies participation, which in turn implies the development of structural mechanisms to achieve such involvement, together with a change in the organisation's culture so that this approach is perceived as valuable. As such, this approach relies on the degree to which senior managers in the organisation are persuaded that this is appropriate and valuable.

Should devolution be increasingly implemented there are considerable implications for the role of personnel practitioners. We have already mentioned the enthusiasm for a consultancy role within the organisation, and the IPD now provides a syllabus in this skill area. However, there are many practitioners who qualified long also and we suggest that continuous professional development has a role to play. We would argue that consultancy and facilitation skills are a distinct set of complex skills which can not be 'picked up as you go', unless there is considerable support from an experienced mentor or coach in the work situation. A further concern is how personnel consultants keep up to date, particularly with legislative changes, if they are not using their other skills (for example, interviewing, disciplinary proceedings, direct training) on a frequent basis. This suggests the constant need to read and pursue alternative approaches to learning, such as professional networks and updating. The consultancy role also distances personnel practitioners from the action, and as a consequence makes this role easier to outsource.

Having considered the progress and implications of devolution of operational personnel activities to line managers, we move on, in the next chapter, to explore another approach to reallocating personnel activities – the decentralisation of personnel tasks from personnel specialists at one level in the organisation to specialists at a lower level in the organisational hierarchy.

References

Armstrong, P. (1991) 'The limits and possibilities of HRM in an age of management accountancy', in J. Storey (ed.) *New Perspectives on Human Resource Management*, London: Routledge, 154–66.

Cabinet Office (1993) *The Effective Management of People*, London: HMSO.

Guest, D. (1987) 'Human resource management and industrial relations', *Journal of Management Studies*, 24(5), 503–21.

Holden, L. and Roberts, I. (1996) 'European middle managers: the search for identity in a conflicting role and an uncertain role', *Contemporary Developments in Human Resource Management*, Paris: Editions ESKA.

Hutchinson, S. and Wood, S. (1995) 'The new experience' in IPD *Personnel and the line: developing the new relationship*, IPD.

Industrial Relations Services (1994) 'The centre can not hold: devolving personnel duties', *IRS Employment Trends*, 6–11.

Industrial Relations Services (1997) 'HR adopts consultancy and business role at Courage', *IRS Employment Trends*, No. 625, February, 14–16.

Kanter, R. (1989) *When Giants Learn to Dance*, London: Routledge.

Keenoy, T. (1990) 'Human resource management: a case of the wolf in sheep's clothing?', *Personnel Review*, 19(2), 3–9.

Kilpatrick, I., Davies, A. and Oliver, N. (1992) 'Decentralisation – friend or foe of HRM?', in P. Blyton and P. Turnbull (eds) *Reassessing Human Resource Management*, London: Sage.

Kinnie, N. (1990) 'The decentralisation of industrial relations? – recent research reconsidered', *Personnel Review*, 14(2), 2–10.

Krulis-Randa, J. (1990) 'Strategic human resource management in Europe after 1992', *International Journal of Human Resource Management*, 1(2), 131–9.

Leach, J. (1995) Devolution of personnel activities – the reality, MA dissertation.

Lowe, J. (1992) '"Locating the line": the front line supervisor and human resource management', in P. Blyton and P. Turnbull (eds) *Reassessing Human Resource Management*, London: Sage.

Mackay, L. and Torrington, D. (1986) *The Changing Nature of Personnel Management*, London: IPD.

Northcott, C. H. (1945) *Personnel Management – Its Scope and Practice*, Hemel Hempstead: Prentice-Hall.

Oswick, C. and Grant, D. (1996) 'Personnel management in the public sector: power roles and relationships', *Personnel Review*, 25(2), 4–18.

Schein, E. (1984) 'Coming to a new awareness of organisational culture', *Sloan Management Review*, Winter, 3–15.

Schein, E. (1991) 'Communicating quality in the service sector', in B. H. Peters and J. L. Peters (eds) *Maintaining Total Quality Advantage*, New York: The Conference Board, 40–2.

Storey, J. (1995a) 'Human resource management: still marching on, or marching out?', *Human Resource Management: a Critical Text*, London: Routledge.

Storey, J. (1995b) 'Is HRM catching on?', *International Journal of Manpower*, 16(4), 3–10.

Towers Perrin (undated) 'Priorities for competitive advantage: a 21st century vision, a worldwide human resource study' (*An IBM Study conducted by Towers Perrin*).

Tyson, S. (1995) *Human Resource Strategy*, London: Pitman Publishing.

Wilkinson, A. and Marchington, M. (1994) 'TQM: Instant pudding for the personnel function?', *Human Resource Management Journal*, 5(1), 33–49.

5

Decentralisation of the human resources function

Introduction

The degree of centralisation within organisations has been an issue since the early days of organisation theory with both Weber (1947) and Fayol (1930) for example, prescribing highly centralised structures in the interest of organisational effectiveness and the most efficient use of resources. More recently, decentralisation in organisations has found much more favour, especially with corporations growing dramatically in size and owning a variety of businesses operating in very different markets. It is against this background that there has been growing interest in the decentralisation of the human resources management function with such major works as Purcell and Ahlstrand (1994) and Marginson *et al.* (1988) both of whom found a shift of power within the function from corporate level to business or establishment level. Although decentralisation appears to be the general trend there is also evidence to suggest some extent of recentralisation within organisations (*see*, for example, Drummond, 1992; IDS, 1991) and we found a small amount of evidence of recentralisation within the function. When we began our research we did not set out, specifically, to investigate this aspect of structure, but as we carried out our interviews, we found some interesting data emerging, and so began to probe this issue further. We also report some Masters level research from others, some of which was carried out in association with one of the authors. In particular, we report the work of Farrell (1997) who carried out two studies – one was a small postal survey of 20 local authorities, and the other was an in-depth case study of one decentralised local authority. In this study, Farrell carried out a total of 24 interviews with central HR officers, department level HR officers, line managers, department heads and heads of directorates (departmental groups).

We begin the chapter by briefly reviewing the issues of organisational decentralisation, as this forms a critical backcloth to what is happening within the function, and following this we will identify the major perspectives on functional decentralisation which we will go on to consider. First, we consider the extent and impact of HR decentralisation from corporate level to business level, and then concentrate on decentralisation of the function *within* the business itself. It is this second aspect, which has received little attention in associated literature, so far, that will be the focus of this chapter.

Decentralisation in organisations and the impact on HR, and HR specialists

There is considerable evidence to suggest that the divisional form of organisation, as opposed to the traditional functional form is now the most common (*see*, for example, Hill and Hoskisson, 1987; IDS, 1991). Associated with this has been an emphasis, in many organisations, on the decentralisation of authority to the divisions/business units themselves and away from the centre, with many organisations referring to themselves as decentralised. However, there are considerable differences in the degree of autonomy which individual business units have gained, and the financial controls to which they are subject by the centre (*see*, for example, Purcell and Ahlstrand, 1994). Indeed, such a variety of arrangements are subsumed under the title of decentralisation that IDS (1991) comment that 'decentralisation is a catchword that defies definition' (p. 4). Individual business units may, at one extreme, only be set profit targets, with considerable autonomy about how these are achieved. At the other end of the spectrum they may also be set specific budget targets, staffing levels, job grading levels, absence levels, and a variety of other targets to meet (as shown, for example, by Colling and Ferner, 1992) which effectively means that they may have very little autonomy. Indeed, Kinnie (1990) makes the point well when he argues that decentralisation of structures is not necessarily associated with the decentralisation of genuine discretion, and some studies have shown that decentralisation does not necessarily reduce central control. A further complicating factor is that business division is often taken to mean a single business unit within the corporate organisation. However, as Hill and Hoskisson (1987) found in their research, divisions may consist of a number of separate businesses. Within this book we will use the words division, business unit and establishment synonymously as this is most often the case (*see*, for example, Sisson, 1995), while recognising that there are other dimensions and further complicating factors in some organisations.

The push behind divisionalisation and decentralisation has been the desire to increase efficiency and performance, particularly in organisations with a very diverse range of businesses. Sisson and Scullion (1985) propose a model which explains the extent of decentralisation in any corporation in terms of its relationship with the degree of diversification. In other words, if the businesses in the corporation are very diverse then there will be a pressure to decentralise, whereas if the divisions are more closely related there will be pressures to centralise. However, whilst Purcell and Alhstrand did find some evidence that greater diversification resulted in greater decentralisation they also found other factors, such as the values and preferences of the chief executive to have an impact on structure. Williamson (1970) provides a thorough analysis of the characteristics of decentralised divisions explaining why they might be considered to be a superior organisational form in some circumstances. While we do not need to concern ourselves with these arguments in any depth it is important to pull out one key characteristic which is pertinent to our explorations in this and other chapters. This characteristic is the separation of strategy from operations; in decentralised organisations the centre is concerned with strategic issues (in terms of portfolio planning and management) while the businesses involve themselves in operations.

It is generally regarded that, from a business perspective, a major advantage of decentralisation is that it encourages local ownership of issues. Whilst this is an advantage there are some concerns that business managers will respond only to the short-term pressures which the business faces rather than any long-term strategic corporate initiatives. There is a fine balance which needs to be struck between divisional flexibility and the degree of corporate integration. Gould and Campbell (1987) found that in conditions of decentralisation managers viewed the business as the priority, rather than the organisation; found rivalry between different business units; found that impositions or interference from the centre were seen as a pressure on the business unit and found a lack of clarity of roles with some duplication. Allegiance to the business unit rather than the organisation as a whole is often viewed as problematic and Prahalad and Hamel (1990) refer to the 'tyranny of the business unit' where the achievement of bottom line results detracts from longer-term corporate needs.

All these issues have a considerable impact on the structure, role and power of the human resource function. Sisson (1995) suggests that decentralisation has profound implications for HRM and in particular for strategic HRM. Keen (1995) argues that organisational decentralisation and budgetary devolution require changes in the structure of other functions, and while she mainly refers to accountancy, there are clear parallels with personnel management. In particular, she identifies a split in functions between the 'corporate' and 'service provider' roles. She also argues that it is important for departments to have alignment between accountability for activities and authority for activities. The logic of the argument goes thus: if the chief executive of the business unit is accountable for unit performance then they need to have some control over the factors that will influence that performance, including direct control over their staff and resources (*see*, for example, Bennett, 1995; Purcell and Ahlstrand, 1994). This implies the need for the human resources function to be located within the division, and a corresponding reduction in the size and importance of the HR function in the centre of the organisation. Sisson and Scullion (1985) suggest that the greater the decentralisation the smaller the role of the central personnel function. Remembering Williamson's characteristic of decentralisation, that the centre is involved in strategy and the division only in operational issues, Purcell and Ahlstrand take this argument further to suggest that a weakening of central HR results in a weakening of a strategic approach to HR. Indeed, Marginson (1993) also noted a reduced size of central HR where an organisation was structured on a divisional basis – not that we can necessarily equate size with power and influence.

There are also other factors which have encouraged the emphasis on HR at business unit level as opposed to corporate level (*see*, for example, Hendry, 1990). The lessening influence of employment legislation and power of the trade unions have also been cited as factors which put less emphasis on the need for the corporate personnel role. Indeed, being based in the business rather than in the centre presents some attractive advantages for HR specialists. In particular Allen (1991) has shown that middle managers view personnel specialists as lacking 'a good business understanding and the ability to support the business', and one consistent theme in literature about the development of the personnel function is the 'ivory tower syndrome' where specialists are divorced from the reality of the business and are hence seen as irrelevant. Being based in the business, as Evans and Cowling (1985) point out, offers the opportunity for personnel specialists to become more widely involved in the management of the business, and demonstrate legitimacy and relevance. Hirsh (1992) also noted that decentralisation was expected to make the personnel function leaner and fitter, although there is some divergence of opinion on this point, and Bach (1995), for example, found decentralisation leading to duplication of activities and the employment of an increasing number of personnel staff.

Thus decentralisation provides some new opportunities for personnel specialists to become more deeply involved in the business, but at an operational rather than a strategic level. However, the neat split between strategy at the centre and operations in the business, explained above, appears much more complex in practice. Sisson (1995), Purcell and Ahlstrand (1994) and others found evidence of strategic activity at divisional level, in terms of strategic choices with long-term consequences, albeit not in the form of portfolio planning. Our research, which we report in Chapter 6, on strategic involvement provides some support for this. In this chapter we concentrate to a greater extent on issues of clarity, role and communication in a situation of HR decentralisation to business unit level. However, as well as these issues, we do consider the strategic/operational divide in our discussion of the decentralisation of HR to *department* level, later in this chapter. Perhaps, in overall terms, the most telling comment is that from Scullion and Sisson (1985) who talk about HR being dealt with 'at the most appropriate level', and we develop this idea later in the chapter.

Another, related, concern with decentralisation is outlined by Colling and Ferner (1992) who suggest that decentralisation of responsibility has created pressures for corporate functions to be treated as services provided for line managers as clients. They go on to argue that if the personnel function was to be 'demand-driven' how could it play its strategic, proactive role with conviction. If indeed HR strategy is little in evidence at the business unit level, or due to the context this is not the most appropriate level for it to be dealt with, then the strategic contribution from the centre becomes particularly important. In such a case, and where the HR function is demand-driven, it would be hard to see how a strategic contribution could be made at all. While we touch on the issue of demand-led service provision in this chapter, we consider it in more depth in Chapter 8 on internal marketing and HR.

Perspectives on decentralisation in the human resources function

We have already made the distinction between devolution of operational personnel activities and decentralisation in Chapter 4. We will not revisit that debate, except to say that while devolution may well produce a 'decentralising' effect, or indeed be a response to business decentralisation, we are concerned in this chapter only with the decentralisation of HR tasks from one level of HR specialist to another level of HR specialist within the organisation.

We have also noted that decentralisation, itself, covers a wide spectrum of arrangements, but what we have only hinted at so far, is that we are going to review decentralisation from two distinct perspectives which have not been explicitly identified in the literature, to date. First, and where most of the research to date has been carried out, there is the decentralisation of the corporate human resources function to an HR unit at business, or establishment level. This level of decentralisation is very much tied up with the level of decentralisation in the organisation generally, as described in the previous section. This area of investigation is critical as it defines the level at which the human resources function operates, and the constraints placed on establishment level human resource management. It is also critical as the level of decentralisation of the human resources function will have an impact on any research into human resource management carried out in a multi-divisional or multi-business organisation. Unless both levels of the organisation are researched, or there is an *explicit* focus on one level as against another, any findings relating to the role and importance of the human resources function might confuse rather than clarify the situation.

Our second perspective on decentralisation of the human resources function is that *within* the establishment itself. In other words, the extent to which authority for human resource issues is decentralised to an HR unit at *departmental* level, from business level. It is most likely that operational personnel activities are redistributed in this way, although, decentralisation may not be restricted to these. It is this aspect of decentralisation which is most often confused with devolution of personnel activities, both in the literature, and in reality. This aspect of decentralisation is important as it has an influence on the extent to which the business unit has a co-ordinated and consistent approach to human resources management, and reflects on the level of ownership of human resource issues. Although decentralisation is about the reallocation of personnel activities from one group of specialists to another, decentralisation may affect the levels and types of specialist employed, career opportunities, and the way in which their role is defined by themselves and others. Hence, there is a potential impact on the personnel management as a profession. In addition, these structural arrangements impact on the nature of HR strategy and operations, and the effectiveness with which these may be implemented.

Decentralisation of HR from corporate level to business unit level

In this section we will consider the research produced by Francis (1995) and then briefly refer to our own findings on this issue. Francis reports an interview-based case study of a recently privatised service sector organisation, with 2000 employees. The organisation had recently decentralised into three separate business units each employing their own HR staff, and Francis focused on the decentralisation of IR, by studying the views of local (business unit level) and central HR staff together with the views of business managers and union representatives. These local HR staff reported directly to the head of the business unit rather than to the head of the central HR unit, which was still maintained even though the directorship role had recently been removed. A series of interviews was held investigating how the system currently worked and how industrial relations, which was not presently decentralised could be organised in this way. The issues identified in this research include lack of clarity; dominance of business need; and lack of communication.

Lack of clarity

Interviewees were unclear of the boundaries between the role of the business HR unit and the central HR unit. Some business managers by-passed their unit HR and went directly to the centre. This lack of clarity also resulted in the duplication of some activities. There were also conflicting views about what the corporate role should be, although the HR staff in the centre had a clear view that their role was to drive the corporate change programme, set standards, carry out benchmarking, and take the responsibility for time-consuming HR projects. The business unit managers acknowledged the centre's role in HR policy, but felt that this needed to be carried out in consultation with the business. The business managers also felt that central HR should act as internal consultants providing expertise and guidance. Both these expectations appeared to be unmet at present. This is similar to, but not as extreme as, Purcell and Gray's finding that 'corporate personnel as currently structured was seen as a largely unnecessary and expensive cost' (p. 219).

Dominance of business need

The advantages of decentralised HR were seen in the speed of response and the ability to focus on the needs of the business. However, the local HR specialists felt pulled in two directions – in one direction by the business and in another direction by central HR. One stated that they found themselves 'sacrificing professional standards for operational expediency'. The trade union officials interviewed identified inconsistency between the businesses in the management of employees, and were concerned about this issue. It was recognised that this situation could be changed by altering the reporting relationships of the unit HR staff from the head of the business to central HR. Business managers, however, did not want the relationship to change. In fact a dotted line relationship had just been introduced linking the unit HR specialist to HR in the centre, where no relationship at all had existed before. In an additional piece of research, Francis visited a separate service business which had decentralised, and the HR manager who was interviewed stated that if the local HR unit were to report to central HR this would 'constitute the failure of decentralisation'. Yet, in spite of the good outcomes this organisation identified from decentralisation they also noted that the HR centre had become isolated. Similarly, the interviewee in a second organisation which Francis visited (financial services) felt that head office HR staff had become 'so far away from reality' that reporting relationships were changed so that unit HR specialists no longer reported directly to the head of the line department but instead to central HR. They also noted that the local HR staff, whom they called field officers, had become isolated as the business managers by-passed them and mainly used them to do the dirty work.

Lack of communication

Francis also found in her case-study organisation that local unit HR professionals felt that corporate HR was not accessible to them and were unhelpful. In addition, they had not been involved in a consultation process as the centre had developed HR policies. However, it is not clear whether they failed to take the opportunity to be involved, or whether the opportunity did not exist. Given the general lack of communication and consultation it is not surprising that corporate HR policies were seen by the business managers as being unrealistic and not related to business needs. Francis concludes that effective communication between central and unit HR is essential in making decentralisation effective.

Central control – imposition and avoidance

In our own research we found HR professionals at business unit level in decentralised organisations played a part in warding off the influence of the centre, but were not necessarily successful. HR specialists found themselves forced into a position where they were imposing tasks on employees in the business – these tasks were often ones that they did not approve of themselves, and which no one in the establishment felt they had any control over. For example, in one establishment in the private sector the personnel advisor we interviewed explained that: 'We have always managed to maintain the distance, our own identify, our own staffing', but who went on to explain that more recently ideas had been imposed:

> Some ideas filter down to use like performance appraisal . . . it's given to us, we're told to implement it, but it doesn't work for us because we are a different culture.

This personnel advisor then went on to describe the problems of implementing this system.

Within central government the head of personnel we interviewed explained how the HR specialists often found themselves saying to line managers: 'Well you may not like it, but we don't either, but we've still got to do it.' Others explained how they tried to avoid central control, or at least keep the centre happy whilst meeting business needs. For example, one HR consultant in the private sector (services) explained that in order to meet centrally-imposed staffing targets they would employ larger numbers of temporary and contract staff as these staff groups were not included in the staffing target. This approach, which had been used over a long time period, had eventually created problems for the business as they lost critical expertise when contract staff left.

Managing the balance between the centre and the business

From the findings above we can see how the tensions between the centre and the separate businesses impact on HR specialists. At one extreme there are those specialists who are so caught up with the business that they feel they are sacrificing some of their professional standards, and at the other extreme there are specialists who feel that they are tools of the centre and as such become implementers of central policy even when they feel that this is inappropriate for the business. Somewhere in between is the art of keeping the centre happy whilst doing the right things by the business.

The business managers, understandably, had a clear preference to manage their own HR unit directly, and were prepared to involve them on this basis. However, where such a relationship did not exist the business managers were quite happy to by-pass the unit officers and go to the centre, if that's where they felt the power lay. The implications seem to be that in the first scenario the central HR unit becomes isolated and in the second the local HR unit becomes isolated. Francis points out the need for better communication between the central HR and the business HR unit and a greater clarity in roles, and Purcell and Ahlstrand demonstrate from their case studies a variety of different ways in which the central and local HR units could work together.

Decentralisation within the business to department level

We only discussed decentralisation within the establishment with a proportion of our interview respondents, so it is not necessarily useful to discuss the numbers of those who had decentralised compared with others. It is more useful to explore the different forms of decentralisation that were in evidence. Bach (1995), similarly identified a range of HR structural options in response to decentralisation within a business (a health trust). We found three major approaches to the decentralisation of the human resource function: two types of physical decentralisation and virtual decentralisation. In the physical decentralisation approach human resource specialists are physically relocated within the department(s) that they serve and in the virtual decentralisation model the human resource specialists remain physically together in the centre, and are allocated specific roles in relation to specific departments with whom they may have service level or customer agreements. It is worth noting that some other researchers (for example, Farrell, 1997) have identified this latter model as centralised. Rather than entering into a debate on terminology we will explore the concept of decentralisation as a continuum rather than an all or nothing approach. For each of the two models above we review the essence of the structure and consider the impact and issues related to that approach to the contribution and delivery of specialist HRM expertise.

Physical decentralisation type A
(Where the HR specialist reports directly to the head of the line department in which they are located)

The strategic/operational divide
The size of the human resource units within departments varied according to the size of department, and sometimes this meant that the human resource unit consisted of one individual. However, we found in all cases that where human resource specialists were physically decentralised to local departmental

level, a central human resources unit, albeit small, still remained in existence. Farrell (1997) in his survey of 20 local authorities and a case study of one particular authority, found the same pattern (in all cases except one), in terms of the existence of a central HR unit at the same time as departmental HR units. It is interesting to note that the respondent in the organisation which had not retained a central HR function stated that they had 'gone a bridge too far'. The parallel existence of such functional groups raises the question of how the roles of each of these groups is defined, and the extent to which these definitions are understood by those both within the function and its users.

Farrell (1997) found definitions of what the respective roles *should* be but also found some confusions in reality. Let us deal, first, with the way the roles are consciously set up. In Farrell's case-study organisation he quotes one central human resources officer who stated that the central unit was there to analyse the needs, aims and objectives of the organisation, develop HR policy and co-ordinate the work of the local departmental HR units. Correspondingly, she felt that the role of the departmental units was to translate the corporate objectives into workable departmental objectives. In our research we also found the central unit being accorded the responsibility for strategy making and the departmental units the responsibility for mundane administration. One director of HR (local government) in our research, stated that:

> We're a relatively small central unit which deals with the main policy issues. The day to day personnel administration is predominantly out in what we call the front line and other services . . . so we've done a lot of work in setting up the policies and practices and they have to be followed, and then the departments carry them through.

This manager went on to explain how there were 10 to 11 professional service units for each sector of the council, and that not only were some of these employing a single person, but that sometimes they had combined roles of personnel and other services, for example, finance. Leach (1995), similarly found that small single person local personnel units within local authority departments were often seen as carrying out administrative and low level tasks.

This separation of strategic and operational activities has consequences for both the human resource function and human resource activities are also reinforced by the type of staff who are located within departments – Farrell in his survey of the 20 local authorities found that departmental HR staff were often labelled 'staffing officers' which he argues is a traditional local authority term for non-qualified personnel staff who carry out more routine administrative tasks. Some local HR units were called 'employee support units' in order to differentiate the role of non-professionally qualified personnel/HR staff, compared with the professional function in the centre.

This dilution of specialist expertise could be seen to have consequences for the image of the function and for the development of specialist expertise and professional human resource careers. Indeed, it almost seems like another version of the line dumping on a central personnel function, people-related tasks in which it is not interested – only the function is now close at hand and easier to dump on! One of our interview respondents, head of personnel (police), made an interesting comparison between the benefits of devolution, as described in the last chapter, and decentralisation of human resource professionals. In relation to devolution he commented that:

> This has been a more important and powerful process than sticking personnel officers in every division.

and went on to explain that they had opted for devolution rather than decentralisation, which they had previously attempted since:

> I don't want people to abrogate their responsibilities on to somebody else when they've been abrogating them to us in the past. I want to make sure it (people management) goes all the way down the line.

Decentralisation then may impede the progress of devolution, even though it is often introduced alongside it in order to locate people decisions close to the source of HR issues and the means of their resolution. Most other evidence to date suggests that centralisation impedes devolution, and yet decentralisation may have the same, or more concentrated effect. This is clearly an issue which requires further investigation.

Farrell, however, makes a spirited argument that, instead of decentralisation representing HR specialists being dumped on further by the line, it represents the central HR department protecting its current power and status. Decentralisation, in the way that it is currently set up, means that the centre can be seen to respond to pressures to decentralise, and yet only give away the routine and mundane tasks so that the centre retains its power and status, and is hence protected. We could therefore make a case that both devolution and decentralisation appear to hand over control to lower down the organisation, but in reality what is given away does not make a substantive difference. In Table 5.1 we compare the experience of the devolution of HR activities to the line with the physical decentralisation of HR specialists.

The strategic/operational divide also reflects in physical form what is happening in many HR departments. In our research we encountered three respondents who explained that there was an 'HR' director but a 'personnel' department. The difference in terminology did not necessarily indicate that the HR director was not a functional specialist – but was seen to indicate that the personnel department were non-strategic and dealt with employee/welfare issues, while the HR director dealt with HR strategy. The disparity in terminology was generally seen as uncomfortable for those within the personnel function, and also an unfair reflection of the work that they did. This division

Table 5.1 A comparison of the different potential impact of devolving personnel activities to line managers and decentralising personnel specialists (at the business to department level)

Aspect of comparison	Decentralisation	Devolution
Line manager role	May have no impact on the activities line managers take on	Expectation that all line managers take on specified operational personnel activities
Line department head/director role	May be more involved in HR matters, in terms of aligning HR activities to fit the department's strategy	Expectation above, but probably less pressure to conform
Line response to this approach to managing HR	General approval from all levels	Often great resistance
HR specialist role	Small number of strategists in the centre. Departmental role is often, but not always operational	HR specialists are consultants to, and trainers of the line. Less emphasis on operational issues more emphasis on strategy
Cohesion of HR specialists	Pressures for fragmentation, both in terms of role, reporting relationships, and physically	Pressures for cohesion
Number of HR specialists employed	Little evidence that the number of specialists is reduced – some suggestion that it may even increase due to duplication of activities	A reduction in the number of HR specialists is often the result (or cause) of devolution
Level of HR specialists employed	Emphasis on lower levels of specialist, and sometimes unqualified staff allocated to HR roles	Emphasis on higher level of staff and more sophisticated skills
Development of HR expertise	Often weakens levels of expertise. Less opportunity for sharing. Dominance of departmental agenda is often a threat to HR professional	Structure encourages the development of expertise and emphasises HR professional values
Development of HR careers	Often seen as restricted due to being trapped in another department. But more opportunity to become involved with other functional areas	Career structure clearer (purist) and less exclusion

is paralleled by Fowler's (1994) explanation of this type of model for the structure of HR specialists – he recognises how the specialist function is split in two with a high status group in the centre operating at a strategic level (and by implication, a low status group located in the departments). Indeed, Farrell (1997) makes the point that in a local government context there was some elitism evident in the central group.

Lack of clarity in decentralised structures

Farrell, however, found that despite the predominant division described above, there was some lack of clarity in practical terms (in the case-study authority) about how the roles were divided and his respondents spoke of a 'blurring of the edges' and uncertainty about the central role. Tensions between the central and departmental units were identified and some line managers were unsure about the human resource management structure, but were much clearer about what to expect from the departmental unit than from the central unit. Farrell finds one explanation for these confusing roles in the incremental nature of decentralisation – thus the roles in themselves changed on a continuous basis. If the central unit had decentralised with a view to protecting their status in this decentralised organisation then they had failed in communicating their special role to many in the organisation, and were to some extent ignored because of this. Heads of departments and directors of departments in Farrell's case study had a very clear view of the role of the departmental HR unit, and one saw it as:

> The human resource function (local unit) has to be seen as an integral part of the department and its objectives. It must be used to help develop strategies which enable the departmental objectives to be achieved.

While the role of the departmental HR unit was seen differently in different departments, depending on the pressures and needs of departments, there was common agreement that they were there to support the department's objectives. While at one end of the scale the human resource unit was perceived to carry out mundane day-to-day tasks and often staffed by someone who was not professionally qualified, at the other end, if qualified staff were employed, with more specialist expertise, they seemed to be drawn into the departmental strategy. As such it was the local HR officers who were seen to add value while the central unit appeared to be in 'no man's land'.

Strategy vs. the service delivery imperative

Although there will be different implications from each of the two scenarios above, there may well be a common consequence of a neglect of the HR strategy of the establishment as a whole. Small groups of specialists, or a single specialist, may be much more susceptible to pressure from the line as they are relatively isolated from other specialists, and they may be especially vulnerable if they are less well qualified and have less support for continuous professional development. While the advantages of closeness, flexibility and responsiveness to departmental needs were identified as an advantage, the HR officer in the department often found themselves in a difficult position. Meeting department needs often brought them into conflict with central HR strategy. In a similar vein, Bach (1995) found conflicts of loyalty expressed by departmental HR staff. Farrell's evidence suggests that on these occasions it was the department which had the greater power, and HR officers aligned themselves with departmental strategy rather than organisational HR strategy when a choice had to be made. This created inconsistencies in the way that employees were managed, which all interviewees acknowledged. There were concerns in the authority that treating employees in different ways was seen to be unfair, laid the authority open to legal challenges and did not provide employees with a sufficient feeling of corporate belonging. A recent article in *The Times* (1997) expressed this situation as a 'time bomb waiting to go off'.

The central HR function in Farrell's case study was accorded, by some of the department heads and directors, a strategic role, and may well have had an HR strategy. However, it appeared to have no mechanisms to implement this, and the impact on departmental practice appears to be varied. Farrell reports that the central unit felt they could not 'impose' initiatives on departments due to the strength of the decentralised paradigm that exists. Whilst Farrell reports that all directors felt that HR was carried out inconsistently, they also felt that the HR strategy was formulated from a centrist point of view and that departmental needs had not been taken into account sufficiently. Many interviewees recognised the need for a two-way flow between central HR and the departments so that departmental needs could inform strategy development, but there was little evidence in Farrell's report of the case study to suggest that anything like this actually happened. This scenario is reminiscent of the ivory tower syndrome – when the personnel department pontificate on what should happen in isolation from the reality of the business. If decentralisation was intended to get HR closer to the business, despite appearances of physical relocation, it seems to have failed.

It is interesting that in Farrell's questionnaire those authorities who had decentralised in a similar manner stated that the main advantages of such an arrangement were that not only did it provide speedy HR responses, allow HR to be tailored to meet departmental needs, encourage managers to own HR issues, but it was also a way that departmental issues could be fed up to central HR. The disadvantages experienced by the questionnaire respondents who had decentralised in this way were: inconsistency in the way that employees were treated; overlapping roles and a duplication of effort: the diminution of the professional role in centre as they had been reduced to auditors and monitors; and the difficulty in sharing experiences and expertise. The reality of decentralisation, it has to be said, seems to result in some serious problems for the whole organisation as well as the specialist function.

Central HR is isolated

The experience of decentralisation of HR to departments described above indicates that the departmental agenda prevails and that the role of central HR has been marginalised and isolated to such an extent that it is unable to have an impact on the establishment. Whilst an HR strategy may well be produced by the centre it seems to have minimal impact on what happens in the departments. As such there is inconsistency in the management of employees. Part of the problem appears to be a lack of communication between central HR, the departmental HR units and the departments generally – as such the strategy produced does not take account of their needs, and is thus ignored or tailored for departmental use. All seemed to recognise this as a problem, and yet department bosses seemed unhappy to relinquish the control they had over HR within their department. Again the HR function is split – but here it seems inappropriate to identify a high status strategic group in the centre (although they may be professionally qualified to a greater extent) – they appear to be just a group with an unclear remit, and with no connection to the rest of the organisation.

Physical decentralisation type B

(Where the HR specialist reports directly to central HR even though they are located in a line department)

While in Farrell's case-study authority the unit HR specialists reported directly to the head of department in which they were located, in our research we also found HR functions which had physically relocated, but which maintained a *direct* reporting relationship into the *central HR function.* One head of human resources in a building society explained how they had wound down the huge HR department in the centre, and how they had 'deployed people out in the field'. He described how four new regional HR centres were created and staff were relocated from the centre. Within each of the regional groups each HR professional then related to a group of specific (geographically defined) branches and clients within that region. He explained how the manager of that specific group of branches would regard the HR consultant they worked with as *their* HR consultant. Yet all HR staff reported directly to the central HR department and not to the managers that they worked with. He described this as a matrix which worked really well. This case also illustrates how different approaches to decentralisation are combined into a particular approach which fits the needs of the individual business, combining, in this case, some physical decentralisation and some virtual decentralisation.

This model of physical decentralisation may well ameliorate some of the problems identified in relation to the physical relocation model (A), above, and in his survey of 20 local authorities Farrell found that this was the most popular structure with ten out of the 20 operating in broadly this way. Indeed, these ten (referred to by Farrell as quasi-decentralisation) variously identified the advantages of their approach as providing a standardised approach, enabling concentration on strategic issues, cost effectiveness, ability to provide expert services, economies of scale and the ability to provide a corporate overview. Indeed, the advantages they identify were the same as those identified by respondents who described themselves as operating a centralised approach. They did, however, raise the difficulties of the blurring of the edges between the department units and the centre, and were concerned about career progression for personnel specialists.

This model appears to have significant advantages and few disadvantages for the operation of HR – however we have to remember that we only have the HR function's perspective of this form of decentralisation, so there may be some disadvantages which have not been recognised.

Virtual decentralisation

Virtual decentralisation is a form of decentralisation of the HR function which does not involve physical relocation, but involves very specific working relationships of named HR professionals with named departments of parts of the establishment. This formation was often accompanied by the idea of 'service contracts' where the personnel advisor agreed to provide agreed services and time allocations to specified departments, sometimes together with agreed performance standards. The personnel advisor may have agreements with more than one department, depending on the size of department and the workload required. It is, as Keen (1995) suggests another approach to decentralisation within organisations.

This model of decentralisation may seem fairly innocuous, and indeed some forms of it appear to be about building a closer relationship between the specialist and the line, and a better understanding of departmental needs. In these cases there were no budgetary implications, and the line specialist relationship was more highly defined in order to stimulate the production of common vision and objectives, and hence efficiency and effectiveness. However, we did find, as Evans and Cowling (1985) predicted that this could result in a demand-led central unit which not only made agreements in terms of which HR specialist would support a specific department, but also marketed and sold services as a means of survival. In these cases there were budgetary implications and the HR function was variously defined as a profit centre or a provider department. This more extreme form of virtual decentralisation has some very different implications and will be explored in detail in Chapter 8 on internal marketing and HR.

Comparing different forms of decentralisation of HR

In this section we will tease out the similarities and differences between all of the different forms of decentralisation of HR which we have so far discussed, starting with decentralisation to line departments and then moving up the organisation to decentralisation to business units.

First, decentralisation of HR from business level to department level can mean many different forms of structural relationship. To some extent decentralisation is best viewed as a continuum, as Farrell suggests, and for a summary of the different forms of decentralisation which we have reported, *see* Figure 5.1.

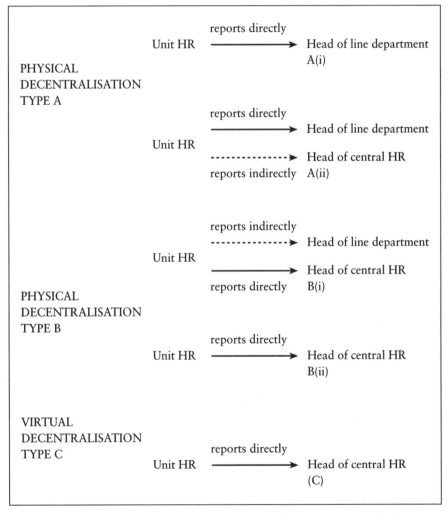

Fig. 5.1 A continuum of decentralisation of the human resources fuction within the business

In Figure 5.2 we have added a second dimension – the content areas of HR which are decentralised – as we found in all cases that a central unit remained and that HR content areas were divided between the two groups. Completing the figure will show the pattern of HR decentralisation within any business. Both figures could also be used for representing the decentralisation of HR from corporate to business level.

	Areas of personnel/HR activity				
	Recruitment	Selection	Training	H&S	Discipline ... and so on
Level of decentralisation					
Physical decentralisation A(i)					
A(ii)					
B(i)					
B(ii)					
Virtual decentralisation					
Centralised					

Fig. 5.2 Patterns of centralisation and decentralisation (to represent the pattern of decentralisation within any specific organisation a matrix similar to the one below would be needed to provide a complete picture)

The implications of decentralisation both for human resource activities and for HR specialists will be heavily influenced by the form of decentralisation adopted. The findings from our research and that of others is that the 'physical decentralisation with departmental reporting' is the most distinct and most extreme form. It is this form where the departmental needs seemed to reign over central needs and where a lack of HR integration at the business level was identified. Even if the central HR unit tried to operate strategically, as there was general agreement at senior levels that they should, there were no mechanisms for gaining departmental commitment and translating the strategy into day-to-day activities. There also appeared to be no mechanism for feeding departmental HR needs into the centre to inform strategy development. Departmental bosses generally, but not always, limited their HR unit to an operational role, and if they were involved in strategy it was departmental strategy rather than central HR strategy.

Changing the reporting relationship of the HR unit from the department to central HR appeared to encourage a much greater degree of HR integration and standardisation, and encouraged a strategic approach to HR. However, some lack of clarity was noted in both models, as were concerns about career progression. While this model may appear to offer greater advantages in terms of people management, combining departmental visibility with a more powerful HR integrating force from the centre, it may be problematic for the unit-based HR specialists in terms of being by-passed by line managers in favour of the centre who are seen to have more clout. The characteristics of the virtual decentralisation model are more similar to the physical decentralisation with central HR reporting model, except that they are not *permanently* located within the department, as they can gain high visibility by spending large proportions of their time there.

The decentralisation choice that any business may make is no doubt influenced by the relative importance of departmental needs over the need for an integrated HR approach. We could argue that the latter equates to business need in which case the choice may seem simple, but clearly organisations do not necessarily equate the two, and the structures put in place no doubt reflect personalities, power, politics and the historical baggage of the different functions. Bach (1995) refers to a power struggle in his research organisation in relation to the exact form of decentralisation of HR. In some establishments we found that the degree of decentralisation was a reaction against a very high degree of centralisation in the past. The political context, in macro terms, must also be a significant influence as the rhetorics of purchaser and provider units, CCT and outsourcing each have decentralising pressures built into them. There is also evidence to suggest that the specific model of decentralisation of HR that is chosen is likely to change to a greater or lesser extent, depending on changing circumstances and the perceived effectiveness of the model in use. Indeed, we did find two organisations which had decentralised some personnel activities – in particular recruitment, and were in the process of recentralising them because the decentralised model did not work. The best we can probably say is that most establishments attempt to gain the decentralisation benefits of both forms of reporting, and constantly tweak the system in an attempt to redress problems.

Moving higher up the organisation it is useful to compare the impact of decentralisation from corporate level to business unit level with decentralisation from business to departmental level (physical decentralisation with departmental reporting model). These two forms appear remarkably similar in terms of impact in the areas of isolation of the centre and a lack of understanding of its role, difficulty of central HR integration, priority of local needs, and lack of clarity in roles. While the *impact* may be similar the *implications* for HR and HR specialists are very different, as is shown in Table 5.2.

While these approaches use the same principles at different levels in the organisation, the differing implications suggest that decentralisation from business to department level is not a logical continuum for decentralisation from corporate to business level. This takes us back to the comments from Sisson and Scullion, who suggest HR needs to be dealt with at the most appropriate level. In order to decide appropriateness we need to decide in what circumstances HR works most effectively in decentralised form and at what level the decentralisation should stop. While we may argue that there are competitive advantages in HR being decentralised to business level as a different culture and type, and employment relationship will match different industry sectors and markets. We may also argue that in terms of geographical location and size, HR decentralisation to business level makes sense – particularly as the opportunity for HR strategy development at this level seems to be increasing (*see* Chapter 6 on strategic involvement). We could also argue that a certain amount of flexibility and immediacy at local level are critical, particularly as employment may be constructed so that employees see themselves as contracted by the business rather than the larger organisation. Trying to apply these arguments to departmental level barely makes any sense, except perhaps in specialised situations. For example, direct services departments (old district works department of the local authorities) are subject to competitive tendering and therefore have to compete outside the council – in these circumstances employees may need to be managed in different ways from other departments, and will have different concerns and different HR needs. However, complications arise as they are locally connected to other departments, employees may see themselves as part of the same council, and legally they are employed by the same council – thus a lack of HR integration and strategy at the local authority/business unit level may cause countless problems.

Moving on from appropriateness of different forms of HR decentralisation in terms of organisational benefits and problems, let us now turn to the implications for the HR function and for HR specialists. Whatever form of decentralisation is adopted, the personnel function becomes split, and it appears that some parts of the function become isolated, depending on the specific arrangements implemented. Yet decentralisation, although it may have been imposed on the function, appears to provide an opportunity for personnel specialists to become more integrated into the business. It seems that managers buy into the part of the function which can immediately satisfy their short-term needs, and exclude the rest. Although politics and power relations in the organisation clearly account for much of the problem, it could be argued that

Table 5.2 A comparison of the implications HR decentralisation at different organisational levels: (i) decentralisation from corporate to business unit level; and (ii) decentralisation from business unit to department level

Characteristics of decentralised HR	Implications when HR is decentralised from corporate to business level (i)	Implications when HR is decentralised from business unit to department level (ii)
Local HR needs dominate central needs	HR supports the business in terms of strategic and operational HR rather than the needs of corporate HR	HR supports the departmental operating/service delivery needs, rather than business level HR strategy
	Long and short term needs can be taken into account	The short term tends to prevail
	Enables the business to compete as tailor-made HR solutions prevail	Enables the department to be effective
Lack of a consistent approach to HR	Different businesses each have a different interpretation of corporate HR strategy/ their own HR strategy to meet business demands	Each department interprets the HR strategy differently/has a different set of HR operating principles
	Employees see themselves as part of the business rather than part of the corporate organisation	Employees see themselves as part of the department rather than part of the business
	Inconsistent treatment of employees can be accommodated as employees can be employed by the business rather than the corporate organisation. Things made easier because businesses tend to be located apart	Inconsistent treatment of employees may be a problem, seen as inequitable and may lay the business open to legal challenge. Particularly difficult as departments tend to be located in close proximity
HR specialists 'go native'	Being absorbed in business as opposed to corporate needs, may be balanced by a sufficiently large group of specialists ensuring that the professional component is not obliterated	HR specialists are often in small groups or alone –experience feelings of isolation and find it difficult to maintain levels of professionalism with little support
	Viable specialist career structures due to size	Career structures difficult due to size, a feeling of having burnt one's bridges, but more opportunity to cross-functional areas
	Possible to develop HR expertise	Difficult to develop HR expertise

the function itself is not doing all that it could to get the best out of the structures that specialists have to work within.

One of the common themes in our research and that of others was the lack of role clarity in different personnel roles and the lack of communication access and support between different parts of the personnel function. The function is almost divided and set against itself – the local unit from the central unit; qualified staff from unqualified staff; careers for some and not for others; strategy development from operations. Different parts of the function failed to share expertise, support one another, and exchange information, despite the many mechanisms that are available to achieve this (*see*, for example, Purcell and Ahlstrand, 1994). The question is why? One explanation might be that in conditions where the expert power of specialists is threatened due to greater line management involvement in personnel activities (*see*, for example, Oswick and Grant, 1996) individuals become more insular in an attempt to protect what little power source they have left. Also some may have an eye to where their future might lie in the organisation, and this could determine where their allegiances lie. This is a fairly bleak assessment, and perhaps applies to a greater extent when decentralisation goes further down the organisation, and local personnel/HR units become smaller and smaller. If personnel specialists are not in a position to (or will not) share information, learning and support, this is not just to their own detriment – the organisation loses out too, in the long run.

While decentralisation to business level may bring more advantages and fewer problems, the balance seems to change (both from the organisation's and the specialist's perspectives) when HR is decentralised within the business.

References

Allen, K. R. (1991) 'Personnel management on the line: how middle managers view the function', *Personnel Management*, June, 40–3.

Bach, S. (1995) 'Restructuring the personnel function: the case of NHS Trusts', *Human Resource Management Journal*, 15(2), 99–115.

Bennett, H. (1995) 'Navigating a bumpy road', *People Management*, 6 April, 29–31.

Colling, T. and Ferner, A. (1992) 'The limits of autonomy: devolution, line managers and industrial relations in privatised companies', *Journal of Management Studies*, 29(1), 209–27.

Drummond, G. (1992) 'Theories of devolution', *Personnel Today*.

Evans, A. and Cowling, A. (1985) 'Personnel's part in organisational restructuring', *Personnel Management*, January, 14–17.

Farrell, B. (1997) *The Effectiveness of Human Resource Management in the Decentralised Environment*, MA dissertation.

Fayol, H. (1930) *Industrial and General Administration*, Geneva: International Management Institute.

Fowler, A. (1994) 'Personnel's model army', *Personnel Management*, September, 34–7.

Francis, C. (1995) *Decentralisation of Industrial Relations*, MA dissertation.

Gould, M. and Campbell, A. (1987) *Strategies and Styles – Role of the Centre*, Oxford: Blackwell.

Hendry, C. (1990) 'The corporate management of human resources under conditions of decentralisation', *British Journal of Management*, 1, 91–103.

Hill, C. W. and Hoskisson, R. E. (1987) 'Strategy and structure in the multi product form', *Academy of Management Review*, 12(2), 331–41.

Hirsch, W. (1992) 'Decentralising the personnel function', *Manpower Policy and Practice*, 12(4), 12–14.

IDS (1991) *Decentralisation*, June, 59.

Keen, L. (1995) 'Organisational decentralisation in local government: a case of middle management autonomy?', *Human Resource Management Journal*, 5(2), 79–98.

Kinnie, N. (1990) 'The decentralisation of industrial relations – recent research considered', *Personnel Review*, 19(3), 28–34.

Leach, J. (1995) *Devolution of Personnel Activities – the reality*, MA dissertation.

Marginson, P., Edwards, P., Martin, R., Purcell, J. and Sisson, K. (1988) *Beyond the Workplace – Managing Industrial Relations in the Multi-establishment Enterprise*, Oxford: Blackwell.

Marginson, P., Armstrong, P., Edwards, P., Purcell, J. and Hubbard, N. (1993) *The Control of Industrial Relations in Large Companies: initial analysis of the second company level survey*, Warwick Papers in Industrial Relations No. 45, Warwick: University of Warwick Industrial Relations Unit.

Oswick, C. and Grant, D. (1996) 'Personnel management in the public sector – power roles and relationships', *Personnel Review*, 25(2), 4–18.

Prahalad, C. K. and Hamel, G. (1990) 'The core competence of the corporation', *Harvard Business Review*, May–June.

Purcell, J. and Ahlstrand, B. (1994) *Human Resource Management in the Multi-divisional Company*, Oxford: Oxford University Press.

Purcell, J. and Gray, A. (1986) 'Corporate personnel departments and the management of industrial relations: two cases in ambiguity', *Journal of Management Studies*, 23(2), 205–23.

Sisson, K. (1995) 'Organisational structure', in S. Tyson (ed.) *Strategic prospects for HRM*, London: IPD.

Sisson, K. and Scullion, H. (1985) 'Putting the corporate personnel department in its place', *Personnel Management*, 17(12), 36–9.

Weber, M. (1947) *The Theory of Social and Economic Organizations*, New York: Free Press.

Williamson, O. E. (1970) *Corporate Control of Business Behaviour*, Englewood Cliffs, NJ: Prentice-Hall.

6

Involvement in HR strategy

Introduction

In Chapter 5 we considered how the structure of the personnel function was often changed in response to a decentralised approach within the organisation, and we noted that this appeared to have a significant impact on the implementation of HR strategy. We now focus on the extent to which personnel specialists in all structural environments are involved with HR strategy. The concept of strategy has received increasing attention both in academic literature and in business practice over the last 20 years. In line with this, and the increasing awareness of people as a valued competitive resource (*see*, for example, Lundy and Cowling, 1996; Schuler, 1992; the nature and contribution of HR strategy has become a focus, and strategic activity is identified as a key part of the HR practitioner's role (*see*, for example, Armstrong, 1992; Harrison, 1993). In spite of its desirability, evidence of the strategic involvement of HR specialists has, so far, been thin on the ground (*see*, for example, Storey, 1992; Monks, 1992). In our research we not only confirmed the desirability of involvement in HR strategy, but also greater evidence of such involvement than has been previously found. We explore the reasons for this.

In terms of format, we first review the concept of HR strategy, and attraction and desirability of strategic involvement for the HR specialist. The complexities of researching HR strategy are highlighted before discussing the extent and nature of strategic involvement in our sample and how this relates to previous studies. In addition, we explore both the internal and external influences on the strategic involvement of the specialist function – in particular, we discuss personnel/HR board level representation, and consider the importance of the chief executive's perspective, the competencies and working relationships of the HR specialist, and the impact of the environment.

Our perspective is the position of the **personnel specialist** and their involvement in HR strategy. We do not therefore fully explore the existence and nature of HR strategy when it is developed primarily by others – although we do make some indicative comments. Also our focus is specifically on HR strategy rather than the involvement of the HR specialist in any aspect of business strategy. All these factors are difficult to disentangle, and we explore these issues in more detail when we discuss the complexities of researching HR strategy.

The concept of HR strategy

In this section we make the connection between an 'HRM' approach and the increasing prominence of HR strategy, and then provide our working definition of HR strategy. We go on to explore the characteristics of HR strategy in the literature, as these form the framework for some of our findings on strategic involvement.

Increasing intensity of competition within global markets has created an environment where human resources are more frequently seen as critical factors of competitive advantage. A strategic approach to the management of human resources, as opposed to the more traditional administrative approach and the implementation of 'best personnel practice', has been perceived as offering added value to the organisation. The rise of the concept of HRM from the 1980s onwards has reinforced this strategic focus to people management, having strategy as a key theme (*see*, for example, Guest (1987, 1989, 1990, 1991; Poole, 1990; Sisson, 1990; Storey, 1989). Beardwell and Holden (1994) comment that 'HRM is about shaping and delivering corporate strategies with commitment and results' (p. 9), and one of the three major perspectives on HRM which Guest identified, in 1994, is 'HRM as strategy, highlighting a strategic perspective being its distinctive feature' (p. 41).

The literature and interest in human resource strategy needs to be set within a context of increasing interest in business strategy, and it is worthwhile stating here that our working definition of the term strategy is based on Johnson's (1987) perspective. He proposes that strategy is likely to involve the long-term direction of the organisation; the scope of the organisation's activities; the matching of the organisation to it's environment, and matching to its resource capabilities.

We have already stated (Torrington and Hall, 1998) that our working definition of HR strategy involves a central philosophy of the way that people are managed in an organisation, and the translation of this into personnel policies and practices, and its integration with business strategy and within itself. This is in line with other definitions, for example, Tyson (1995) has described human resource strategy as 'a set of ideas, policies and practices which management adopt in order to achieve a people management outcome' (p. 3) and sees HR philosophy as a philosophy of management which results in different types of employment relationship. Handy *et al.* (1989) and Hendry and Pettigrew (1986) both draw out the themes of a central philosophy and integration. Handy notes that this requires a strategic view of the role of personnel management in the organisation.

Using the above definitions, the concept of HR strategy suggests that deliberate choices can be made and implemented concerning the way that employees are managed, and that the selected choices will be related to the competitive needs of the business over the longer term, and implemented in a consistent manner.

Much of the HR strategy literature emphasises the critical need to fit HR strategy with business strategy (sometimes referred to as vertical or external integration). There has been a wealth of literature prescribing the content of HR strategy and how this can be fashioned to meet the needs of the organisation. Fombrun, Tichy and Devanna (1984) explicitly describe organisational strategy as determining HR strategy, and Schuler and Jackson (1987) produce a model which describes the behaviours required and personnel policies needed, to support three strategic organisational positions based on Porter's competitive strategies. Miles and Snow (1984) develop an alternative model which relates HR strategy to three basic relationships which the organisation has with its product market–defenders, prospectors and analysers. On a broad level, Legge (1989) argues that there are difficulties in matching HRM policy to business strategy, and the specific models developed have been criticised. For example, Fombrun *et al.*'s fit model has since been criticised on the basis of being unitarist, assuming a passive workforce, and ignoring other stakeholders and influences (Boxall, 1992). More adventurous models suggest that HR strategy can drive business strategy (*see*, for example, Butler, 1988) and Purcell (1995). Some sophisticated models of HR strategy still utilise the idea of fit but take a more interactive and processual approach (*see*, for example, Hendry and Pettigrew, 1992). Our research focuses on the process side of HR strategy but we do pay attention, in general terms, to evidence of fit or otherwise with business strategy.

A second theme in HR strategy relates to internal integration – in other words the need for HR strategy to be consistent and mutually reinforcing within itself. Lengnick-Hall and Lengnick-Hall (1988) discuss the need for two types of fit – external integration (as described in the paragraph above), and internal or horizontal fit between all aspects of the HR strategy itself. Kochan, Katz and McKersie (1990), and Baird and Meshoulam (1988) also emphasise the importance of the different components of HR strategy being mutually reinforcing. We explore the concept in internal fit in our interviews.

The ideal model of HR strategy has generally been portrayed as a vertically and horizontally integrated entity, planned rationally in advance, which exists in material form – written down so that it can be examined. A more sophisticated model of this ideal is of a fully integrated business strategy which incorporates HR strategy in a seamless manner as the whole is developed together rather than separately. In this sense HR strategy ceases to exist as a separate functional strategy.

We have already referred, above, to some of the more critical literature in relation to HR strategy, but two more issues are worthy of note. First, on a more practical level, a lack of attention to implementation of HR strategy has been identified (For example, Beaumont, 1992; Lundy and Cowling 1996; Hall and Torrington, 1996), while this was not the focus of our research, we recognise this as a gap which needs addressing with some urgency.

Second, some of the difficulties with the fit models lie in the use of the traditional perspective of strategy as a rational process. Alternatively, Stacey (1993), for example, sees strategy as order emerging from chaos, rather than as a rational long-term plan, and Mintzberg (1987) characterises strategy as a pattern of behaviour which has evolved over time rather than being rationally designed and then implemented. He argues that it is constantly adjusted through experience, changing circumstances and information rising up through the organisation. Although an organisation may have a written strategy, it is constantly changing, and the fact that there is no written strategy does not mean that a strategy does not exist. Strategy is formed, he argues, not formulated, and thus can be seen with more clarity in retrospect. Similarly, Boxall (1992), in an HRM context, sees strategy as something which helps us make sense, post hoc, of the choices made.

This leads us to question whether the term 'human resource strategy' could be used in a different way than the term 'strategic human resource management'. The first suggests strategy as an entity in the form of a comprehensive rationally derived plan, whereas the second is more suggestive of a frame of mind and an interactive process. We would agree with Boxall (1994) who suggests that it is the stream of strategic decisions which we need to focus on, not a strategy. Tyson explains strategy as a process (1995a) and Whipp (1992) comments that 'the ability to see strategy as a process can not be emphasised too strongly'. Rothwell (1995) similarly views strategy as a complex interpersonal process. We approached our research with an openness to both perspectives, and our results confirm the value of understanding strategy as a process rather than an entity. We return to these two perspectives on strategy when we discuss the complexities of researching HR strategy, but first we consider why HR professionals are attracted by the prospect of strategic involvement.

The attraction of strategic involvement for the HR specialist

Strategic involvement can be seen as a way of emphasising a function often perceived as marginal and ambiguous (*see*, for example, Legge, 1978; Watson, 1977), and a function whose contribution to the business has often been questioned (*see*, for example, Hunter, 1957 and Niven, 1967). Fernie (1994) identifies a search for legitimacy for a personnel function which, in the past has been accused of not serving organisational goals. Beyond a search for legitimacy there is a search for status, as Purcell and Ahlstrand (1994) express it, 'strategy presupposes importance'. Guest (1990) and Kamoche (1994), among others, have noted the attraction of strategy in the function's quest for status. Hendry and Pettigrew (1990) argue that 'what HRM offered was a focus for challenging deficiencies in attitudes, scope, coherence and direction – of existing personnel management' and it is interesting to note that an emphasis on HR strategy appears to provide a remedy for each of these perceived ailments. On a more practical level, Schuler (1990) predicts an increase in status for the function if it can successfully link personnel/HR practices with the organisation's strategic goals, and Bevan and Thompson (1991) suggest that the goal of the personnel function should be to move from 'a reactive functionalist welfare model towards a more proactive strategic facilitator model'. In addition, the adoption of a strategic role rather than an operational one changes the nature of the 'customer' or 'client' of the HR function. It is the managers of the organisation who become the key customers of the HR function, and hence members of the HR function will spend their time interacting with managers rather than all employees. In personnel/HR management texts, strategic involvement is seen to be, almost without exception, 'a good thing' (Armstrong, 1992; Walker, 1992; Harrison, 1993, among others).

Strategic involvement has also become enshrined in the qualification structure for the personnel profession. The Lead Body Model of personnel management includes strategic involvement in their core units and in their key statement of purpose for personnel (PSLB, 1993), and strategy is a very visible component of the IPD syllabuses. This visibility in itself can have a powerful influence over the aspirations of IPD members and those undergoing the qualifications process. However, Gibb (1995) argues convincingly that this does not mean that this is an accurate picture of what practitioners actually do, but a consequence of stakeholder attitudes in the PSLB process, and perhaps the desire to reflect their own perceived level of importance.

Our interview respondents without exception saw involvement in HR strategy as a positive thing, and had accepted the rhetoric of strategic involvement, regardless of the extent to which they were currently involved:

> What we **should** be here to do is to set the policies, or help the business set the policies and identify the long term issues, like in 10 years' time we're going to need this skill . . . not the day to day issues.
>
> (HR manager, electronics)

Many were apologetic in tone if they thought they were not doing as much as they should, and had plans to increase their involvement and 'do it better' in the future. Strategic involvement appeared to be how they measured their personal success, their view of the legitimate role of the personnel function, and how they added value to the business, rather than by any operational contribution. The issue of contribution to the business, status, interaction with managers and distancing from the welfare role are all evident in the following quote:

> Everyone in the department thinks we are an HR function, because we are not a tea and sympathy function, it's very much getting the strategy and big ideas and making it go through – but still maintaining gentle face. You (ordinary employees) can come and talk to us, but we're here to support the policies of the company and develop plans that will develop the company . . . We're here for management, to help them do the job and the staff shouldn't need to run to us every two minutes if their managers are doing a good job.
>
> (Head of personnel, publishing/retail)

Another spoke of involvement in strategy as 'driving the organisation forward' rather than being in just a support role, and here there is a sense of the function having the opportunity to lead rather than merely to follow.

The level of strategic involvement appeared to weigh heavily on the minds of our interview respondents, and some demonstrated a self-questioning approach to the value of their work. They almost asked themselves questions like: Do I come up to scratch? Have I made as much progress as I could have done? After answering a question on strategic activities of the HR function, one respondent (who had given us some clear examples of his strategic involvement) commented:

> Is this really strategic? – the answer is that hitherto 'not as strategic as it could be'.
>
> (Head of retail HR, building society)

We were convinced from the interviews that the rhetoric of strategic involvement was accepted and that it was a desirable end to strive towards. This does not reflect on the achievability of strategic involvement, or whether it is an appropriate aim in individual circumstances.

Complexities of researching HR strategy

So far we have largely considered the concept of HR strategy, in terms of the characteristics of its 'idealised' form and the attraction which it may hold for personnel specialists. But we have also alluded to strategy as a process. Research into the existence of HR strategy is problematic in a number of ways:

1 Strategy is not a single concept. First, we are influenced by our own understanding of what is meant by HR strategy and our own perspectives and interests. This determines the questions we ask and the ways that we understand the answers. In our research we have a broad view of strategy which accepts that strategy is therefore not necessarily a written document, even if it is written it is likely that it will exist in different places, each source written at a different time; and that it is not necessarily comprehensive. We

are inclined to view strategy as a process as much as a thing, and evidence of strategic thinking and strategic decision making, as expressed by Boxall (1994) in respect of HR strategy. The words 'strategic human resource management' more closely capture the essence of what we are looking for, rather than 'an HR strategy', although we certainly did not ignore the second. This interpretation of strategy makes its existence, or otherwise, more elusive and difficult to pin down, and puts a heavier weight on our interpretation of what our respondents tell us.

2 Second, what we find will be influenced by the interpretations that our respondents have of strategy. Particularly in the questionnaire we may find overoptimistic results in terms of strategic involvement as the word strategic may be interpreted by respondents very loosely. We have also noted how desirable it is for personnel managers to be seen to be involved in strategy and this will no doubt consciously or unconsciously affect their responses. In addition, aware of Marginson's (1988) finding, that although eighty per cent of personnel chiefs claimed to have an overall HR policy, very few when asked could describe it, we aimed to probe the initial responses we were given. Thus, in the interviews we aimed to understand our respondents' definitions by asking them for examples of their strategic involvement. In many cases this gave us confidence that our definitions were broadly the same, but it has to be noted that some of our respondents' definitions varied widely. We have tried to separate out those responses where their interpretations were very different from the general characteristics of strategy which we have accepted, based on Johnson, as our working definition, such as a long-term perspective. For example, when we asked about involvement in HR strategy some respondents gave us examples such as producing new employee handbooks, new safety manuals, and relocation packages in response to a geographic and structural reorganisation; or a description of the operational activities of the function. One commented that: 'We develop an annual training strategy' (General manager, local government).

Such different interpretations have most probably resulted in an overoptimistic picture, of strategic involvement in the questionnaire results, but the ability to probe in the interviews and ask for examples to back up assertions should also mean that such overstatement is less likely in the interview results.

3 Third, the ultimate ideal of HR strategy is often identified as full integration with business strategy, which Baird, Meshoulam and De Give as early as 1983 describe very clearly, arguing that:

Human resources can not be integrated as a separate element into the organisation strategy, because there is no organisation strategy without the inclusion of human resources.

Clearly this type of integration is an ideal and implies that strategy is developed in a holistic way from the outset rather than being formed of separate functional strategies which are then brought together. If this ideal is reached fully, or even partially, is it then possible to disentangle HR strategy from organisation strategy, in order to identify whether or not it exists? In this case the fact that it does not exist independently is surely evidence of a more, rather than less, sophisticated approach to HR strategy.

4   Fourth, as we are interested in strategic HRM as a process, then we are interested in *who* is involved in strategic HRM and *how* they are involved. We only collected questionnaire data from, and interviewed, personnel specialists (bar two interview exceptions). Our perspective is that of the specialist – the extent to which the HR specialist is involved in HR strategy. There are two implications of this reflecting pressures acting in opposite directions. First, that this tells us about the *minimum level* at which strategic HRM exists in these organisations, as sometimes the contribution of others in this area will be excluded. Second, previous research (*see*, for example, Burack, 1985) suggests that HR specialists perceive the extent of their involvement in given activities to be greater than the extent perceived by others in the same organisation.

Strategic involvement of the HR specialist

As a backcloth to analysing the involvement of HR specialists in HR strategy in our research, it is useful to recapitulate on the results of previous studies relating to evidence of the existence of HR strategy and evidence of the strategic involvement of HR specialists. Until recently, despite the rhetoric on the importance of HR strategy, researchers found little evidence of its existence. Whipp and Clark (1986) comment that:

> Case studies completed in the 1970s showed just how alien was the notion of strategy in the personnel and industrial relations functions across different industries.

Later, Hendry *et al.* (1989) found that: The claim that UK firms are well positioned to adopt something called 'strategic human resource management' looks decidedly suspect.

In 1992 Storey found only modest evidence of a strategic approach to HR in 15 in-depth case studies of large organisations in the UK carried out between 1986 and 1988. However in a more recent article reporting further work with the same case-study organisations (Storey, 1995) he comments that 'we were impressed by the extent to which by 1993–4 the case companies had begun to take a strategic view of HR management' (p. 10). This comment, however, gives no indication of who is involved in developing the strategic view, and line management involvement in HR strategy has emerged as a key theme. Brewster and Hegewisch (1994) found only fifty per cent of UK companies had a written HR strategy but, as Tyson (1995b) points out, it does depend on what you mean by a written HR strategy.

If, as Fowler (1987) suggests, 'HRM represents the discovery of personnel management by chief executives,' and one of the key aspects of HRM is HRM strategy, then we may speculate that senior and general management might dominate the development of HR strategy. Indeed, Storey (1992) found that the personnel function was often overlooked in the development of HR strategy in favour of line management involvement. Guest (1990) argues that the implication of the concentration on the importance of people in organisations is that 'HR is too important to be left to personnel managers but is instead a key strategic issue demanding the attention of all managers' (p. 378). Freedman (1985) found that organisations where there have been a significant number of HRM innovations line managers were more likely to be involved.

So far, in the UK context, the extent to which HR practitioners are involved in strategy, appears to be minimal. Monks (1992) in an Irish study identified only nine out of the 87 organisations surveyed in 1989–90 as having personnel functions which were regarded as important and which had long-term plans. Storey (1992) reporting on his 15 case studies identified four distinct types of personnel function roles. He found that in only two of the case studies did the personnel function approximate to the strategic and interventionary roles of 'changemaker'.

In our research we found that the HR function was involved in strategy to a greater extent than previous research has generally indicated. Table 6.1 shows the results of a question which asked respondents to select the one, closest, type of strategic involvement that the HR function had in a range of different areas of HR. Five choices were available to describe the involvement in each area. Putting aside the differences between the content areas, there are two clear messages in this table. The first is that in each area (with the two exceptions of quality initiatives and work design) only a small percentage of personnel functions felt that they had no strategic involvement. For example, in recruitment and selection, and in employee relations only five per cent reported no strategic involvement. The second is that if we follow Mintzberg's (1994) division of strategy and planning and compare the two choices which clearly focus on strategy development (columns 1 and 2) with those which focus on to a greater extent on planning issues – that is implementation of strategy and information input into strategy development (columns 3 and 4) – then the emphasis is on strategy development as opposed to related activities. In all content areas, except for work design, the combined percentage from columns 1 and 2 exceeds the combined percentage from columns 3 and 4. In terms of content areas most strategic involvement was in the area of employee relations (72 per cent), followed closely by training (70 per cent), management development (67

Table 6.1 Personnel roles in HR strategy. Answers to the question, 'Which of the following most closely describes the nature of the personnel function's involvement at a strategic level in each of the areas listed below?'

	Develops strategy alone	Develops strategy with the line	Provides information to inform strategic decisions	Implements strategic decisions	None
	Percentage	Percentage	Percentage	Percentage	Percentage
HR planning	9	49	26	6	10
Recruitment and selection	15	49	14	16	5
Work design	2	25	24	13	35
Performance management	7	44	23	10	16
Quality initiatives	4	38	17	11	29
Training	10	60	12	7	11
Management development	10	57	10	7	16
Career planning	7	50	16	6	22
Communications	10	53	17	10	10
Employee relations/ involvement	16	56	15	7	5
Health and safety	13	38	15	14	21
Reward	8	45	17	14	17
Redundancy and dismissal	11	46	23	14	6

Row total = @ 100% (+ or – rounding).

per cent), recruitment and selection (64 per cent) and communications (63 per cent). It is interesting that these are the traditional bread and butter areas of personnel management, and correspond to those areas which our interview respondents identified as most important to the business.

This level of strategic involvement is, in some ways, reinforced by the interviews, in that two-thirds (21 out of 30) were able to give at least one example of strategic involvement. One HR director stated that:

> My role is in setting the direction and making sure the resources are there in terms of specialist capacity to continue to meet that direction and meet the (business) strategic demands.
>
> (Director of HR and corporate affairs, NHS Trust)

He spoke of the separate HR strategy which was designed to turn business plans into practice, and that the strategy was:

> Not a strategy in terms of numbers, it talks about trends – more of this, less of that and picks out the threads of direction and pace. But it's not a huge book – it's only three to four pages.

In explaining what issues the strategy addressed this director spoke of the balance between different types of staff, skill mix, pay, recruitment, employee relations and staffing levels. Along similar lines an HR director in the pharmaceuticals industry commented:

> We have got a strategy that's the first thing – we actually sat down and tried to articulate what it was that we thought we should be doing and our most pressing concern is a flexible multi-skilled workforce – that is what I'm here to try and achieve. We are doing it by investing quite a lot in training and development . . . we are investors in people here . . .

This director went on to talk of a picture that managers in the organisation had of a Greek temple supported by pillars. The roof of the temple was their version of quality management and to support this there were some pillars representing manufacturing systems and others representing a variety of human resource issues and systems. They visualised progress by building up each pillar at the same pace, because if there was too much progress on some pillars and not enough on others the roof would become unbalanced and collapse. In another organisation the head of personnel explained that:

> There is an HR strategy in that we want to have a committed, developed, multi-skilled workforce, but that's easy to say, it's got to be put in the context of what the business is doing . . .

He went on to explain that the senior managers are committed to this, and that as there is a board director for personnel then the strategies and policies are discussed at top level, and generally accepted, although they change rapidly as the business changes. In one establishment there was an HR strategy produced by the head of personnel which was regarded more as a discussion document, and used for departmental development days. This statement linked the eight strategic goals of the organisation to the strategy of the HR function. However, although the HR strategy existed, and indeed was read by one of the authors, it was not an 'official' document because the organisation's strategy to meet the eight goals had not been developed and the HR strategy had not been ratified by senior management. Here was an example of an HR department pushing at the boundaries. It also raises the issue of the value of such a strategy if it is not owned and implemented by the whole organisation. As Duberley and Burns (1991) put it, 'what's the point of having wonderfully strategic human resource policies if they bear no relationship to what's happening in the organisation?'

To provide a balanced view of our findings we quote, at the other end of the spectrum from the general affairs manager in a manufacturing business. This manager, who was the most senior person responsible for personnel matters, had previous HR experience in other companies, had staff reporting to her who were studying for the IPD, but did not have a personnel/HR job title, commented:

> Well there's not too much strategic activity – the attitude here really is that we (personnel staff) just do what we're told . . . Basically we are perceived to be people who do, not the people who are consulted or involved . . . It's getting slightly better because we have a new deputy chairman and he certainly involves me a lot more, which is good, but the overall strategy which involves us, as personnel and payroll, is minimal.
>
> (General affairs manager, manufacturing)

Although our research identifies many differences between organisations, it provides evidence that the strategic involvement of the HR function is both real and increasing – a finding which is at odds with Purcell (1989) and Sisson (1995) who argue that HRM as a strategic activity peaked in the 1980s. It is also a finding which provides a more positive picture than for example, Storey (1992). One reason for this difference may be the perspective; ours is from within the function whereas Storey's data was largely from a general management perspective. Similarly the way in which we reached our respondents may well skew our sample towards those organisations which have a greater commitment to the personnel management profession, and which are therefore more likely to support the involvement of personnel practitioners in HR strategy. Another explanation for this difference may be the date of the research. Storey reports on what was happening in 1986–8, whereas our findings reflect data collected in 1994–5 – in other words the situation on the ground really is changing. There is support for this explanation from a number of sources. First, the personnel practitioners interviewed often described the way that their involvement in HR strategy was either beginning or increasing, and that it was expected to continue to increase. Similarly there was evidence to suggest that the role of the personnel function in business strategy as a whole was gradually beginning to increase. Second, some interviewees identified changes in business demands which had resulted in the necessity for a more strategic approach from the personnel function – an issue which we shall return to later in this chapter.

A further point to consider in relation to our findings is the level of the organisation (establishment/business unit level) at which we carried out our research. The literature and research we have reported in Chapter 5 suggests that the importance of the HR function at corporate level is declining, and that the function at business level is likely to be more prominent. While some writers have argued that strategy is not appropriately formed at business level, there is increasing evidence to suggest that strategy development does happen here and there is the opportunity for HR specialists to be involved at this level.

The nature of HR strategy: internal and external integration?

However, the positive picture painted above does not mean that all 21 organisations had an internally integrated HR strategy, and we have so far accepted a relatively broad definition of HR strategy. Only five respondents were able to give any indication of anything like an integrated HR strategy, and most respondents spoke about HR programmes, initiatives or individual areas of strategy which may have been developed with long-term perspectives and had long-term consequences for the business. For example, a typical response was:

> Currently we're just responding to changing circumstances. We've no integrated HR strategy.
>
> (HR manager, electronics)

from an HR manager who explained this in an apologetic way. He then went on to explain how the product strategy had changed from a small number of generic products to a larger number of customer specific products. The outcome of this would be more production teams, with more team leaders needing different types of skills than in the past. He explained how his HR team was involved in developing the new organisational structure and the development programme to make sure that the line had the team leaders with the appropriate skills when needed.

When asked whether the HR strategy was integrated, or just based around individual issues one HR director stated:

> I think, if I'm honest it would be very much on an individual, broadly we're saying that the three areas that we're looking at are reward, performance and training and development which we're doing a lot of work on now. So if you say yes, this is where we're going, but they've all been plucked out because those are the concerns of the trust, rather than me saying, maybe we should have this umbrella strategy.
>
> (HR director, NHS Trust)

The picture was one of a piecemeal rather than holistic approach; generally reacting to separately identified issues rather than having a more proactive open-ended approach. It appeared that strategic involvement focused on those issues identified by the business as requiring a strategic contribution from the personnel function.

However, a few were embarking on the beginnings of a more integrated approach. One HR manager explained how the new chief executive was: 'coming back with loads of things in terms of management style and culture and the way we manage our staff that we hadn't heard before', and went on to explain that in the HR function:

> now we can take all our existing HR policies and practices and techniques right across the HR function and say do they really line up with every single thing the CE wants?
>
> (Head of personnel, building society)

Another explained how:

> We've asked them all (the business level HR committees, which include the senior personnel person in the business) to move into an integrated strategy – they haven't been doing that . . .
>
> (HR adviser, services)

Another indicator of the lack of an integrated approach to HR strategy can be found in the questionnaire results. When looking across the responses for each single establishment in respect of every area of potential strategic involvement a very inconsistent pattern was displayed – with high involvement in some areas and none in others. This pattern suggests that either the strategy in these areas was being developed elsewhere or that they were neglected in terms of strategy development, indicating that the approach to HR strategy was not comprehensive or consistent.

While the evidence for the development of internally integrated HR strategies was limited and the general picture was one of a piecemeal rather than a holistic approach, there was much more evidence of external fit with business strategy. Most establishments portrayed a picture of HR strategic involvement being focused on those issues identified by the business as requiring an HR strategic contribution, and in this sense HR strategy was business driven. Many respondents spoke of strategy as being 'commercially driven' or 'marketing driven'. One manager explained his view:

> that (HR) can't shape strategies but we can be the key to implementing strategies . . . the business managers lead the business. What we can do is take their vision and implement that bit of the vision that impacts on the human resource side of things – which is almost all of it because you can't really have a strategy that doesn't involve HR in the organisation.
>
> (HR manager, electronics)

All but two respondents were clear of the direction of fit – that business strategy determined HR strategy. The two who indicated the potential of the HR strategy to drive the business strategy were both in service sector establishments with a high proportion of business costs being allocated to pay. One respondent, referred to above, had developed a form of HR strategy, which was designed to meet business needs but as yet was not agreed strategy across the business.

Accepting that textbook definitions of the fully integrated HR strategy are few and far between, we have found forms of HR strategy clearly related to business strategy and which have long-term consequences for the relationship between the organisation and its employees. Strategy, albeit piecemeal, appears to be a reality at business unit level, and irrespective of the extent to which the personnel function was currently involved in HR strategy, over half the interviewees felt that they should be doing more in terms of strategy and had plans to increase their involvement in the future. Many were in a transitional stage of increasing involvement. Almost every interviewee (n = 26) explained that their personnel function was devolving personnel responsibilities to line managers. Some respondents, as we explained in Chapter 4 on devolution, made the explicit link of shedding the day-to-day operational personnel work and spending the time gained on strategy.

The nature of strategic involvement

So far we have considered to what extent HR specialists are involved in HR strategy and what form that strategy takes, we now turn to issues of how and with whom that strategy is developed. Evidence suggests that the participation of line managers and HR specialists in HR strategy development does not have to be an either/or question. In a US study Martell and Carroll (1995) found that line managers play a role in HRM policy making in partnership with personnel specialists. Towers Perrin (undated) report that in 1991 their survey respondents all indicated that HR strategy was predominantly defined by HR departments (39 per cent) rather than shared with the line (28 per cent). The respondents projected however that this situation would be reversed by the year 2000. Twenty-seven per cent identified the HR department as solely responsible for HR strategy in 2000 compared with 50 per cent identifying that responsibility would fall to a line/HRM partnership (p. 89). This apparent trend presents a conflicting picture to a traditional view which characterises the personnel function as being isolationist, operating from an ivory tower, trying to impose its views on the organisation without any real understanding of business pressures; or on the other hand being isolated from the business, for example, Nkomo (1988).

Returning to Table 6.1 there is a clear indication that HR strategy is co-determined with the line rather than being the province solely of the personnel function. In every content area shown on Table 6.1 the percentages in column

2 (showing strategy development in partnership with the line) was always greater than that in column 1 (showing the personnel function developing HR strategy alone). In the most extreme case column 2 was over 12 times column 1 (work design), but was more typically around six times that in column 1, as, for example, in performance management and training. The smallest multiple was health and safety, with just under three times that in column 1.

The interviews provided us with many illustrations of how this works in practice. On an issue basis many interviewees reported that line colleagues were involved from the outset in discussing HR policy/strategy decisions, in order to incorporate their critical input. Other organisations had formed cross-functional semi-permanent groups where key personnel issues would be debated. Some organisations arranged away days and policy conferences involving line managers where HR strategy would be discussed. In other organisations the process was less formalised and less focused. In these cases senior personnel staff would use political and campaigning skills on a continuous basis with senior and line managers to develop a joint understanding of the HR strategy that was needed to be developed, anticipating that this process would take years rather than months.

As one HR director commented:

> I would like to be influential, but I think we should be less solely responsible, and I think the way to achieve things is to get a much closer partnership with line managers . . . that is going to make my job and our job more difficult but it is bound to be beneficial in the long run, I'm sure.
>
> (HR director, pharmaceuticals)

In another organisation the personnel manager reinforced this:

> That's why the organisation's got to be clear about some of those strategic issues because we will not be solely responsible for those strategies – we will contribute with change management – it would be ludicrous for us to be solely responsible.
>
> (Personnel manager, police force)

This same manager went on to explain how a cross-functional approach to HR strategy development mirrors (as in some other organisations) a cross-functional approach to business strategy, where HR has been involved along with other functions:

> In the past it would have been a case of somebody somewhere would be charged with drawing up a policy document – they would have gone into a cupboard somewhere and emerged back six months later and said 'here's a fully formed policy', two weeks before it came into action . . . Now . . . there's a more cross-functional approach to it. So whenever there's a major strategic issue being debated you're more likely to find multi-function teams being put together to take it forward.
>
> (Personnel manager, police force)

This applied to HR issues as well as other business issues. In another establishment a more ambitious project was underway, where a cross-functional team was brought together for 18 months to work on overall strategy for the establishment and who operated as an adjunct to the executive board.

> . . . the team that has been formulated, members have been extracted from engineering divisions, from personnel and the marketing and sales areas, and each of them have an equal say in the overall strategy.
>
> (Divisional personnel adviser, insurance)

The interviews revealed that the extent to which the personnel function was involved in organisational strategy was very mixed, ranging from those being heavily involved to those who had no involvement whatsoever.

The process of strategy formation clearly has an impact on the nature of the resultant strategy. Strategies that are jointly developed across functions are more likely to integrate HR and business issues, and we found evidence of a changing approach towards strategy development generally which emphasised integration rather than functional separateness, and sometimes HR is seen as the integrating factor:

> It seems to be written by five functional leaders and it didn't read very well – it wasn't very integrated, so it almost said human resources will do this, finance were going to do this, production were going to do that, and maybe someday in the future they would meet and regard themselves as a team. So, we have started again for this one. We are not having separate ones . . . Let's integrate the activities so we have the theme of human resources just running through what everyone else is doing . . . That seems to improve things – this version for this year.
>
> (HR director, pharmaceuticals)

Other evidence of HR at least having the opportunity to be an integrating factor is in one establishment where the head of personnel had just been allocated a second major role – that of co-ordinator of the organisation's strategy.

Not only is strategy development cross functional, in a few cases it involves all levels of the establishment. For example, there may be working parties involving representatives from a range of departments and of differing levels to discuss the implementation of a strategy. We had examples of task teams working on specific strategy areas. In one organisation all staff were divided into groups and each group made a video of suggested improvements which were watched by the chief executive and senior management team. Another organisation had 'talkbacks' – a live version of the previous idea but not necessarily involving all staff. In the same organisation management review seminars were run where the directors presented their perspective and were 'put on the spot' to answer difficult questions. Not all these activities were identified as strategic, but there was clear input of these into strategic thinking in the organisation.

Influences on strategic involvement

Board membership

For some time, the status of the most senior personnel/HR person, in terms of whether or not they are a director and member of the board, has been identified as one of the major influences on whether the personnel/HR specialist is involved in any aspect of strategy. Board membership is seen as important as it enables the personnel specialist to be in a position where they can be involved in strategy development at the outset rather than being involved at a later stage to implement a strategy which has already been decided by others. Sisson (1995), for example, argues that if personnel specialists are not there when the key decisions are taken then 'personnel issues are almost inevitably condemned to second-order status' and the personnel contribution is limited to 'dealing with the implications of implementing such decisions' (p. 97). Such was the perceived importance of Board membership, that it was almost taken for a proxy for strategic involvement. We will, therefore, briefly consider the evidence to date on the existence of personnel/HR board membership.

In 1984, together with MacKay, we carried out a survey similar to the one which we are reporting in this book. The survey was similar in terms of the way in which we contacted our respondents and in terms of the representation of different sectors of the economy, although there were some differences in organisational size (*see* Appendix 5). In this survey 21 per cent of establishments had personnel board level representation (Mackay and Torrington, 1986). Higher figures have since been found by other researchers, for example, Millward *et al.* (1992) found that in 69 per cent of establishments the personnel function was represented at board level. Similarly, Brewster and Smith (1990) found 63 per cent of corporate personnel functions were represented on the main board, and Poole and Jenkins (1996) report that two-thirds of their respondents stated that the most senior personnel/HR manager was on the board, or top policy committee. In the analysis of our current research, board membership reaches high proportions with 63 per cent of functions being represented at board level, as shown in Table 6.2. This demonstrates a considerable increase on the 21 per cent we found 12 years ago.

All these figures suggest increasing levels of board membership; however, Purcell (1995) found declining board membership in his nine longitudinal case studies. In addition, the figures produced by Millward had changed little since 1980 and included non-personnel specialists representing the personnel function (specialist representation was 40 per cent in 1990), and it has been argued that board membership is now declining (*see*, for example, Tyson, 1995). It is interesting that when conducting the interviews we found a more complex picture than a simple increase. Two organisations had previously had an HR director on the board, but no longer had one. In one organisation the title of

Table 6.2 Representation of the personnel department on the establishment's board. Answers to the question, 'Does s/he have a decision-making place on the board (where you work), if applicable?' Please circle category

Nature of role	Number of responses	Percentage of responses
Yes, a decision making role	85	53
Yes, place on the board but not as a decision maker	16	10
No place on board	58	37
Total	159*	100

* Fifty-five establishments are not included in this analysis. This is because there was no board at establishment level, or in a few cases, because an unclear response was given to the question.

HR director was held by someone outside the function. We also discovered establishments where there the most senior personnel person had previously been a board member, but when they left the new appointee to head the personnel function was not automatically given a place on the board – they first had to earn their spurs. In these establishments the new appointee was, a few years later, having gained credibility and trust, then appointed to the board. Figures of board membership can be misleading. While board membership may well have stabilised, there is insufficient evidence based on small numbers of case studies to claim that it is declining.

However, while board membership is clearly a beneficial position, doubt has been shed on the relationship between board membership and strategic involvement. For example, Brewster and Bournois (1991) and also Purcell (1995) who found that the most influential HR directors in his research cases were those with a close personal working relationship with the chief executive, argued that corridor power was more in evidence than functional authority. Tyson (1995a) concludes that those with HR responsibility are exercising a much more political and flexible role. We also found that board membership did not guarantee a strategic approach to HR, as did Sisson, and in one establishment the existence of an HR director did not seem to have stimulated any involvement in HR strategy.

Whilst we found that board membership did have some impact on involvement in strategy, there were a number of other influences making this a complex relationship. The dangers of not being represented on the board can be summed up by:

> There is a principal steering group (like a board) – a sort of executive committee and I am not represented on that which I think is quite a serious problem. I report to the

financial secretary, and he is represented on that. He is actually quite good at raising personnel issues but he doesn't always see the personnel implications until too late.

(Personnel manager, education)

However, we found clear evidence of HR strategy and a commitment to people issues in organisations without a board director representing the personnel function. One of our interviewees explained this well when he talked of the impact of the mindset of the chief executive:

I'm not entirely convinced of the argument which says that there's got to be an HR director on the board. I think it's very much down to the mindset of the chief executive and to what extent he's basically got an HRM mindset.

(Head of retail HR, building society)

In this organisation, although there was no HR director, the chief executive had identified three high-level critical success factors for the organisation, and one of these was about people.

Levels of board membership then appear to have stabilised. Although being a board member can be beneficial in terms of strategic involvement, it does not automatically guarantee this, and alternatively, lack of board membership can not be taken to infer a lack of strategic involvement. There are too many other influencing factors for board membership to be taken, simply, as a proxy of strategic involvement. It is to these other factors which we now turn.

Impact of the environment

The interviews revealed that not only is the content of HR strategy driven by the business and reactive, but the extent to which the personnel function was involved in strategy was also heavily influenced by the circumstances facing the business.

Six of the 30 interviewees explicitly expressed a view that the current role and importance of the function (and this included specifically their involvement in strategy) was affected by the business environment. The impact of this was in all cases that they had become more central, more important and more involved. Consequently, the argument was also made that if the circumstances changed then the role and importance of the function would also change, especially their strategic role. These interviewees represented a range of sectors – manufacturing (two organisations), local government, central government, communications and the health sector. The following quotes typify how interviewees felt:

In terms of where the business is going, it's very much a marketing company, but personnel are right at the beginning of the concept stage, are involved in the implications for the people side of the business. It's not a question of picking up the pieces – it used to be . . . When we're discussing for instance the introduction of a new product and the need to produce that on a shiftworking basis, the meeting sort of stops and they turn to me and are prepared at that stage to listen to the implications.

When asked why the change in role had taken place:

We didn't have the change. Certainly not the rate of change to deal with. There were less variables and less impact on the people.

(Company personnel manager, food manufacturing)

Another head of personnel, this time from the public sector commented that:

I think it puts us at the centre of things. I think that of all the issues that are going to occur with the reorganisation, the HR issues are going to be the big ones . . . You can see it's quite an exciting time really. I wouldn't say that we wouldn't have an important role – but there would be greater pressure on us to reduce our costs.

(Head of personnel, local government)

The director of personnel in an NHS Trust argued that the increasing importance of the personnel function had come about due to three factors. First, that a less central structure was provided now that the Whitley councils were gone, and that the personnel function was needed to help the organisation interpret where it needed to go from here. Second, the influence of senior employees who had been appointed from the private sector and who had greater expectations of the role that the personnel function should play. And, third, that the Trust's agenda was that 'they are employers in their own right and have to develop their own relationship with the staff'. Other interviewees raising the same issue, commented on how changes being currently experienced were bringing HR issues to the fore and hence the personnel function was seen as key within the organisation. Some could see circumstances changing yet again to those where HR would no longer be such a key focus.

In general the function's position in the organisation seems to be constantly on the move which is well exemplified by the following:

But it's at a real crisis point (the personnel function). Either it goes forward and actually takes on a much more strategic role than it has been able to do up until now or it gets pushed down again.

(Personnel manager, education)

Influence of the chief executive and business relationships

A further important factor in HR strategic involvement was the relationship of the most senior personnel person with the chief executive. In some cases a direct formal reporting relationship was found to be helpful, and in others the building up of a good working relationship:

. . . time spent with her (the CE), discussing issues gets HR onto her agenda, gets her agenda onto the HR side as well, so we know what's in her mind, and given the way this organisation revolves around the chief executive . . .

(Personnel manager, TEC)

For others it was the perspective of the chief executive that was important:

I think the CEO really believes that sustainable competitive advantage can only be derived through people.

(Head of personnel, building society)

This was a very different environment from the many where specialists talked about selling ideas to the chief executive – not that this approach was ineffective in operating at a strategic level and:

trying to work with the business . . . they've got to understand (line managers) . . . and that's why we've got to sell ourselves.

(Head of personnel, retail)

In addition, those specialists who build informal networks to test ideas and get the support of key managers appeared to have greater involvement in strategy.

Individual characteristics of the HR professional

Another key dimension was the skills and personality of the most senior HR person – they were often involved, not because of their formal role but because of their individual skills and the potential they have to offer to the organisation. For example, in the insurance company referred to above all members of the strategy team were not expected to return to their original jobs, but to move on within the company after their developmental experience. One personnel manager had the confidence and skills to 'gatecrash' board meetings, and others talked of constantly influencing other managers and campaigning in respect of personnel issues. When asked if their contribution to the HR committee (which dealt with strategy) was proactive one personnel adviser stated that:

It depends who you've got on the committee and how loud you are . . . you've got to get them to trust you.

(Personnel adviser, services)

Another director of HR and corporate affairs (NHS Trust) stated that: 'So I guess it's more personality and personal skills than it is a function', and 'most of it's down to personality' stated another head of department from retailing. Creating opportunities was seen as important by others, for example:

My responsibility as head of department is to see where there is an opportunity for us (HR) to intervene.

(Head of personnel, central government)

Additional responsibilities gave senior personnel specialists further entrées – in one establishment the personnel manager had been made responsible for organisational strategy and in another the personnel director was also director for corporate affairs. One HR director was also responsible for the TQM initiative, something he had brought with him from his previous role in the establishment, which was outside the personnel function. Martell and Carroll (1995), in the USA argue that despite a modest view of the importance of the role of the HR function, general managers considered HR professionals as valuable members of their management team and 58 per cent of these general managers considered HR professionals as full strategic partners – in other words it is the individual rather than their functional label which is most important.

Conclusions

Our evidence suggests that personnel/HR specialists are increasingly involved in HR strategy, and we have already discussed some explanations as to why this involvement is greater than in previous research. We are not suggesting, however, that the establishments we visited had proactive, fully formed, vertically and horizontally integrated HR strategies. What we did find was evidence of strategic thinking, as a response to business need.

Few organisations looked towards the personnel function to produce an integrated HR strategy in response to business needs, but tended more to look towards a strategic response to identified key business issues. HR strategy thus tended to be in many cases reactive, in Ansoff's (1975) terms, rather than proactive, and was built up in a piecemeal rather than holistic way. This is similar to Guest's (1990) summary of US research findings. None of our interviewees identified HR strategy as driving business strategy, but there were many who identified business strategy as driving HR strategy. The question is whether this is such a bad thing. It demonstrates the personnel function being responsive to business need, and does move us on from the ivory tower syndrome where the personnel function know best irrespective of what the business thinks or needs. As Duberley and Burns (1991) put it, 'what's the point of having wonderfully strategic human resource policies if they bear no relationship to what's happening in the organisation'. Chapter 5, using the research of Farrell and Francis, we identified the importance of relating HR strategy to perceived business need, otherwise it is marginalised.

One approach to achieving this relationship depends on the whole organisation operating in a more integrated manner. A number of organisations had begun to see HR strategy as essentially integrated into the business, and there were examples of how business issues were addressed strategically in an integrated, rather than functional manner. Similarly, some more adventurous organisations were seeking to develop an overall integrated business strategy where every function was involved at the outset. From our evidence we suggest that the idea of functional strategy is nearing its sell-by date, and some singled out HR as the key to integration. Thus the nature of the business approach to strategy has critical implications for the nature of the personnel approach to HR strategy. The evidence from our research supports a process of evolution of strategy, as described by Mintzberg for both the business as a whole and for the function.

Whether or not HR strategy was developed in an integrated way with business strategy, there were strong indications (both from the questionnaire and the interviews) of HR strategy being determined not by the personnel function alone, but in partnership with the line. This supports similar findings (e.g. Towers Perrin, undated), and places the personnel function in a very different role than previously. In some ways, this evidence of *partnership* is our most important finding. The interviews revealed that personnel practitioners were wholehearted in working together with the line rather than apart from it. It reflects a change of stance away from the imposition of functional best practice towards co-determination of the most appropriate way forward on HR matters for the business, thus substituting realism for idealism. In one sense this limits the freedom of the function to provide a distinctive perspective, but in another sense it is more likely that their efforts will be translated into business functioning rather than being sidelined through pressure of business need. In the previous chapter we saw how, in a decentralised environment, department managers would tailor or avoid the business level HR strategy if it did not fit with their immediate business need, partly because they felt they had not been consulted or involved in the strategy development process.

Working in this way also makes different demands on personnel professionals in terms of skills and competencies required. In addition to functional expertise, other skills are absolutely key, such as strategic thinking, business awareness and understanding, influencing and political skills. This partnership with the line and interactive process of strategy formation also leads us to question whether Mintzberg's strict division between strategy visioning and implementation is helpful. Our evidence suggests that the stages of visioning and implementation are to some extent merged through the interactive processes used.

Storey (1992) identified the change in role of personnel practitioners as largely a result of pressures from outside the function. We also found that the business imperative and the perspective of the chief executive largely drives the extent to which personnel practitioners are involved in HR strategy, but the practitioners as individuals have been another major influence. Circumstances are providing a window of opportunity for the personnel function to make a greater contribution – and many individuals have grabbed this with both hands. The personal skills and competencies of individual personnel managers, and their working relationships, particularly with the chief executive, have in many organisations been critical. We found, as Pettigrew (1977) argues, that strategy is the result of a political process. If blessed with a position on the board these skills have enabled personnel managers to make the most of it. These skills have also enabled those in a different hierarchical position to circumvent the formal constraints and still have an important influence. Having a seat on the board is helpful, but not critical. Having a seat on the board does not automatically mean the strategic involvement of the personnel function – what matters is what the individual makes of their position. Real effectiveness comes from having an HRM 'mindset' – a shrewd understanding at a strategic level of the issues involved in HRM, which may have been developed through specialist personnel expertise and knowledge or otherwise. In other words the 'mindset' is more critical than the specialist skills.

In summary, the involvement of the personnel function in HR strategy has increased, and this increase has been influenced by the business imperative, critical personal skills of personnel practitioners and the perspective of the chief executive. Personnel practitioners are increasingly being viewed as partners in the area of strategy. However, it would be foolish to be swept away by the sense of achievement so far. There were indications in the research that if business circumstances changed the role of personnel would be reconsidered. Strategic involvement may be seen as key at present, but may be seen as unimportant in the future. Similarly where involvement was heavily based on the individual personnel practitioner's skills – what happens when they leave? – is it possible for another just to pick up where they left off. Our research suggests that this is difficult, and that every individual has to establish their contribution independently through their own actions – this was clearly shown when HR board directorships were not automatically offered to new heads of the personnel function, until they had proved their credibility and worth. This seems to indicate that strategic HR involvement is an optional extra rather than being seen as a basic minimum. Finally, the mindset of the chief executive also appears to be critical. It has been recognised that major changes occur with the appointment of a new chief executive – how do we know that the next chief executive will have an HR mindset?

All this suggests that the increasing involvement of the personnel function in HR strategy is more about business need and individuals, and less about changing the status of the function itself. Strategic involvement may well be yet another stage in the development of the function, and may pass. This suggests two ways forward for those in the function. One is working to ensure that where possible strategic involvement is maintained and exploited – through reappraising the skills and competencies needed of personnel practitioners, and through influencing the mindset of chief executives. A second is considering what the function can offer apart from strategic involvement – in other words what is the next type of contribution which the personnel function needs to develop. Heavy pushes to devolve HR responsibilities to the line are cutting much of the operational workload. We are not debating the value of devolution here, and this approach may well be very appropriate; however, it does squeeze the function and puts more pressure on clarifying its distinctive contribution.

References

Armstrong, M. (1992) *HRM Strategy and Action*, London: Kogan Page.

Baird, L. and Meshoulam, I. (1988) 'Managing two fits of strategic human resource management', *Academy of Management Review*, 13(1), 116–28.

Baird, L., Meshoulam, I. and De Give, G. (1983) 'Meshing human resource planning with strategic business planning: a model approach', *Personnel*, Sept./Oct., 60(5), 14–25.

Beardwell, I. and Holden, L. (1997) *Human Resource Management*, 2nd edn, London: Pitman.

Beaumont, P. B. (1992) 'The US human resource management literature: a review', in G. Salamon (ed.) *Human Resource Strategies*, London: Sage, in association with OUP.

Bevan, S. and Thompson, M. (1991) 'Performance management at the cross-roads' *Personnel Management*, 23(11), 36–9.

Boxall, P. F. (1992) 'Strategic human resource management: beginnings of a new theoretical sophistication?', *Human Resource Management Journal*, 2(3), 60–78.

Boxall, P. F. (1994) 'Placing HR strategy at the heart of business success', *Personnel Management*, July, 32–5.

Brewster, C. and Bournois, F. (1991) 'Human resource management : a European perspective', *Personnel Review*, 20(6), 4–13.

Brewster, C. and Hegewisch, A. (1994) *Policy and Practice in European Human Resource Management*, London: Routledge.

Burack, E. H. (1985) 'Linking corporate business and human resource planning: strategic issues and concerns', *Human Resource Planning*, 8(2), 133–45.

Butler, J. E. (1988) 'Human resource management as a driving force in business strategy', *Journal of General Management*, 13(4).

Connock, S. (1991) *HR Vision – Managing a Quality Workforce*, London: IPD.

Duberley, J. P. and Burns, N. D. (1991) 'Organisational configurations: implications for the human resource/personnel management debate', *Personnel Review*, 22(4), 26–39.

Fernie, S., Metcalf, D. and Woodland, S. (1994) 'Does HRM boost employee–management relations?', *LSE Working Paper*, No. 548.

Fombrum, C., Tichy, N. M. and Devanna, M. A. (1984) *Strategic Human Resource Management*, New York: Wiley.

Fowler, A. (1987) 'When chief executives discover HRM', *Personnel Management*, May.

Freedman, A. (1985) *A New Look at Wage Policy and Employee Relations*, Report No. 865, Conference Board Inc.

Gibb, S. (1995) 'The lead body of personnel management: a critique', *Human Resource Management Journal*, 5(5), 60–74.

Guest, D. (1987) 'Human resource management and industrial relations', *Journal of Management Studies*, 24(5), 503–21.

Guest, D. (1989) 'Personnel and HRM: Can you tell the difference?', *Personnel Management*, January.

Guest, D. (1990) 'Human resource management and the American dream', *Journal of Management Studies*, 27(4), 377–97.

Guest, D. (1991) 'Personnel management: the end of the orthodoxy?', *British Journal of Industrial Relations*, 29(2), 149–75.

Hall, L., Allen, C. and Torrington, D. (1996) 'Human resource strategy and the personnel functions', *Contemporary Developments in Human Resource Management*, Paris: Editions ESKA.

Handy, L., Barnham, K., Panter, S. and Winhard A. (1989) 'Beyond the personnel function', *Journal of European Industrial Training*, 13(1), 13–18.

Harrison, R. (1993) *Human Resource Management: Issues and Strategies*, London: Addison-Wesley.

Hendry, C. and Pettigrew, A. (1990) 'Human resource management: an agenda for the 1990s', *International Human Resource Management Journal*, 1(1).

Hendry, C. and Pettigrew, A. (1992) 'Patterns of strategic change in the development of human resource management', *British Journal of Management*, 3, 137–56.

Hendry, C., Pettigrew, A. and Sparrow, P. (1989) 'Linking strategic change, competitive performance and human resource management: results of a UK empirical study' in R. M. Mansfield (ed.) *New Frontiers of Management*, London: Routledge.

Hunter, G. (1957) *The Role of the Personnel Officer*, London: IPM.

Johnson, G. (1987) *Strategic Change and the Management Process*, Oxford: Blackwell.

Kamoche, K. (1994) 'A critique of a proposed reformation of strategic human resource management', *Human Resource Management Journal*, 4(4), 29–43.

Legge, K. (1978) *Power Innovation and Problem Solving in Personnel Management*, London: McGraw-Hill.

Legge, K. (1989) 'HRM: a critical analysis', in J. Storey (ed.) *New Perspectives on Human Resource Management*, London: Routledge.

Lengnick-Hall, C. A. and Lengnick-Hall, M. L. (1988) 'Strategic human resources management: a review of the literature and a proposed typography', *Academy of Management Review*, 13(3), 454–70.

Lundy, O. and Cowling, A. (1996) *Strategic Human Resource Management*, London: Routledge.

Mackay, L. and Torrington, D. P. (1986) *The Changing Nature of Personnel Management*, London: IPD.

Martell, K. and Carroll, S. J. (1995) 'How strategic is HRM?', *Human Resource Management*, Summer, 34(2), 253–67.

Miles, R. E. and Snow, C. C. (1984) 'Designing human resource systems', *Organisational Dynamics*, 13(1), 36–52.

Mintzberg, H. (1987) 'Crafting strategy', *Harvard Business Review*, July/August, 66–75.

Mintzberg, H. (1994) 'The rise and fall of strategic planning', *Harvard Business Review*, Jan./Feb., 107–14.

Monks, K. (1992) 'Models of personnel management: a means of understanding the diversity of personnel practices?', *Human Resource Management Journal*, 13(2), 29–41.

Niven, M. (1967) *Personnel Management 1913–1963*, London: IPM.

Pettigrew, A. M. (1977) 'Strategy formulation as a political process', *International Journal of Management and Organisation*, 7(2), 78–87.

Poole, M. (1990) 'Human resource management in an international perspective' (editorial)', *International Journal of Human Resource Management*, 1(1), 1–15.

Poole, M. and Jenkins, G. (1996) *Back to the Line? – a Survey of Managers' Attitudes to Human Resource Management Issues*, London: Institute of Management.

PSLB (1993) *In touch: Newsletter of the PSLB*, Issue 1, PSLB.

Purcell, J. (1989) 'The impact of corporate strategy on human resource management', in J. Storey (ed.) *New Perspectives on Human Resource Management*, London: Routledge.

Purcell, J. (1995) 'Corporate strategy and its link with human resource strategy', in J. Storey (ed.) *Human Resource Management: a Critical Text*, London: Routledge.

Purcell, J. and Ahlstrand, B. (1994) *Human Resource Management in the Multidivisional Company*, Oxford: Oxford University Press.

Rothwell, S. (1995) 'Human resource planning' in J. Storey (ed.) *Human Resource Management: a Critical Text*, London: Routledge.

Schuler, R. S. (1990) 'Repositioning the human resource function: transformation or demise?', *Academy of Management Executive*, 4(3), 49–60.

Schuler, R. S. (1992) 'Strategic human resources management: linking the people with the strategic needs of the business', *Organisational Dynamics*, Summer, 18–31.

Schuler, R. S. and Jackson, S. E. (1987) 'Linking competitive strategies with human resource management practices', *Academy of Management Executive*, 1(3), August.

Sisson, K. (1990) 'Introducing the Human Resource Management Journal', *Human Resource Management Journal*, 1(1), 1–11.

Sisson, K. (1995) 'Human resource management and the personnel function' in J. Storey (ed.) *Human Resource Management: a Critical Text*, London: Routledge.

Stacey, R. (1993) 'Strategy as order emerging out of chaos', *Long Range Planning*, 26(1), 10–17.

Storey, J. (1989) 'Introduction', in J. Storey (ed.) *New Perspectives on Human Resource Management*, London: Routledge.

Storey, J. (1992) *Developments in the Management of Human Resources*, Oxford: Blackwell Business.

Storey, J. (1995) 'Is HRM catching on?', *International Journal of Manpower*, 16(4), 3–10.

Torrington, D. and Hall, L. (1998) *Human Resource Management*, Hemel Hempstead: Prentice-Hall.

Towers Perrin (undated) *Priorities for Competitive Advantage*: a 21st century vision, a worldwide human resource study (*An IBM Study conducted by Towers Perrin*), Towers Perrin.

Tyson, S. (1995a) 'Human resource management and performance', *Paper presented at*

the Seminar on Human Resource Management and Performance, held at Tinbergen
Institute, Holland, 22 September 1995.

Tyson, S. (1995b) *Human Resource Strategy*, London: Pitman Publishing.

Walker, J. W. (1992) *Human Resource Strategy*, London: McGraw-Hill.

Watson, T. J. (1977) *The Personnel Managers*, London: Routledge and Kegan Paul.

Whipp, R. (1992) 'Human resource management, competition and strategy: some pro-
ductive tensions', in P. Blyton and P. Turnbull (eds) *Reassessing Human Resource
Management*, London: Sage.

Whipp, R. and Clark, C. (1986) *Innovation and the Auto Industry: Product, Process
and Work Organisation*, London: Frances Pinter.

7

Outsourcing

It is now some years since the English language was corrupted by taking the noun 'resource' and turning it into the verb 'to resource', meaning to find and recruit the people or human resources that the business required. A further development has been the term 'outsourcing', which means finding the human resources or services you need without taking them on to the payroll. This is part of the general process whereby flexibility slims down some businesses and creates others.

A common theme in all our interviews was a certain uneasiness about the number of activities that were no longer carried out 'in-house'. Many respondents felt that they were losing something valuable if they relied on outside suppliers rather than providing the resource from within. This, however, is how economies develop and new businesses are created. Forty years ago it was commonplace for companies to employ their own security personnel, but now it is an unusual business that does not use the services of a specialist security company. Thirty years ago most company catering was provided by in-house catering employees; now more than half of all catering services come from specialist suppliers.

The outsourcing of personnel activities presents a potential problem of throwing out the baby with the bathwater. There is a clear need for expertise to deal with the great variety of matters that are involved in effective human resource management, and it would be extravagant to attempt to hold all the necessary expertise in-house. Apart from the cost in terms of salary and benefits, there would be a potential loss of edge through not using the expertise of those who work in a number of different situations. One of our research interviewees gave an illustration.

> We already outsource significant parts of what we used to do and have therefore been able to reduce our fixed costs. The logical extension is to outsource more, especially recruitment and selection. We are shrinking and shrinking the HR function. Eight weeks ago we had 35 people, today we have 27 and by the end of next year we will be down to 22.
>
> (Head of retail HR, building society)

On the other hand there is a risk in moving too much outside. It is the usual core/periphery argument. Core expertise needs to be retained and developed. Peripheral expertise that is important but only needed infrequently can be called upon when needed. As with all management activities, the tricky bit is getting the balance right.

Current reliance on external expertise

Some activities are now conventionally sub-contracted. We have already referred to the two examples of security and catering. It is usual for a company to retain the services of a firm of solicitors to provide legal expertise in instances, for example, of alleged unfair dismissal. It is also usual for the company medical adviser to be a part-time rather than full-time employee. These are all activities where there is acknowledged expertise, qualified independently and operating independently of personnel work, although occasionally relevant to it. Sometimes the expertise is core personnel work, and this is where the balance becomes problematic.

We asked our research respondents about the extent to which they had used external consultants in the previous year. The percentages saying that they had used consultants in that time varied from single figures to nearly 60 per cent, according to the activity.

Table 7.1 Answers to the question, 'In the last year have you used external consultants in any of the following areas at your place of work?' Please circle as many as are appropriate

Activity	Percentage of respondents using
Training	58.4
Management development	38.3
Recruitment and selection	32.5
Outplacement	24.9
Health and safety	24.4
Quality initiatives	18.7
Job evaluation	18.2
Reward strategies and systems	14.8
Performance management	13.9
Redundancy and dismissal	12.9
Employee relations	9.6
Human resource planning	9.6
Communications	6.2
Work design	5.7
Careers	2.4

In considering those replies a number of interesting points arise about the types of activity on which external expertise is sought.

Training and management development

Two-thirds of respondents used external expertise in this general area. A further question was related to the sources of training provided in the same year for different broad categories of employee.

Table 7.2 Answers to the question, 'In the last year have you provided training through any of the following means for the various categories of employee?' Please circle as many as are appropriate

Means of training	Manual	Non-manual	Managerial
Personnel/training officer	41.4	62.4	59.0
Line manager	40.5	55.0	39.5
Training consultant (tailor-made course)	27.6	55.7	69.0
Training consultant (off-the-peg course)	13.3	35.7	45.2
Professional body	3.8	41.4	51.0
Technical college/university	20.5	61.9	61.0
Distance learning	9.5	41.0	38.6
Outward bound	2.9	7.1	14.8
Commercial management college	0.5	7.1	20.5

There initially appears to be some inconsistency here, with the percentages for external consultants in the second table being higher than those in the first, but the overall import is clearly that there is greater use of outside resources than of internal resources in each of these areas.

Some of the external sources are inescapable and appropriate since the training provided by professional bodies, technical colleges and universities usually leads to an external qualification. This will generally have greater currency in the labour market than in-house training, although there are a few stunning exceptions, like Marks & Spencer who are still regarded as providing the best available training for a career in retail management. There are also often strategic reasons for using external courses, such as the MBA. The person who has great potential but for whom there is not yet the right opening may be sent on an MBA course to discourage a move to a different employer. The intrinsic value of the MBA to the student is more debatable and the value to the employer even more debatable. Standards vary enormously and the 'value' is often more a feature of the reputation of the provider than the specific skills acquired or capacities developed.

Skills which are both specific and identical regardless of work location are logically sourced externally. Keyboard speed is best trained and tested in a commercial management college with specialist tutors. Many of our respondents gave examples of courses run by professional bodies like the engineers, chemists and builders to deal with very specific technical matters that were common to a number of employers.

NVQs are slightly different, as these are intended to be workplace based, but employers have generally been unwilling to devote the time and effort involved, so that collaboration with a local college has become the most common form of NVQ training.

In contrast, the training kept in-house tends to be of two types: induction and procedural:

> I would love to farm out induction, but it is obviously unrealistic when we are trying to get people established *in* the company. We don't do it well because we can not get our more senior people to devote the time that is needed. We can always wheel out some impressive looking person to talk for half an hour in terms that most of the newcomers do not understand, but real induction tends to be gossip with one or two of the old hands during coffee break, and God knows what they say.
>
> (Personnel manager, insurance)

Procedural training is about how the business is going to deal with an external event. Data protection legislation is the best example. Staff can attend external courses on the law and the principles, but the practice requires adjustment to internal procedures, which staff then have to be trained to understand and follow. Many issues of unlawful discriminatory practice are attributable to procedural failings. Jill Earnshaw (1997) carried out research for the Department of Trade and Industry on the part played by procedural defects in unfair dismissal claims. Dismissal needs to be based on a fair ground but also fair in the circumstances. Nearly half of the cases examined with procedural defect went in favour of the ex-employee.

In the area of training and development we therefore have a picture of extensive outsourcing because of the range of specialist expertise that is needed ('Outward Bound type training can only be done by people who really know what they are doing'), the efficiencies of specific skills being handled by specialist agencies ('Sight and Sound can do it better, quicker and more cheaply than we ever could'), and the benefits of the wider view that external bodies can provide:

> It's the same old story. There are three reasons for going to conferences. You get a day away from the office, you make useful contacts over lunch and in the bar, and you hear something discussed from different perspectives. If you are really lucky, you also learn something about the conference subject!
>
> (Management development manager, chemicals)

Matters that are organisation specific have to be kept in-house, but this does not mean that the only in-house training function is running induction and procedural training. The training officer is a training needs analyst, buyer of training and a monitor of training provided. That requires an expertise all of its own.

Recruitment and selection

After training and development the most significant use of external consultants was in recruitment and selection, with a third of respondents reporting their use. A later question asked about methods of recruitment that had been used in the previous 12 months and we have selected from those data to see the use of particular agencies. A similar survey by the authors 10 years earlier (Mackay and Torrington, 1986) asked an almost identical question and the figures in brackets are from that survey, so that comparisons can be drawn. All figures are in percentages.

Table 7.3 Answers to the question, 'Which of the following methods of recruitment have you used in the last year for the various categories of job?' Please circle as many numbers as are appropriate

Method of recruitment	Manual	Non-manual	Managerial
Selection consultants	0.9 (1.7)	14.2 (10.6)	33.0 (31.1)
Executive search	0.5 (0.3)	1.9 (3.4)	22.6 (23.7)
Job centres	55.7 (40.6)	64.2 (47.7)	12.7 (26.3)
Employment agencies	17.9 (13.7)	36.3 (41.7)	14.2 (12.0)

Apart from a change in the reported use of Job Centres, the figures show remarkable consistency across the ten-year divide. At the time of the earlier survey Job Centres were rather differently organised, so the wording in that questionnaire was, 'Professional Executive Recruitment (PER)/Job Centres', whereas in the later survey it was simply, 'Job Centre'. That could partly explain the disparity, together with the improved labour market, so that more people were being taken on at the time of the second survey than the first.

Terminology is a problem, as we now have recruitment consultancies emerging as a general term to cover what we previously knew as employment agencies and selection consultancies. Many people will still think of the company Manpower as an employment agency, but nowadays it sees itself as a recruitment consultancy.

The recruitment industry is developing like a form of match-making, with a number of firms acting as the go-between between job seekers and employee seekers. The most rapid growth has been in shortage areas of specialised skills, such as information technology, although there has long been a convention of using agencies when seeking work as a secretary in Central London. Recruitment consultancies are also central to the processes often involved in obtaining the services of people to cover short-term needs, where someone is required to deal with a very specific task that will take a week or a few months. They don't come on to the payroll, but have a contract for services. They are therefore a source of supply for the personnel function. Potential applicants will be approximately matched to the company requirements and will then be coached for the company's selection process.

The advantages are that the process is quick, as there is no need to advertise, and initially painless, as there will be half-a-dozen CVs to read rather than dozens or hundreds of letters of application to handle. The problem is that recruitment consultancy sees itself as a high intensity sales operation and their coaching of candidates emphasises how they should sell themselves in the interview. This also leads to an attempt to control the situation.

Although understandable, any personnel specialist knows that the candidate trying to take control is usually an interference with the central personnel task of forming an accurate judgement of the candidate's potential for the vacancy that is to be filled.

Apart from its cost – up to a third of the first year's salary of the appointee – the personnel specialist probably loses little by the development of this new industry. It is best seen as an alternative to recruitment advertising, although that industry is also booming:

> According to figures published by the Advertising Association, revenue in the market grew by 18 per cent in 1996 and is set for further growth of 23 per cent in 1997.
>
> (Howard, 1997, p. 4)

Later in his comments, Simon Howard points out that the total number of recruitment advertisements grew by only 3.4 per cent. That is a better measure of recruitment activity.

The process of deploying whatever expertise is regarded as appropriate in making the selection decision remains firmly in-house, and this is the sort of expertise which personnel specialists claim to have and to need:

> We can only contract out those aspects where the expertise is general – like knowing the labour market, or very specific – like recruitment advertising. When it comes to assessing the suitability of candidates to work here, in our culture, we have to do it.
>
> (HR manager, electronics)

Release from the organisation

This bland euphemism for getting rid of people covers those who used consultants to assist with outplacement as well as redundancy and dismissal, although the significance of the personnel role in those two is markedly different. In outplacement the decision has been made that the employee is leaving. It may have been very painful with a lot of bad feeling and lawyers involved, but even if it was amicable, the contract of employment has ended and the individual employee's future is best handled in conjunction with an outside agency. All that the previous employer does is to pay the consultant's bill. There is no continuing HR role for the personnel function to manage.

Redundancy and dismissal require very positive management by the personnel function and the involvement of external consultants has to be minimal and low profile. The interviewees in our research were clear that the external assistance sought was usually legal advice. The management of the process was retained in-house. Making people redundant against their will, or dismissing them, is probably the most unpopular job for personnel people to do. Not only is it an unpleasant task, but there seems no way of doing it properly. Those who have been made redundant frequently nurture for years a deep sense of anger about the way they heard the news. It was too abrupt or it was too drawn out. It was in writing or it was not in writing. The reasons were explained and were unacceptable, or they were not explained and that was unacceptable. The personnel specialist and other managers will have a concern about the effect of the news on those who are not going as well as on those who are. It is as unrealistic to outsource the central features of redundancy and dismissal as it would be to outsource induction.

Health and safety

Twenty-five per cent of respondents calling on external assistance with health and safety initially seems a high figure. Surely this is a core activity? In fact much of the external assistance is on purely technical matters rather than policy or strategy: civil engineers and industrial chemists coming to assess particular risks or to discuss their alleviation. This heading includes the catch-all concept of stress, which seems to affect so many people nowadays. There is also the small, but growing, number of companies that run employee assistance programmes. The counselling and advice is nearly always provided externally and would lose much of its value if it were provided in any other way.

Quality initiatives

Total quality management has been one of the popular management approaches of the last ten years or so and is a sufficiently specific 'bag of tricks' that it can be introduced as a package. Several companies had been obliged to introduce it in order to keep key customers, who made it a condition of their contractual arrangement, and it has all the attractions of the flavour of the month that was lasting a bit longer. It is not an HR-type initiative, although

David Guest (1992) is one of several commentators who see a logical link between the needs of HRM to be effective and the opportunity that TQM provides. Adrian Wilkinson (1994) provides a strong argument to say that TQM will only prosper if it develops from its engineering base to give more emphasis to such factors as commitment, self-control and trust.

Here we see a different situation from the other types of external assistance. This is not the risk that the personnel function may lose its effectiveness, but that collaboration with this type of external facilitation could enhance the personnel contribution to overall HR effectiveness.

Job evaluation, reward and performance management

Performance management is put here under the same heading as the two pay matters, as so often it is the term used to describe what is only performance-related pay. The reason for using external assistance with job evaluation is largely connected with the newly-developed – and proprietary – computer programmes that have become popular in recent years. There is also some interest in using the consultants to do the basic leg-work that is involved. Reward and performance management assignments are often connected with trying to get out of the mess that most performance-related payment schemes seem to get into within a year or so of being launched. There was a short-term enthusiasm for the tax avoidance opportunity of profit-related pay, but this will presumably cease now that the tax advantages have been withdrawn.

There are two concerns here for the personnel function.

Although it may make sense to use the consultant's people to do the leg-work of job evaluation, it may be a short-term benefit if one is then locked in to a proprietary job evaluation system. It has to be said, however, that hundreds of employers have been quite content to be 'locked in' to the Hay-MSL job evaluation system for many years.

Using consultants to develop performance-related pay is a different matter, as there is an invaluable role for the external specialist to advise and guide, on the basis of expertise gathered from other companies. Performance-related pay is, however, such an important matter, and so easy to get wrong, that it is undoubtedly a core activity for the personnel function, not to be handed over to the consultant because it is such a hot potato.

Other topics

Table 7.1 showed small percentages for human resource planning, employee relations, communications and career planning. The background to the human resource planning score is that most of those applications are to do with computerised personnel record systems, most of which have some HR planning features. Employee relations and communications applications are usually about team-briefing exercises or working out the implications of new legislation of EU membership. In some ways the real surprise is the negligible attention given to career planning. It is conventional wisdom that careers are not what they used to be and that we all have to view our working lives as the process of maintaining our employability rather than our employment:

> No longer will a career mean climbing the ladder of jobs in an organisation. For one thing, there will not be more than three or four rungs on the ladder. No longer can one expect to sell 100 000 hours of one's life to an organisation. No longer will your job title define you for life, or even for very much of it.
>
> (Handy, 1994, p. 170)

It seems as if the implication of this scenario have not yet been absorbed. If people are to plan their careers it is unlikely that they will rely on their friendly, local personnel manager, who would seem not sufficiently independent. Independent counselling is needed, but so far there seems less willingness to provide counselling for careers than there is for employee assistance programmes or outplacement.

The rationale and methods of outsourcing

The main justification for outsourcing is likely to be cost-saving. However sensible that reasoning may be, it is insufficient in itself and may miss some of the hidden costs, such as management time and opportunity costs (Bennett, 1992, p. 98). It also carries with it the usual problem of looking at the personnel contribution as a cost rather than as an investment; and the best thing to do with costs is to eliminate them. There have to be further reasons, and one relates to skills or competencies. It is widely commented that the range of expertise in human resource management is extensive and it may make very good sense indeed to concentrate on developing some personnel skills at the expense of others. This was the reason for contracting out security and catering. If your business is one of low staff turnover and little likelihood of headcount expansion, it may well make sense to scale down your in-house recruitment in order to develop further your in-house skills at performance management and training. Centrally driven initiatives in those two areas could increase the flexibility, commitment and effectiveness of the existing workforce, reducing still further the need to recruit.

A similar argument relates to the specialised skills that are needed rarely. If the job evaluation procedures are to be overhauled for the first time in ten years, that will require a level of activity that would be high for a short time and then reduce significantly in the medium term. There will therefore be a strong case for outsourcing much of the initial work, so as not to have in-house specialists twiddling their thumbs afterwards.

Much depends on environmental aspects, especially the state of the labour market. Hegarty (1992, p. 19) gives examples of large numbers of applicants for specific vacancies:

> The British Red Cross received 1200 replies to a single advertisement.
> Save the Children Fund received 400 replies to a single advertisement.
> A county fire service received 5000 applications for 20 vacancies.

These numbers were reported at a time when the labour market was much less buoyant than it is in the late 1990s, but some employers still receive large numbers of applications for posts that seem secure (like the fire service), are attractive because of their purpose (like charities) or are widely understood (like personnel managers).

The initial reaction to this level of application may be to rejoice at how easy it will be to make a good appointment. On the other hand there is a large processing job to be done that will have problems. With five applicants you may not have a wide choice, but you have only four people disappointed. With 500 you potentially have 499 disappointed and perhaps disgruntled at the way the application was handled. Conversations in pubs include comments like:

> 'Never had a reply from them. I think it's disgusting.'
> 'Just a standard rejection letter. 'Dear Sir or Madam (please delete which does not apply.)'
> 'After a month I rang up and just got the brush-off. They didn't want to know.'

The company is perceived negatively by a large number of people, who may buy its products or use its services. There is a strong case here for using an intermediary, such as a recruitment consultancy.

A further aspect of rationale for outsourcing is the re-shaping of the economy. There is a steady process of change in the supply chain, as in-house activities are moved out to an independent supplier. In HRM, the same thing happens with individuals. The expert employee becomes the external source of expertise. This may be a clear career choice of the individual or it may be a choice made as a result of redundancy or early retirement. The effect is the same:

> A growing number of businesses are buying skills from exactly the same people they have used in the past – but as supplier rather than employee. A business and one of its employees might wish to part company – on the initiative of either party – but still recognise a mutual need. Early retirement, redundancy, itchy feet – whatever the reason, if the real business need still remains to be filled, then the individual switches from being an employee to being a supplier.
>
> (Wheatley, 1994, p. 10)

This can be a way of smoothing the path of redundancy and usually the work needed is work that will not be needed for long, probably no more than a year, but sometimes the supplier develops a vigorous business with a growing list of customers.

Where the skills needed are re-interpreted, then there can be a different type of outsourcing opportunity – or threat. The interest in the profit-related pay schemes introduced by the Conservative governments of the 1980s brought firms of accountants in to this area for the first time. What HR professionals saw as a reward issue was re-interpreted in some companies as a cost-saving and tax avoidance issue. In many instances the financial argument was considered to be the main consideration and employee compliance was taken for granted.

The huge growth in recruitment consultancy in the 1990s is seen – by the consultants – as a selling activity, so that job applicants are coached to sell themselves in interview. While this has always been a tendency, HR professionals see it as a nuisance, because they are interested in understanding who the candidate really is in order to determine the true potential and suitability. This involves getting beyond the façade of the 'pitch' and the carefully rehearsed presentation.

All outsourcing opportunities involve drawbacks. Any external input needs to be managed and monitored. That requires some management time, sound judgement and considerable management expertise. No external supplier can make strategic decisions about what is needed and what can be afforded. No external supplier can truly assess the organisational culture and know what can be done and what can not. No external supplier can assume management responsibility for things that may go wrong. They can sometimes be useful to take the *blame* when things go wrong, but the responsibility for success and failure remains with the management. There is something else that is as real as it is intangible:

> We buy in very little apart from technical stuff. If personnel means anything it means the heart, spirit and being of the organisation, and that's what we like to think we are.
> (Head of personnel, local government)

It is also important to avoid over-extending the external involvement. Exuberant recruitment consultants may present candidates with strong endorsement, but only the HR people and other in-house colleagues can make the selection decision, for which they will need both time and expertise.

There is always some scepticism about the value of using external consultants.

> The naive might have imagined that as management disciplines matured and executives increasingly mastered them, the need for outside advisers would fade. Think again . . . the global consultancy market is now worth around $40 billion . . . and employs upwards of 100 000 of the most highly-qualified people in the world.
> (Caulkin, 1997, p. 33)

Daily fees frequently are £1000–£3000 per person per day, with the occasional superstar asking five times that amount. When companies are paying out sums like that, you would expect vigorous justification about the payment of sums that would make in-house people drool with envy, but it is unusual to find situations when there is enthusiastic endorsement of the consultant's contribution. The typical comment is exactly the opposite. Simon Caulkin quotes Lord Weinstock and Anita Roddick:

> (Lord Weinstock) Consultants are invariably a waste of money. There has been the occasional instance where a useful idea has come up, but the input we have received has usually been banal and unoriginal, wrapped up in impressive sounding but irrelevant rhetoric.'

> Anita Roddick says that having consultants tramping through the Body Shop was the most uncomfortable period in its history.
>
> (Caulkin, 1997, p. 34)

Some personnel activities are undoubtedly best undertaken by consultants. An example is the use of personnel tests in selection. These have been available for many years as a means of making selection more systematic and objective, yet their use remains limited and is sometimes misguided. Few employing organisations are big enough to have a scale of recruitment *for similar posts* that produces a large enough set of results for analysis and comparison to be fruitful. The Royal Air Force selects trainee pilots using a battery of tests developed over many years. There is also a wealth of evidence from tests and subsequent performance, for the ability to fly an aircraft to be predicted with reasonable accuracy from test results alone. Few other employers can accummulate enough evidence to make comparable predictions, but specialist firms of consultants can, at least theoretically, produce occupational norms to provide useful performance indicators from test results.

The management of outsourcing

In managing the outsourcing process, it is sensible to keep most, but not all, options open at the outset:

> In identifying the areas of work suitable for outsourcing, it is interesting to look at the areas which have been kept in-house. This often shows that there is in fact very little which can not be undertaken externally. Essentially the core personnel and training team must maintain jurisdiction over the strategic direction of the function and the ability to take a lead role within the organisation. They must also retain responsibility for devising policies and for quality and standards. Outside of these areas, however, some level of external input is worth considering.
>
> (Croner, 1994, p. 6)

The qualifications there are important. Although there is very little that cannot benefit from some level of external input, the in-house team must retain both competent jurisdiction and the credibility to take a lead role internally, devising policy and monitoring standards.

David Burnett (1992) suggests a simple three stage process in recruiting external resources.

The first stage is *initial screening*, which will be the scrutinising of a brochure from the supplier. Here the purchaser will look for indicators like turnover and financial performance, structure and numbers of personnel, including the depth of resources behind those fronting the business. It will also be helpful to see lists of previous clients and the nature of services provided.

The next stage is to *interview* alternative suppliers. This assumes there is a choice, and not all practitioners believe that to be true. Hall (1995) quotes a BT executive as saying:

> There are plenty of firms well placed to take on outsourced recruitment and payroll, as one would expect, but there is not a huge range of people doing the more esoteric stuff like internal communication, management development and strategic thinking in the personnel area . . . It is one thing to decide you want to outsource a particular function. It's another to find someone out there to do it.
>
> (Hall, 1995, p. 33)

This makes the useful point that it is the 'safe' topics that are easy to put out, as the task for the external supplier can be isolated and identified quite precisely. What is described as 'the more esoteric stuff' is much more fully integrated in the ebb and flow of everyday working, networks of responsibility, working relationships and power struggles. This is where it is all too easy for the consultant to become like a bull in a china shop.

The purpose of the interview is initially to probe certain aspects of the brochure and uncover exactly what the resources and experience are, but also to test out the 'chemistry' and decide whether the people representing the consultancy are the sort it is possible to do business with.

The third stage is to specify and cost your *requirements*. Here the purchaser has to deploy considerable skill in specifying exactly what is required and providing enough information for a sound tender to be submitted. A possible method of approaching this is taken from another of our publications (Torrington and Hall, 1998).

(a) Describe the problem

What is the matter about which you might seek external assistance? Working through an issue can show that the real matter needing to be addressed is not what is immediately apparent. If, for example, the marketing manager leaves abruptly – as they often seem to do – the immediate problem will present itself as, 'We must find a replacement', but worrying about finding a correct description of the problem could suggest that the presenting cause is easy to deal with because young X has been waiting for just such an opportunity for months and all the signals suggest that X would be ideal. The 'real' problem may turn out to be what caused the marketing manager to leave, or whether there is a string of other 'young X's' waiting in the wings. It could require attention to succession planning, reward strategy, management development, career planning or many more alternative possibilities.

(b) Formulate an approach

The next step is to rough out an approach to the problem, with the emphasis here on 'rough'. If you knew the answer you would not need further help; if you have no idea of the answer you cannot brief a consultant. What is needed is a clear but not inflexible strategy so that you can go through the remaining stages of making up your mind without putting the consultant, and yourself, in the wrong framework. If you decide that the problem behind the departure of the marketing manager is a combination of succession planning and remuneration policy, the approach you would then formulate would be based on ideas about how those two issues could be tackled, without an absolute commitment to a single method or technique.

(c) Work out how you could do it in-house

Before going any further, how would you do it without recourse to external sources? What would you do? How much it would cost. How long it would take and what would the implications be, such as stopping work on something else?

Whether one is specifying a brief for an outside consultant or coming to terms oneself with a problem that has been presented, there is a need for some device to describe the problem as a preliminary to formulating an approach to solving it. Priestley and his colleagues (1978, p. 28) suggest a simple '5 W-H' method which is What? Who? Where? When? Why? and How? A typical problem could be approached thus:

What is the problem?	Communications in the office are poor.
Who is involved?	Everyone, but most problems are at the level of first-line supervision.
Where is it worst?	In accounts and in the print room.
When is it worst?	At the end of the week and at the end of the month.
Why does it happen?	Because of an erratic flow of work between the two departments, which is worst at those times.
How could it be tackled?	By getting the first-line supervisors to tackle it, smooth out the flow of work, helping them to appreciate the effect of their work flows on the other departments, etc.

This is a very simple problem with a minimal number of questions serving to do no more than illustrate the method. Each question would probably have dozens of supplementaries in order to fill out the details of a complex problem.

The main value of the consultant at this stage is the ability to raise questions that those close to the matter have not thought about. This is not because consultants are more clever, but because they have a different pattern of experience and take for granted different things from those who are looking at the presenting problem every day.

(d) Find out how it could be done by consultants

Provided you have done the first two steps satisfactorily, it should be possible to brief one or more potential outside suppliers of expertise, so that they can bid for the business. If the problem is not correctly described there may be bids for the wrong things, and if the approach is not accurately formulated, the consultant will be obliged to carry out a preliminary study, at your expense, to formulate an approach for you. When this happens you are beginning to lose control of the operation.

The main questions to ask of the consultants are again how it would be done, how much would it cost and how long would it take.

(e) Decide between the alternatives

A set of alternatives from which to choose gives you the opportunity to compare relative costs, times and likely outputs, as well as implications. In making the final decision the most important point to remember is that the responsibility is inescapably yours. If the consultant can produce the 'best' outcome, have you the resources to implement it? Can you wait? If you can save £10 000 by relying on your own staff and time, will you produce an outcome that adequately meets the needs of your rough-cut approach? The eventual outcome is all that matters.

The extent to which the success or failure of consultancy initiatives rests with the internal management can be demonstrated by a comparison of the impact of the same scheme 'installed' by the same team in two different companies, one directly after the other. We are unable even to hint at the identity of either, nor to describe what the initiative was, but follow-up research gave some interesting commentary on the degree of effectiveness by recording the percentage of employees who answered 'yes' in a questionnaire about the initiatives.

Question	Company A	Company B
1. Do you understand the new scheme?	87%	44%
2. Have you had targets set?	77%	29%
3. Have you had management feedback?	87%	41%
4. Have you had the training?	53%	24%
5. Do you understand the pay plan?	44%	38%

There can be all sorts of explanation for the variable response, but there is at least a very strong indication indeed that the internal management of the initiative had a bearing on the apparently different level of effectiveness. It is ironic that both companies are outstandingly successful in their respective fields, by almost every conceivable criterion.

References

Bennett, L. (1992) 'Managing "just-in time" human resources,' *Human Resources*, 8, Winter 1992/93, 97–100.

Bird, J. (1992) 'IT goes out', *Management Today*, April, 80–3.

Burnett, D. 1992, 'Making the right outsourcing decisions', *Government Purchasing*, December, 8–10.

Caulkin, S. (1997) 'The great consultancy cop-out', *Management Today*, February, 32–8.

Earnshaw, J. M. (1997) 'Tribunals and tribulations', *People Management*, May, 34–6.

Guest, D. (1992) 'Human resource management in the UK', in K. Sisson (ed.) *Personnel Management*, 2nd edn, Oxford: Blackwell.

Hall, L. (1995) 'Moving out', *Personnel Today*, 23 May, 32–5.

Handy, C. B. (1994) *The Empty Raincoat*, London: Hutchinson.

Hegarty, S. (1992) 'Avalanche of hopefuls', *Personnel Today*, 29 September, 19–20.

Howard, S. (1997) 'Broadsheets reap reward of jobs boom', in *Annual Review of the Recruitment Advertising Industry, 1997*, London: Institute of Personnel and Development.

Mackay, L. E. and Torrington, D. P. (1986) *The Changing Nature of the Personnel Function*, London: Institute of Personnel Management.

Priestley, P., McGuire, J., Flegg, D., Hemsley, V. and Welham, D. (1978) *Social Skills and Personal Problem-solving*, London: Tavistock.

Torrington, D. P. and Hall, L. A. (1998) *Human Resource Management*, 4th edn, Hemel Hempstead: Prentice-Hall International.

Using External Suppliers in the Personnel and Training Function, London: Croner Publications, 16 May 1994, 4–6.

Wheatley, M. (1994) 'Is nothing sacred?', *Human Resources*, 13, Spring, 8–12.

Wilkinson, A. J. (1994) 'Managing human resources for quality' in B. G. Dale (ed.) *Managing Quality*, 2nd edn, London: Prentice-Hall International, 40–7.

8

Internal marketing of HR activities and the HR function

Introduction

The concept of internal marketing (hereafter referred to as IM) has been increasingly discussed in the marketing literature, as an essential precursor to the external marketing process, being a means of focusing all employees on the importance of meeting customer needs and providing a high quality service. As such, marketing ceases to be a function but rather, a way of doing business (McKenna, 1991). There is a variety of definitions of IM, some of which have a general impact on the way the human resources function behaves (in common with the effect on other staff functions) within the organisation in terms of marketing its services to other departments and a charging for those services delivered. The second group of definitions is more specific to HRM itself in that IM has been defined, by Kotler (1991) for example, as 'the task of successfully hiring, training, and motivating able employees to serve the customer well'. Foreman and Money (1995) suggest that a more cynical perspective on this is to see IM as 'merely a synonym for good human resources (HR) management' (p. 756). In this chapter we will first look at the attractions of IM for HR specialists, and then consider how IM in HR relates to our previous themes of devolution, decentralisation and strategic involvement. We will then consider in more detail the various interpretations of IM using a model developed by Foreman and Money (1995) and will use our own research and case studies reported by others to plot how each segment of the model can be related to the HR function including the marketing tools which may be used by HR specialists. The chapter is concluded with a critical review of the implications for HR specialists of adopting an IM approach.

Attraction of the IM approach

The attraction of IM for the organisation as a whole rests upon improving competitive advantage by developing the organisational capability for providing value added customer service which meets customer needs and preferences (*see*, for example, Varey, 1995). It operates on the premise that everyone in the organisation has a customer, and that IM stimulates everyone to examine their own role, adopting a customer and service orientation. By improving internal market relationships in this way the organisation can be more flexible and responsive and the needs of external customers can be more effectively met. Thus organisational effectiveness can be increased by improving internal market relationships (*see*, for example, Berry, 1981).

From the perspective of the HR specialist there are a number of reasons why adopting an IM approach might be seen as an advantage, and we discuss these below:

From 'can't do' to 'can do'

Much of the history of personnel management has been dogged with the perception that it was a department which prevented line managers from doing what they wanted to do. For example, immediately increasing staffing levels if the full establishment of staff had already been reached; sacking staff, if the proper procedures had not been followed; paying staff more or less than specified in the grade range on which they were appointed; and deviating from the contract of employment by asking staff to work more, less, or different hours than specified. The tag of the personnel function as 'policeman' was referred to by four of our interviewees, and was explained by one personnel manager (TEC) as the reason for desiring to change the name of the personnel department to a human resources department – to 'get away from the old image of administration, policing and pain in the backside'. Other interviewees explained how the personnel department was excluded from decision making and marginalised because they constantly told managers what they couldn't do rather than what they could do. As one personnel advisor put it:

> We get an awful lot of negative feedback, I think it's part of the culture of us telling them what they could or couldn't do.
>
> (Personnel adviser, insurance)

One operations manager (who had previously been a personnel specialist) we spoke to described a situation where the personnel function supported the manager, rather than the other way around (which was how it used to be). The adoption of an internal marketing approach can be seen as symbolic in identifying the line manager as a customer of the personnel function, and the desire to create customer satisfaction. As IPD (1992) report, in relation to changes made at Wessex Water, the focus moves from 'you can't do that because of our personnel policy' to 'how can we help you achieve your goals?'

Demonstrating added-value

Another difficulty which has always plagued the personnel function is finding ways in which specialists can demonstrate their contribution to the organisation – in other words what value does the function add? The difficulty of this task has generally resulted in its avoidance, as there are no obvious ways of separating out the personnel contribution and evaluating its impact. For example, one of our interviewees expressed a concern with establishing the 'true cost of personnel provision' (general manager, local government), and five spoke of the need to demonstrate the added value which the function brings, as one HR director stated:

> I think you have to constantly demonstrate, in these service functions, the added value of what you do.
>
> (HR director, pharmaceuticals)

There has been an increasing trend to try and assess the contribution in terms of bottom line results, for example Connock (1992), and to benchmark personnel activities by comparing them with similar organisations, an activity in which five of our interviewees were involved. However, neither of these approaches, alone, has the immediacy and directness of personnel specialists developing their relationships with the line by exploring and defining specific needs and contracting to meet these, often at a specified cost, or in terms of person hours to be allocated over the forthcoming year. The related concept that the line manager is not forced to accept the offerings from in-house personnel specialists, but may go elsewhere to buy services to meet their needs, makes explicit the relationship between money spent and service acquired – in other words demonstrates the value for money which the personnel function is offering.

Getting closer to the line

The type of approach outlined above demands that the personnel specialist gets closer to the line, is in a position where they can better appreciate the perspective of the line, rather than being isolated. The ivory tower syndrome has always been another (misguided?) perception for the personnel specialist to change, where they are seen as pontificating 'best practice' from on high, and out of touch with the concerns and the realities of the business – another reason for being marginalised. One operations manager explained the problems in the past as based around the line's perception of the personnel role exemplified in such questions as:

> What is this guru called personnel? Where is this ivory tower in which they live? Why is it that no-one understands what they do and what they talk about?
>
> (Operations manager, financial services)

Another personnel officer admitted that:

> We are not close to the line, we don't understand, perhaps, some of the problems of day to day running . . . we don't appear to be integrated into the organisation.
>
> (Personnel officer, local government)

Others spoke of the need to be more interactive with the line, and that the 'ultimate aim should be integration' (HR director, health). While physical decentralisation may be an effective way of addressing this issue, employing an IM approach more explicitly demands an interaction between the line manager and the specialist. If this interaction is constructed with the line manager as the customer, it behoves the specialist to understand the line's perspective and priorities in order that they may meet the line's needs as closely as possible.

Raising the profile of HR

IM can be adopted as a way of raising the profile of the HR function and in particular of what HR has to offer to the business. This can work in two ways – first, IM can be used to highlight, explain, and discuss HR initiatives with both managers and employees alike. This not only raises the profile of what the HR department does but also goes someway towards gaining commitment to initiatives and changes. Second, it can be used to raise the profile of the HR function and what it has to contribute in future situations. This may be especially appropriate where the HR function is attempting to change its role. In Leach's research on devolution of operational personnel tasks to the line, different line managers had a different understanding of why this change in role was being made and some did not even appear to know that there was any change! One personnel officer in our research commented that:

> Line managers see us as a necessary evil. Some line managers, the more progressive ones, do see that we can provide a useful service for them.
>
> (Personnel manager, central government)

and another that:

> There are different perceptions across the organisation of what the personnel role is. There is always scope for selling our service – some don't know, some understand but simply dont like it.
>
> (Head of personnel department, central government)

Getting the message across is an issue that could be addressed by IM.

Reviewing these four aspects above it appears that an IM approach solves some of the perennial problems identified with the specialist personnel role in organisations. However, it is important to consider the extent to which they fit with other generalised attempts at changing the personnel role, and to consider critically the implications of adopting an IM approach. In the next section we relate the use of IM back to other changes within the human resource function which we have identified in previous chapters, and draw out consistencies and contradictions. At the end of this chapter we provide a critical review of the implications of an IM approach.

The relationship between IM and other trends in HR

IM sits reasonably comfortably with the process of devolving operational personnel activities to the line. If devolution is about making line managers accountable and responsible for their HR decisions, then there is a logic in providing choice in respect of the expert HR services and facilities which they define as their needs. The fit is closest when line managers are allocated devolved budgets in respect of their HR needs, as it is only then that the line manager has a real choice to use the in-house personnel function, at a cost, or to seek to satisfy those needs externally. Where a budget has not been allocated line managers may not have a real choice as to which personnel 'product' or 'service' to buy, but may have a greater influence on the in-house service provided, as they have a greater decision-making role and are in a better position to ignore the dictates of a central personnel function. Indeed, they may use other budgets to purchase personnel expertise by employing a personnel specialist within the department or buying services elsewhere.

All this suggests that an IM approach by the HR function may be an appropriate response to a situation where choice is vested in the line manager. By raising their profile, understanding the needs of the line, providing the support that line has identified, and demonstrating value for money, the personnel function may persuade the line that all their HR needs can be met effectively in-house. However, this argument, in concentrating on meeting client needs, fails to take account of the way in which these needs are met by personnel specialists, and whether this is the most appropriate expression of their expert role – we come back to this issue later.

We turn now to another trend we have discussed, that of outsourcing. In Chapter 7 we analysed the extent to which personnel activities were outsourced in our research sample. There is, however, a fundamental difference between the nature of outsourcing described in that chapter (when the HR function play a part in making the decision to outsource and manage the outsourcing in a practical sense), and the nature of outsourcing described above (where outsourcing is a consequence of devolved HR budgets, and is therefore arranged and overseen by line managers). In the first scenario IM appears to have little to contribute – except perhaps in stimulating the debate on what should be outsourced – whereas in the second, as we have already argued, it has potentially a major role to play.

In relation to a decentralised HR structure IM may have a considerable role to play, yet there is little evidence of its implementation. In Chapter 5 we identified the differences between physical decentralisation of HR with line reporting (type A), and physical decentralisation of HR with reporting to central personnel (type B). In the first scenario we found that the central personnel unit became isolated from the business, and that most line managers did not have a clear view of the remit of the central role. In addition, the edges were blurred between the local and central HR units and there was some duplication of activity reported. In this scenario too, there was considerable inconsistency in the way that employees were managed in the different departments. The use of IM would appear to be an appropriate tool for the central HR unit to use to address some of these issues. Using IM to raise their profile and highlight their role could be a positive step, and using IM techniques to overcome their isolation from the business and to better integrate themselves with line perspectives and concerns. Using an IM perspective it could be said that this form of HR decentralisation may have brought *part* of the HR function closer to line managers, but this appears to be at the expense of the remainder of the function who appear to have become more distant. The central unit may well produce a strategy, but this tends to be seen as an irrelevance and not appropriate to line needs, and this leaves them tinged with the 'can't do' label, rather than the 'can do' label which the local HR unit may have achieved. Also, given the distance between the central unit and the line, they are in no position to demonstrate added value. Not only might an IM approach be useful in these respects, but also in relation to the central HR unit and the local HR units. Thus IM within the HR function may have a role to play as was attempted in the DSS (IPD, 1992), who used an awareness-raising exhibition and roadshow to enhance the communication and understanding between the central and local training units. They felt that 'some form of centralised marketing is essential in a large, geographically separated HR function, to keep the component parts in touch with one another' (p. 68). In our research one HR manager stated that:

> We've got to get across to HR that *your* function is to show the line how to do these things.

> (HR manager, financial services)

This argument may similarly apply in a situation where HR was decentralised from corporate headquarters to business unit level.

In the case of virtual decentralisation of HR an IM approach would appear to fit well in a context where centrally based HR specialists contract with different departments to provide a specified level of service, over a given period, often for a specified cost. It is within this model where the personnel function (perhaps along with other staff functions) has been declared a provider department with a remit to supply the purchaser departments, that a formal internal market has often been constructed. Indeed, Colling and Ferner (1992) comment in general terms that the decentralisation of responsibility in organisation has created pressures for corporate functions to be treated as services provided for line managers as 'clients'. It is this type of structure, which has become particularly common in public sector organisations due to government influence, where IM would appear to be an essential function of the HR department. Our interviewees who operated in these circumstances often spoke of the need to market and sell their services, how the HR department is customer based, and how:

> HR has got to sell its services through being efficient and effective and providing good quality services on time.
>
> (General manager, local government (1))

and:

> Personnel are driven to taking the initiative – setting their prices right and providing the right service.
>
> (General manager, local government (2))

Hendry (1990) similarly comments that in conditions of decentralisation, if training activity survives as a central function it is organised on a cost recovery or profit centre basis and is forced to become 'customer led'. One of our respondents argued that:

> If we're interested in something we have to have an eye on whether it is marketable. This applies to training courses, if it doesn't go well we drop it – if the customer wants them they go ahead, and if the customer doesn't want them the services stop.
>
> (General manager, local government (1))

Having been declared a profit centre, with an expectation of seeking additional customers outside the home organisation, external marketing may well also become a critical activity. We found one HR function in an education setting which sold vacancy lists to potential teachers, a subscription to 'keeping in touch' services for teachers on career break, and cheap training courses to the general public. Yet, as Colling and Ferner go on to say, if the personnel function is demand-driven, how can it play its strategic, proactive role with conviction? We return to this issue at the end of the chapter.

It is, indeed, in respect of strategic involvement described in Chapter 6, where the greatest conflict comes with an IM approach. The emphasis for personnel specialists in strategic involvement was in acting as a partner with the line, and this is different from acting as supplier to an internal customer. Kessler and Purcell (1994) note that:

> The partnering orientation for HR is different from the popular internal customer model . . . partnering connotes *mutual obligation*; that is the true nature of contracting for a new HR role.

The customer–supplier relationship, on the other hand is customer-driven, rather than mutual, and fails to provide an environment where the HR specialist is in a position to challenge perceptions.

Different interpretations of IM and how each might apply to HR

Whilst IM is a key theme in current marketing literature, there has been a lack of attention to the detail of what IM represents and some uncertainty about its meaning (*see*, for example, Hales, 1995) as such the literature about IM in an HR context similarly lacks precise definition. Foreman and Money (1995) explain different perspectives in the literature as:

> . . . IM is not only seen as something which the firm (in totality) does to its employees (in totality). Indeed there is much evidence that IM is frequently not performed by the whole firm, but by departments, groups, or functions within it. Similarly the majority of employees are frequently not the target of IM efforts – rather only one department, group,or function may be focused on and marketed to. (p. 760)

They go on to draw up a four-cell matrix representing each combination of the above characteristics, and this is shown in Figure 8.1. Below we briefly explain each of the four resulting types and consider how each may be applied to the HR function, using examples from our own research and other published case studies.

Who is doing the marketing?

	Group	Whole organisation	
Group	*Type I*	*Type II*	Group
Whole organisation	*Type III*	*Type IV*	Whole organisation

Who is being marketed to?

Fig. 8.1
Source: Adapted from Foreman and Money, 1995, p. 760.

Type I

In this type a specific function markets itself to another function. As Hales (1995) states this means 'reconceptualising organisational relationships as *if* they were market ones' (p. 53). It is this type of relationship which was explored above in connection with decentralised environments where sub units operate as cost or profit centres. In our research we found a number of examples of HR functions operating in this way, in both the public and private sectors. There was a clear view that line mangers would seek their personnel services elsewhere if the in-house offering was not to their satisfaction:

> We are so much of a service function that if they get the service better somewhere else they go and buy it somewhere else, so it's down to us to prove we have the expertise.
>
> (Head of personnel, distribution and retail)

and:

> Managers have threatened buy personnel services from other places – so far they haven't – but we're all under the microscope.
>
> (Personnel adviser, insurance)

and:

> Things are changing now so that personnel have to market their services against external contractors.
>
> (General manager, local government (2))

As Hales explains a key aspect of this type of market relationship is producing the right product at the right price (as our interviewees have stated, above), and agrees that this is typical of organisations that have been reformed on a market basis or of internal services.

We found that this was not restricted to the public sector, although it was particularly prevalent there. The type of IM techniques that may be used in this context are customer service contracts with the managers of groups of departments; customer satisfaction surveys; market research; and market testing of new products, such as a training course. These can be used informally as well as structured on a formal basis, and in one of our interview organisations the operations manager who used personnel services stated that:

> Personnel have their own standards by which we appraise them – there are two ways in which we've broken down the ivory tower thing – regular meetings and visits and the chance to give real feedback.
>
> (Operations manager, financial services)

Indeed, these approaches may also be argued to be appropriate as a key tool for all HR specialists in understanding the line's priorities and concerns and in communicating the potential contribution of HR to the line. They need not be used exclusively in organisations which operate formal internal markets. This type of IM would also include efforts of the HR function to market the HR role to members of the function itself, as a precursor to marketing this to other groups in the organisation. We spoke to one head of personnel in the police force who had organised 'away days' with members of his department in order to focus on the old and new roles of the personnel function in the organisation. He showed the researcher an OHP of the new role of the function, which was 'strategic, consulting, supporting, facilitating, empowering, devolved and integrated'. He used the same slides when he presented to groups on training courses at the Police Staff College.

Type II

This type reflects the situation where the organisation as a whole markets itself to specific groups, or departments within itself, with the intention that 'the group will engage in behaviour which supports or enhances some organisational initiative' (p. 761). This may be applied to the HR function when it represents the whole organisation, rather than specifically the HR function, in its communications. An example of this experienced by one of the authors was in a hospital setting where there was a high turnover of nurses who were difficult to replace. A nursery scheme was set up on site to care for the children of nurses, and to persuade them to stay via this inducement. Nurses with small children were targeted and sent publicity information about the nursery. Other areas where this may be appropriate are in publicising early retirement schemes to employees in specified age bands. Communications in Type II will centre around HRM messages and activities supported by the whole organisation, and where the HR function is in the best position to deal with the matter in an operational sense. The main marketing techniques here include the use of focus groups with members of the relevant groups, targeted attitude surveys and publicity campaigns.

Type III

In Type III a specific group in the organisation market themselves to the whole organisation. A good example of how this might apply to the HR function is demonstrated by Whitbread Inns plc (IPD, 1992) who marketed a new pension scheme to all employees. They conducted market research with all employees to find out what problems were perceived with the new scheme and why some employees continued to arrange their pensions externally. They found from their results that the problem was not with the scheme itself, but the lack of personal support in explaining the implications of the scheme on an individual basis. As a result members of the HR function began to provide this support to all employees. Similarly, counselling services or other services which were offered by the HR function and available to all employees could be marketed.

Marketing tools which would be appropriate here could include general publicity campaigns, focus groups, attitude surveys.

Type IV

The last type identified by Foreman and Money is the situation where the whole organisation markets itself to the whole organisation – that is to all employees. This is particularly relevant in times of change. It is this aspect of IM which Hales concentrates on, and he describes how employees can be seen as customers of the organisation, and that the organisation's mission, strategy, culture, structure, jobs and conditions of employment must be marketed. As much of this is within, or related to, the province of the HR function it would seem appropriate that the HR function, would represent the organisation in this respect on some occasions. An example here may be marketing new systems via training courses, which involves all employees. Other tools might involve focus groups, help desks, roadshows, and exhibitions.

Critique

There is clearly a great attractiveness for the HR function in the IM approach, in that it provides a way of symbolising support for the business, getting close to the line, demonstrating added value and raising the profile of the function. Berridge (1992) identifies 'personnel management' as supply-driven and HRM as demand-driven, and in some respects IM exemplifies this distinction, and therein probably lies a further attraction. However, we have already hinted at some problematic areas. The major difficulty appears to be in organisations which have taken the concept so far that they operate in a formal internal market, where the HR function only appears to survive by providing exactly what the customer requires at the right price. We referred, above, to areas of activity that the HR function may feel are important, like a specific training course, which will be ditched if the customer is not interested, irrespective of the HR function's view of organisational need. There are a number of concerns related to this. The prioritisation of customer need at the expense of professional judgement, may superficially demonstrate attending to the line's needs – but the perception of needs depends on where you are standing and the time-span in question. An example which one of the authors came across was in the context of education, where schools purchased their personnel services from the local authority. The personnel officer who had been contracted to work for a number of schools found that many did not provide absence and appraisal records as they had agreed, and was reluctant to press for them too often as she was worried this would prevent the schools from giving the contract for services to her in the following year. Similarly, with those schools who submitted records, she was reticent to comment or criticise on areas that she identified as problematic and she considered, in her professional judgement, needed attention. Meeting the needs of the line in a mechanical way can lead to short termism and may not, in the final event, be in the best interests of the line, or the organisation as a whole. Challenge appears to be precluded, and a dialogue of equal partners may be a more appropriate way of addressing the issue.

This brings us to the next concern – that being demand driven at all levels of the organisation almost precludes HR from taking on a strategic and proactive role. Fowler (1994) argues that the purchaser–provider split represents a simple view of the function – the personnel function is seen as a wholly support function, carrying out what has been agreed in the service level agreements, and takes the human resource function out of the strategic role. Partly because HR professionals are forced to react purely at all levels of the managerial hierarchy, and partly due to accepting a more submissive role, the function seems in no position to offer an independent perspective or proactive advice. Around half of our respondents talked about offering and selling a service. It is this word 'service' that causes the problem – a word that conjures up the idea of being 'in service' – a servant to betters. It threatens the independence and autonomy of HR professionals – if they don't come up to scratch in the eyes of their masters they're sacked. There appears little room for challenge, and differing perspective and a debate between equals. It all depends on who has the money.

It is interesting that the service role is almost a complete opposite to the policeman role from which personnel specialists are so keen to escape. Using, in a general sense, Berne's model of transactional analysis, when the personnel specialist is the policeman they are the adult and the line manager the child. Alternatively, when the personnel specialist is the servant to the line manager, the specialist becomes the child and the line manager the adult – similar to master/servant relationships of old where the master always knew what was best for the servant to do. Neither of these forms of relationship is satisfactory, and we will progress to offering a more acceptable solution. However, it is worth pointing out at this stage that although the 'policeman' role has such a bad press, it has emerged from the same root as 'policy' – and there is surely some value in having a framework which guides action. A framework in which the personnel specialist not only states what can not be done, but also explains what can be done. Perhaps it is *how* the role is played by the specialist that is the critical difference. In some respects the policeman role is the strategy role *if* it is played carefully and well.

Alternatively, it has been argued that an HR department which operates effectively at the service level is actually gaining in credibility, which will eventually open the door to being involved at a more strategic level:

> We talk a lot in HR these days about strategic involvement but no one is going to
> trust us with strategic decision making until we can run our own function as a

professional and efficient business. And that includes learning to promote ourselves and the value we add in our market place.

(British Aerospace, IPD, 1992, p. 79)

But quite how a function can move to a different position so dramatically in an organisation has yet to be explained. We are more sympathetic to other routes to credibility such as listening to, and understanding business and line needs, providing needed expertise, developing skills which are valued and used confidently, and being prepared to network and use the politics of the organisation.

There are problems too with the operation of the internal market in the way that it forces HR professions to spend their time. A number of our interviewees clearly spent time constructing HR packages that forced line managers to buy larger rather than smaller amounts of their services and they also spent time creating contingency plans if the managers complained about what was on offer. The bureaucracy and form filling involved in internal markets is also time consuming – Kessler and Purcell (1994) argue that if service level agreements are charged this creates bureaucracy – also it diverts attention to those aspects of the personnel function which can be pre-specified. This again diminishes what the function can offer.

The recent changes in the health service highlight some of the problems faced by formal internal markets with which we are concerned. Leaving on one side the issue of equality of healthcare, internal markets in the NHS are seen to cause increased bureaucracy and administration involved with the process of cross charging. Frank Dobson, Minister for Health (reported in *The Times*, 1997), clarified even more critical issues when he stated:

We will end competition and replace it with a new statutory duty of partnership so that local health services pull together rather than apart. (p. 1)

The *Guardian* (1997), on the same day, comment on the long-term nature of the new forms of service agreement as opposed to the old contracts. The idea that the internal market works against partnership and longer-term relationships could be applied equally to the HR role in the organisation. Partnership is preferable to either the service or the policeman role, as in Berne's terms this is an adult-to-adult relationship between equals.

We could summarise by saying that IM diverts the attention of the HR function from what really matters, and constrains their role both of which are unhelpful to the organisation. However, these problems seem to be mostly (not completely) associated with the creation of formal internal markets, and there is a strong case to argue that IM in other circumstances can enhance the role and credibility of the function.

References

Berridge, J. (1992) 'Human resource management in Britain', *Employee Relations*, 14(5), 62–91.

Berry, L. L. (1981) 'The employee as customer', *Journal of Retail Banking*, 3(1), 33–40.

Colling, T. and Ferner, A. (1992) 'The limits of autonomy: devolution, line managers and industrial relations in privatised companies', *Journal of Management Studies*, 29(2), 209–27.

Connock, S. (1992) *Personnel and the Bottom Line*, London: IPD.

Foreman, S. K. and Money, A. H. (1995) 'Internal marketing: concepts, measurement and application', *Journal of Marketing Management*, 11, 755–68.

Fowler, A. (1994) 'Personnel's model army', *Personnel Management*, September.

Hales, C. (1995) 'Internal marketing as an approach to human resource management: a new perspective or a metaphor too far?', *Human Resource Management Journal*, 5(1).

Hendry, C. (1990) 'The corporate management of human resources under conditions of decentralisation', *British Journal of Management*.

IPD (1992) *Marketing the HR Function*, London: IPD.

Kessler, I. and Purcell, J. (1994) 'Strategic choice and new forms of employment relations in the public service sector: developing an analytical framework', paper presented to ERU Annual Conference, Cardiff Business School, September.

Kotler, P. (1991) *Marketing Management: Analysis, Planning, Implementation and Control*, 7th edn, Englewood Cliffs, NJ: Prentice-Hall.

McKenna, R. (1991) *Relationship Marketing*, London: Century.

Varey, R. J. (1995) 'A model for building and sustaining a competitive service advantage', *Journal of Marketing Management*, 11, 41–54.

9

Roles and styles in personnel management

The early research about the personnel function (for example, Anthony and Crichton, 1969; Crichton, 1963; Watson, 1977) concentrated on the sort of people personnel managers were and how they viewed their role. The reason for this was the interest in them as actors in industrial relations and the place they held in an industrial society. More recently that interest has waned, but this chapter re-visits the topic to report on what our research demonstrated.

Personnel and HR roles

Replies to an early question in our questionnaire established that 89 per cent of the respondents worked where there was a personnel/HR function. In view of the one or two isolated specialists who responded to the questionnaire (18 per cent of respondents did not have anyone reporting to them and 30 per cent had only one or two), we can take this as virtually unanimous. Bearing in mind how the research was framed and directed, this is not surprising, but it is important to note the wording of the question, 'Is there a specialist Personnel/HR department where you work?' Earlier in the questionnaire there was emphasis on data being collected about 'the specific place where you work'. In research about workplaces, this was obviously an important emphasis, but it was interesting that there was a specific department in 90 per cent of all the workplaces. Whatever the academic soothsayers may be claiming, this suggests that the Personnel/HR function is virtually a universal phenomenon.

The title of the department showed that 'personnel' titles outnumbered 'HR' titles by about two to one, but it is worth reviewing the actual titles that were reported, and their frequency. We have divided them in three groups: personnel, HR and others.

Title of personnel department	Percentage of respondents	Title of human resources department	Percentage of respondents
Personnel department	38.1	HR dept	19.0
Personnel and training department	9.9	Human resource unit	1.6
		Retail HR	1.1
Personnel section	4.2	Directorate of HR	1.6
Personnel directorate	2.1	HR directorate	0.5
Personnel services	2.1	HR section	0.5
Personnel and services department	1.4	**Total HR titles**	**23.8%**
Personnel and staffing	1.4		
Personnel function	1.1	Title of miscellaneous department	Percentage of respondents
Regional personnel department	1.1		
Personnel and administrative services	0.9	Civilian management unit	1.6
District personnel unit	0.9	Administrative department	1.1
Personnel and facilities	0.9	Management services	1.1
Personnel office	0.9	Staff planning unit	0.5
Divisional personnel	0.5	Accounts	0.5
Personnel management unit	0.5	Staff office	0.5
District personnel department	0.5	Common services support group	0.5
Group personnel	0.5	Chief executive's	0.5
Personnel and administration department	0.5	**Total miscellaneous titles**	**6.3%**
Personnel management	0.5		
Chief Staff Office (Personnel management)	0.5		
Education personnel management	0.5		
Corporate personnel services	0.5		
Administration and personnel	0.5		
Total personnel titles	**69.5%**		

The preference for the term 'personnel' is quite clear, but the range of titles incorporating that term indicates how long it has been current and the breadth of its coverage. Several indicated an existence as part of something else, or in conjunction with something else, such as administration or facilities. None of the HR titles carried that sort of connotation.

Three further questions asked for the job title of the person in charge of the function, the title of the person to whom the respondent reported and the title of the respondent.

The job titles of those in charge of the department are split into four categories. First are titles that include the term 'personnel' with no other functional indicator than another aspect of personnel work, such as personnel and training manager. The second category is the same except that the lead term is 'HR'. The third category is those where personnel or HR is combined with something else, such as 'Head of HR and facilities', and the fourth grouping is those whose titles exclude any specialist personnel/HR reference at all, like chief executive.

Personnel titles	58.0%
HR titles	23.6%
Mixed titles	7.8%
Non-personnel/HR titles	10.4%

Apart from a similar preference in title for personnel rather than HR, the mixed titles are interesting as they are predominantly a combination with some sort of administrative, service or support function, with three examples of a combination with TQM. Of the non-personnel/HR titles there is a puzzling mixture, as there is only one chief executive, no managing director, no general manager and no chairman. Of the personnel or HR titles 39, approaching one in five, include the term 'director'.

There were no fewer than 59 different job titles reported for the person in charge of the function. When it came to the job titles of those to whom the respondents reported, there was a total of 85 and the job titles of the respondents themselves was 93: a quite bewildering array. The replies to this question are presented in the same way as for the person in charge of the function.

	To whom you report	*Yourself*
Personnel titles	30.6%	60.2%
HR titles	8.7%	10.4%
Mixed titles	11.7%	15.8%
Non-personnel/HR titles	48.6%	13.3%

Here we can see some evidence of the decline of strict hierarchy. Nearly half the respondents reported to people without a personnel/HR label. The most common titles of those to whom the respondent reported were:

General manager (or comparable title)	9.1%
Managing director	8.7%
Personnel manager	8.7%
Chief executive	7.2%
Director or directors	5.4%
HR director	3.4%
Deputy managing director	2.9%
Human resource manager	2.9%
Director of personnel	2.4%
Personnel and training manager	2.4%

There are five non personnel/HR titles, all sounding to be of considerable authority, and constituting 33 per cent of those to whom the respondent reports: a very different picture than that which is shown by the replies to the earlier question, 'What is the job title of the person responsible for this department?'

When scanning the individual responses, the reason for this apparent inconsistency becomes clearer. As was indicated in the chapter on decentralisation, the personnel/HR department or function does not comprise all the personnel people, many of whom operate in an individual, freelance role. There were three organisations where there was an HR director, but a personnel department. In the later, one-to-one interviews with questionnaire respondents, they explained that the membership of the personnel function was only a proportion (although usually a large proportion) of those in the business with a clear personnel role. This is a neat illustration of the way in which the firm hierarchical principle in organisation has been modified by the various 'flattening' initiatives of recent years, making the organisational formalities of accountability and responsibility much more fluid. Although the evidence does not demonstrate a comprehensive change, there is certainly a significant proportion of businesses where something that is probably called 'central personnel' is absolutely vital to the business, but mainly in an administrative or support role, while other personnel or HR specialists are operating individually, detached from that administrative core, and carrying out mainly advisory or consultancy activities.

The titles of the individual respondents provide us with no fewer than 93 different job titles to analyse. We have already seen that 70.6 per cent of these are personnel or HR titles, but we break that proportion down one stage further to show those that are generic (such as personnel director, human resource manager, personnel officer or assistant, human resources) and those that show some degree of specialisation (such as career development officer, pay projects manager, recruitment consultant, or personnel and training manager).

Generic personnel/HR title	46.0%
Training and development specialism	10.3%
Administration/systems	7.8%
Pay and benefits specialism	2.3%
Employee relations specialism	2.3%
Recruitment/resourcing specialism	1.9%
Total	70.6%

In the 'mixed' category, where the title shows a combination with an area that is not explicitly a personnel/HR activity, the largest single response was a combination of personnel with quality.

We can not be too forthright in drawing conclusions from these specialist titles, as the generic titles often concealed a high degree of specialisation in the activities of the job holder, but interview respondents generally confirmed a picture of personnel professionals holding broad portfolios. We conclude that there is a significant move to outsource the more specialised aspects of personnel work, as was explored in Chapter 7. Also, the main remaining specialist emphases on in-house personnel posts are training and development, and administration and systems. There are clear reasons for this.

Training has had a great deal of attention in recent years and many training specialists have been reluctant to identify with the more generalised terms of personnel management or human resource management. The amalgamation of the two professional bodies is recent and the identity of a specialism in training and development that is distinct from general personnel work has a robust tradition. The development of computerised personnel information systems has developed the significance and use of the central personnel database. Employee relations does not have the high profile that it did and recruitment is much reduced as a specialist activity, although – as we shall see in the next paragraphs – they remain a major general feature of personnel work.

We asked respondents to report the relative amount of time spent on different activities and to rank those activities in terms of importance in contribution to the business. We were able to compare this information with that provided in the comparable study 10 years earlier.

Table 9.1. shows the relative amount of time spent by respondents on 13 different activities; the most time-consuming is the first and the least time-consuming is the last. This is then compared with the answers to a similar question posed a decade ago, although the topics were not exactly the same.

Table 9.1 Answers to question, 'Approximately what percentage of your time is spent on the following matters?', compared with answers to a similar question 10 years earlier

Perception of relative time spent on key personnel activities

Rank order NOW (mid-1990s)		Rank order PAST (mid-1980s)
Recruitment/selection	1	Employee relations
Training	2	Recruitment/selection
Employee relations/involvement	3	Training
Human resource planning	4	Organisation and management development
Payment administration	5	Payment administration
Discipline/grievance	6	Discipline/grievance
Quality initiatives	7	Changes in work organisation
Redundancy/dismissal	8	Manpower planning
Appraisals	9	Health, safety, welfare
Health, safety, welfare	10	Redundancy/dismissal
Job evaluation	11	New technology
Career planning	12	Appraisals
Fringe benefits	13	Job evaluation

Table 9.2 is the result of asking respondents to rank key personnel activities in terms of their importance in delivering the contribution to organisational objectives in the last three years. There is thus an attempt to elicit a longer-term, reflective perspective than an immediate reaction to the current situation.

It is certainly striking that recruitment/selection, training and employee relations are the three most time-consuming and, with human resource planning, are regarded as the most significant in terms of their contribution to the business at both ends of the decade. It became apparent in interviews that the activity of human resource planning was often interpreted as a planning approach to human resource matters, rather than the more specialised type of quantitative forecasting that textbooks describe.

Quality initiatives are relatively time-consuming but not highly rated in terms of the personnel contribution to the business. This may be due to their being owned by others. Discipline, grievance, redundancy and dismissal have all declined in importance, although they still take about the same amount of time as they used to. Health, safety and welfare still rank quite low and career planning does not take much time nor appear very important, despite the recent attention paid to it.

The overall picture that emerges from these data is:

1 A personnel department as a distinct, functional entity is found almost universally, but this does not include all the specialist personnel activity in the business.

Table 9.2 Answers to the question, 'How would you rank the following activities in terms of their importance in the contribution made by the personnel function to organisational objectives in the last three years?'

Perception of importance to the business

Rank order NOW (mid-1990s)		Rank order PAST (mid-1980s)
Recruitment/selection	1	Employee relations
Human resource planning	2	Recruitment/selection
Employee relations/involvement	3	Training
Training	4	Manpower planning
Communications	5	Discipline/grievance
Management development	6	Changes in work organisation
Appraisal	7	Organisation and management development
Performance management	8	Redundancy/dismissal
Discipline/grievance	9	Appraisal
Redundancy/dismissal	10	Payment administration
Reward strategies and systems	11	Health, safety, welfare
Health, safety, welfare	12	Job evaluation
Quality initiatives	13	New technology
Career planning	14	Fringe benefits

2 Personnel/HR specialists outside the personnel department tended to report to a more senior person than the person in charge of the department itself.
3 'Personnel' titles were used much more widely than 'HR' titles, with no apparent difference in activity or emphasis between them, except that 'HR' titles were not associated with some other function.
4 Where job titles indicate a specialism or specialist emphasis, training and development or administration and systems are the most common.
5 The staple fare of personnel work remains recruitment, training and employee relations.

Over thirty years ago, Crichton and Collins (1966) carried out a survey which showed the range of job titles used at that time to describe members of the personnel profession. They used what now seems a bizarre distinction between technologists, but they also reported on the titles that were written in by respondents. There were 585 technologists, who were regarded as having jobs which involved building and maintaining the organisation, and 1689 technicians, who had narrow and very specific duties.

Table 9.3 Personnel roles in 1966, taken from Crichton and Collins, 1966

Titles for technologists

Included in questionnaire

Personnel director	Personnel manager	Personnel officer
Personnel assistant	Staff manager	Employment manager
Labour manager	Labour officer	Recruitment officer
Industrial relations manager	Employee relations manager	Labour relations manager
Negotiating officer	Welfare manager	Education manager
Education and training officer	Management development manager	Training officer

Written in by respondents

Manager, personnel services	Personnel superintendent	Personnel controller
Staff director	Staff personnel officer	Administration and staff manager
Head of staff section	Staff controller	Head of staff section
Staff assistant	Women's staff supervisor	Women's supervisor
Supervisor (females)	Establishment officer	I/C salaries and establishment
I/C staff recruitment	Industrial relations director	Consultation and administration officer
Training superintendent	Distribution training officer	Training and education officer

Titles for technicians

Included in questionnaire

Apprentice supervisor	Instructor	Training assistant
Safety officer	Safety engineer	Medical officer
Nurse	Accident prevention officer	Trainer

Written in by respondents

Apprentice training and recruitment manager	Safety superintendent	Fire officer
Rescue man	Accident investigator	Safety and fire prevention officer
Safety and hygiene technologist	Physiotherapist	Chief nursing officer
Nursing sister	Ambulance room attendant	Nursing superintendent
Suggestions secretary	Pension and insurance officer	Pensions secretary
Sports and social officer	Job analyst	Sports and social club secretary
Internal publicity assistant	I/C internal publicity	Personnel record officer
Hostel warden	Travel officer	Work study manager
Manager, administration	Labour and security officer	Welfare and training officer

How things have changed! Now we have much less reference to employee relations and none to industrial relations, which is almost extinct as a term to describe what happens inside companies. Not one of our respondents had an explicit involvement in health, safety or welfare. The clear references to different categories of employee – staff and labour – is no more and nowadays women are not described as a separate category.

Going further back, to 1943, Moxon listed five functions of the personnel department:

> Employment, education and training, wages, negotiation and consultation, health and safety, and employee services.
>
> (Moxon, 1943, p. 11)

Some current titles and roles explored

We now move to examine some of the current roles that personnel specialists occupy and the nature of the responsibilities involved. We cannot say that every person with one of the following titles necessarily operates in the way described. The proliferation of titles that we have already demonstrated shows that titles are more to satisfy the need for personal identity and a sense of status than to describe accurately what the job holder actually does. Some job titles are clearly informative. Plumber, primary school teacher, lecturer in Greek, psychiatric nurse, company secretary and driving instructor all mean much the same, wherever they are used, and give an accurate message to the outside world. In management, this is not found. We use these titles, therefore, as a means of classification of the roles, not as a reliable description of jobs.

Personnel or human resource director

The nature of this role is heavily strategic in its emphasis and general in its orientation. It is sometimes held by someone without any professional personnel training, but with well-developed management expertise and skilled at strategic thinking. It is a top management role, as part of a board of directors, or similar body, that is charged with the responsibility of making the business succeed. Most of the other directors will have a functional responsibility, such as finance, marketing or operations, and the personnel director will represent human resource considerations in all the strategic decision-making and management discussion.

The personnel director will represent '. . . human resource considerations . . .', which is not by any means the same as representing the interests of the employees. The nature of this representation has been a topic of discussion for many years. Over 40 years ago a study group wrestled with what they saw as the central dilemma:

> How could he (the personnel officer) manage to be seen as unbiased . . . whilst acting as management's agent and representing their viewpoint? And how could he be identified with the management group whilst reminding them of the workers' views? Should he seek concessions on employees' behalf? The study group argued that his role was that of 'remembrancer', so that workpeople's views would be taken into consideration in making policies, but not their representative.
>
> (Hunter, 1957)

Peter Anthony regarded this as a ludicrous proposition:

> Personnel specialists are often paid for their 'expert' knowledge of union methods and attitudes; this expertise may encourage a feeling that they represent those for whom they are required to develop a sympathetic understanding; they are no more entitled to represent them than is an ambassador the citizens and officials of a foreign capital.
>
> (Anthony and Crichton, 1969, p. 153)

Both those quotations date from a time when the arena of personnel work was relations between employers and employees: customers were someone else's problem. The representation dilemma remains. Trade unions may now have a more marginal role and employees of all grades dutifully subordinate their own interests in the service of the almighty customer, but as employees become better educated, from more diverse backgrounds, and more assertive, they will not deliver the goods in a climate of rapid change and cultural sophistication if they do not support management action. One of the buzz words of contemporary management is 'commitment'. All employees have to have it and it is up to management to make sure they've got it. It is a simple fact of human nature that people will not commit themselves for long to that in which they have no confidence. This is expressed in strong terms by two American writers:

> Studies of work flow suggest there is five times more opportunity to experience joy in the workplace on a daily basis than in the home environment, if it is a home environment that is in tune with the soul . . . Once we have a community of fully nurtured souls the possibility of creativity is enormous.
>
> (Wright and Smye, 1996, p. 248)

The personnel director will represent human resource considerations, which will include the likely reaction of employees to management initiatives, but will also include assessments of how to deal with unfavourable reactions, whether the nature of existing skills and competencies can be developed satisfactorily with existing people, how commitment can be achieved and a range of ethical issues. The Royal Dutch/Shell Group of Companies rely largely for their international effectiveness, on the values shared by all their companies and employees. No new venture will be developed unless the partner company accepts them.

> The business principles are a set of beliefs which say what the Shell group stands for, and covers in general terms its responsibilities to its principal stakeholders, its shareholders, employees, customers and society. They are concerned with economic principles, business integrity, political activities, the environment, the community and availability of information.
>
> (Haddock and South, 1994, p. 226)

Personnel manager

This is the general manager in charge of the personnel function or department, who acts as its figurehead and main spokesperson, representing personnel issues in all senior management discussions and policy-making. There are usually one or more specialist responsibilities attaching to the post, such as employee relations or management development. This is the role, together with most of those that follow, for which the Institute of Personnel and Development's membership examinations provide the most appropriate and widely regarded qualification. It is most unusual for someone to be placed in this position without significant experience in personnel work.

While the personnel director is a member of a close-knit senior team with shared responsibility for cross-functional matters, the personnel manager is the leading member of a different group, one of specialists with varying types and levels of responsibility. The emphasis is more on strategy implementation, rather than strategy formulation, although that distinction is easier to describe in theory than to see in practice. Implementation involves working things through with other members of the function and a great deal of planning and monitoring. There is also a major activity in consulting and negotiating with people across the business and outside the organisational boundary.

It would be misleading to say that personnel managers wait for things to happen before taking action, but they have an important reactive role, in that there is a lot of fire-fighting that has to be done and coping with matters as they arise. It is fashionable for managers to aim to be proactive, rather than reactive; going out and making things happen, introducing change and keeping everyone on their toes. It is fatal for personnel or HR people to move too far in that direction, and personnel managers properly spend significant chunks of their time dealing with things that they had not anticipated when they set off to drive to work in the morning. One of our research respondents moved to a new job soon after we interviewed him and his previous employer has subsequently been strongly criticised for being slow to deal with the problems of pension mis-selling. Our respondent may not be altogether dispassionate in his judgement, but his commentary is:

They have not followed through properly. They have decided what to do on three separate occasions, but they have not then followed through and made sure things got done. When they encountered an unforeseen problem my successor didn't react to the situation and manage a way through it, she simply convened another meeting to discuss the problem. She's gone now, but the company has lost eighteen months and a lot of business.

Personnel managers are managers of operations, making things happen, getting round problems and constantly networking to find better solutions to practical problems.

Personnel officer

In most establishments this is the title of the person who deals with all personnel issues, being a second type of generalist role, but not having the same range of responsibility and authority of a personnel manager. Alternatively, it can be a specialised role, with the specialism coming in brackets afterwards. Personnel officer (pay and benefits), personnel officer (administration) are examples. Their background and experience is likely to be the same as that of personnel manager, whose job they are probably aiming for.

Employee relations manager

Although it is most often a feature of the specialist responsibilities carried by the personnel manager, or director, one specialist role is that of dealing (note the reactive language!) with the collective relationship between management and employees, especially where this is formalised through union recognition and procedure agreements. It may also include responsibility for pay issues, employee involvement and communication. The distinctive feature is that employees are aggregates, not individuals. Although the role is a product of a time when unions were more active, there remains a range of activities where there is a management interaction with the workforce as a whole.

In most businesses there will be a degree of consultation, negotiation or bargaining that the management needs to undertake with representatives of employee opinion. Many would argue that that this is because they have a right to such consultation as major stakeholders in the business. Managers of a different persuasion will usually acknowledge that employees can cause trouble if they are not consulted, and they might well have useful suggestions, so that consultation can improve management decision-making and avoid a breakdown of commitment. Those who believe that the management have a right to manage that which cannot be gainsaid could take note of two disputes in 1997. British Airways attempted to impose new conditions of employment on cabin staff, which they regarded as unfair. The outcome was a strike that cost the airline (according to the chief executive) at least £125m. At almost the same time Barclays Bank introduced a new pay and grading structure without the agreement of the main staff unions. Industrial action was begun by the unions in October and so far the dispute is not resolved. The employee relations manager is the person who represents the management in all such collective matters, at least at the outset, although the most senior figures in the company will also be involved from time to time.

The employee relations manager knows the union rules and procedures for any unions represented in the undertaking, will assist managers at all levels in dealing with day-to-day issues as they arise, and will advise senior management regularly on comparative terms and conditions of employment elsewhere in the industrial sector and in the locality. There is also a general responsibility for monitoring the use of procedures, such as grievance and discipline. In some companies there is a much more proactive role in taking initiatives to improve communications and mutual confidence.

Training and development manager

Another strong tradition is to concentrate responsibility for training and employee development in the hands of a specialist manager. The increasing tendency to deal with development matters by heavy reliance on outside facilities, such as consultants, means that this role is mainly concerned with analysing training needs in the business and managing the contractual arrangements with outside suppliers to meet those needs. There is less likely to be a large staff of in-house trainers and instructors to be co-ordinated. There is also often a focus on management development rather than on employee development to emphasise the responsibility of individual managers for developing their staff.

The interaction with the outside is not only in contracting with training suppliers, but also in monitoring government initiatives in the training and education field. The development of the national skill base continues to be a prime preoccupation of government, together with a commitment that it is 'industry' that alone can solve the problem. Initiatives like NVQs and Investors in People require close monitoring to ensure that the business picks up on the opportunities presented, as well as meeting its civic obligations.

Training and development consultants

Training officers have similar responsibilities to personnel officers in that they may be single trainers with general training duties in an establishment, or they may be charged with specific training tasks, like operator training. The term 'consultant' is increasingly being used instead of 'officer' to ensure that the work is used as a consultancy by managers to arrange the training they want rather than what the training officer has organised. Formal qualifications in organisational or occupational psychology are often held by training specialists, and IPD qualifications devote a large proportion of their standards and total syllabus to this area.

Recruitment and selection manager

These posts are not as widespread as they were and usually these duties are the regular part-time responsibility of several people in a personnel department, yet the work remains highly skilled and many large organisations still retain specialist personnel, usually with an occupational psychology background expertise.

Just as there are many outside sources of training expertise that have changed the nature of the training function, there is also a rapidly growing industry in recruitment, so that HR people specialising in recruitment retain the core skill of selection but increasingly have to deal with suppliers of candidates.

Human resource planner

This is a much less clear job title with many variations, used to describe someone whose expertise is basically in human resource planning and statistics, and who will do much of the preliminary work on working out future human resource needs of the business, how they will alter and what the implications will be of those changes. Only in very large organisations is this a discrete role. Usually it is an aspect of what someone does alongside a different lead responsibility.

Organisation development consultant

This role specialises in enabling the organisation to adapt to its changing environment and its members to develop their roles to meet the new challenges and opportunities that are emerging. It is a job with few administrative features and is usually held by someone with an independent, roving commission, reporting into the central hierarchy at a pretty high level. It is a somewhat vulnerable role, because the role holder has no clear base in the business and always looks expendable. The person doing this job needs to be extremely capable and self-reliant, with well-developed political skills.

Safety officer/welfare officer

The area of health, safety and welfare is one where there are strong legal constraints on employer action and the safety officer is not always a part of the personnel function at all. Our research suggests that few, if any – of our respondents held this type of portfolio. Large organisations often have one or more welfare officers to deal with general issues of employee support and there has recently been an increase in employee assistance programmes, which perform part of the welfare function through the use of an outside agency.

Personnel administration manager

The final role in this sample list is a longstanding one, which is changing direction. There is some tendency for personnel administration to increase, and a part of the expanding numbers in personnel departments is in the clerical/administrative/keyboard area, with the demands of such tasks as statutory sick pay and the need to maintain a personnel database on the computer. This part of the operation is run by someone who used to be called 'office manager', but who is now more to be described as 'personnel administration manager'.

Style

What is the management style of the HR/personnel specialist? The answer to this question is partly governed by the type of person who opts for this line of work. There is no doubt at all that many people are drawn to it because of its conventional association with 'helping people'. Ever since it began as a specialism the professional training has been dominated by the social science disciplines and their lessons in how to assess people, social justice, legal rights and so on. Many of the people who take it up – perhaps most – are looking to avoid the sharper edges of commercial life. That has shaped the development of the personnel function and still provides its distinctive characteristics. Management is not homogenous in style. Marketing people tend to have a style which is markedly different from operations people, and both have a style that is different from accountants. Although these are crude stereotypes, with innumerable individual differences and variations, they remain potent in our informal dealings with people.

The HR/personnel style can manifest itself in four broad ways.

Service style

This style is one of dealing with things as they arise and responding to the needs of colleagues and others, by providing an efficient, conscientious and principled service to the business and its people. Many of the people who are keen to stake out the strategic role of personnel regard this attitude as the kiss of death, but it remains almost the ideal for some roles, such as personnel administration manager.

Furthermore, it is the style for the entire function that is still widely favoured by practitioners. Well over half of our interview respondents were quite clear that the success criteria for the HR function were the extent to which it provided an effective service to the rest of the business:

> There is always scope for selling our service, and we must never lose sight of our primary service role. Providing a service is not simply doing what anyone may want, it

is providing a service in response to demand, but in a skilled and creative way. We must know better than the internal customer what needs to be done and how.

(Head of personnel, central government)

Our problem is not to get rid of the service idea, but to promote it! Service is such a dominant ethic in the NHS, that only by being seen as being 'of service' can one have any street credibility at all. Mostly they think we are a pain and we have to remember that they understand how to use pain killers.

(Director of HR and corporate affairs)

Advisory style

This style is one of helping colleagues by providing well-informed and constructive advice on matters where the colleague does not have the necessary expertise. Safety officers are in this role, as are the organisation development consultants, and success requires not only expertise that other people seek, but also persuasive skills and a continuing proactive search for advisory paths to follow. Not many people can adopt this style and then sit back waiting for the panel patients to make appointments.

I read somewhere that we should give advice like an expert solicitor rather than like a well-intentioned mother-in-law. I always remembered that because my mother-in-law is a solicitor. I only partly agree, as the advice we give must be sufficiently expert that people realise they could not have worked it out for themselves, but it must also be well-intentioned and competent in the sense of having a real feeling for the situation and a personal concern for getting things right.

(Regional HR manager, recently-privatised utility)

Political style

This style involves the understanding and manipulation of the power that exists within the organisation:

If everyone were perfectly agreed on ends and means, no-one would ever need to change the way of another. Hence no relations of influence or power would arise. Hence no political system would exist. Let one person frustrate another in the pursuit of his goals and you already have the germ of a political system; conflict and politics are born inseparable twins.

(Dahl, 1970, p. 59)

The organisational politician is one who understands these processes and seeks to get things done through that understanding. The employee relations manager is inevitably working with that style, but many other personnel specialists adopt it as well.

Leadership style

This style is the fashionable right way to operate. This is not responding to circumstances, nor avoiding real responsibility by simply giving advice to other people who make the decisions and take the risks. It is not manipulating the forces at play in a continuing power struggle. It is taking a lead, accepting responsibility for what one does and enthusing others to catch your own vision and make things happen that otherwise would not. This style is a *sine qua non* for those in senior managerial positions, but it can also be found in people holding much more humble positions.

References

Anthony, P. D. and Crichton, A. (1969) *Industrial Relations and the Personnel Specialists*, London: Batsford.

Crichton, A. (1963) 'A persistent stereotype? The personnel manager: the outsider.' *Personnel Management*, December, 160–7.

Crichton, A. and Collins, R. G. (1966) 'Personnel specialists: a count by employers', *British Journal of Industrial Relations*, July.

Dahl, R. (1970) *Modern Political Analysis*, 2nd edn, Englewood Cliffs, NJ: Prentice-Hall.

Haddock, C. and South, B. (1994) 'How Shell's organisation and HR practices help it to be both global and local' in D. P. Torrington (ed.) *International Human Resource Management*, Hemel Hempstead: Prentice-Hall International.

Hunter, G. (1957) *The Role of the Personnel Officer*, London: Institute of Personnel Management. (Quoted in Anthony and Crichton, 1969, 199–200.)

Moxon, G. R. (1943) *The Functions of a Personnel Department*, London: Institute of Personnel Management.

Watson, T. J. (1977) *The Personnel Managers*, London: Routledge and Kegan Paul.

Wright, L. and Smye, M. (1996) *Corporate Abuse*, New York: Macmillan.

10

The training and development of personnel specialists

In this chapter we intend to review how the training and development of personnel and HR specialists has developed and to consider the implications for further training of our research findings. As it has a long tradition, it is important for us to understand how and why personnel management training has developed in the way that it has. It is firmly embedded in the higher education system, for reasons we will explain. Anything which is so firmly embedded has advocates convinced of the value of what they are doing and resistant to radical change that appears to undermine the contribution that has been made.

Through its long-standing association with certain universities and its readiness to accept the findings of researchers in the social sciences, personnel work has a long tradition in the training and development of its practitioners. The technology of the specialism was developed in the early years after the First World War, with a further boost in the years after the Second World War. The Institute of Personnel and Development is one of the largest of the qualifying associations in management, and many universities and colleges run first-degree courses, masters' and professional programmes that are geared to IPD membership requirements. How should these be developed? Do they provide the most appropriate preparation for people working in this area? Are there alternatives, and how do people keep up-to-date after initial qualification? Our research enables us to explore some of these issues.

Staffing and qualifications of personnel staff

We have already seen that the existence of a personnel or HR department was almost universal in the businesses represented in our research sample, although not all of those with HR/personnel responsibilities worked within its purview. Having asked our respondents whether or not a specialist department existed, we than asked the numbers of people working in it.

Table 10.1 Answers to the question, 'How many people work in the department?'

Numbers in the department	% of respondents
5 or less	43.6
6 to 10	20.0
11 to 15	9.0
16 to 20	5.5
21 to 25	8.0
26 to 30	2.0
31 to 35	1.5
36 to 40	0.5
41 to 45	2.0
46 to 50	1.5
51 and over	6.4

Of those reporting numbers over 50, 8 reported numbers over 100 and 1 reported 300. The total number of staff reported in all the respondents' departments was 3454. A further question was: 'Of these, how many people have professional and/or educational qualifications in personnel/ personnel related matters?' This total number was 884, or 25.59 per cent. Eighty-two per cent of the respondents themselves were members of the IPD.

The full list of replies to this question shows a very wide range of other professional qualifications. The Institute of Administrative Management, The Institute of Mechanical Engineers and The Chartered Institute of Bankers all showed two memberships. The remainder were single memberships reported of various bodies.

The level of educational qualification achieved by respondents after leaving school was as follows:

PhD	1.5%
MA/MSc. Personnel/HRM	1.5%
MBA	3.6%
IPD postgraduate diploma	8.1%
Other IPD qualification	22.0%
	36.7%
Other postgraduate qualification	5.6%
First degree in business/management	2.0%
Other first degree/HND	33.4%
	41.0%

Further answers showed first how long respondents had been in their present job:

Less than 1 year	17.8%
Less than 3 years	58.2%
Less than 5 years	79.3%
Less than 10 years	93.9%
Less than 20 years	97.7%

and how long they had been working in personnel:

Less than 1 year	8.4%
Less than 3 years	28.6%
Less than 5 years	43.8%
Less than 10 years	71.4%
Less than 20 years	89.7%

This again shows the fact that a number of respondents did not see themselves as being a part of 'the personnel/HR department', although they had a clear personnel/HR role in the business.

Respondents were then asked, 'Have you worked in any other departments or managerial roles? If so, which?' The responses here were so varied as to make analysis problematic. Forty-three per cent of the respondents answered that they had not had other roles. The other replies can be grouped as follows:

General management	20.0%
Administration	15.5%
Accounts or finance	12.7%
Training	11.8%
Operations	10.9%
Management services	6.3%
Marketing	3.6%
Miscellaneous	19.2%

The 'miscellaneous' category defied further classification, as it included such answers as civil service, British high commission, librarian, VAT and consultancy. The overall picture is therefore one of varied prior experience, although half of the respondents had been within the function throughout their careers. An interesting comparison can be made with an analysis by Crichton, writing in 1961:

> Personnel work can be done by two groups of people, the one specialising in human relations aspects of management all their lives and getting their experience by moving from one personnel post to another; and the other kind staying with one company and learning to take responsibility in many aspects of management, personnel management being only one in a series of these experiences.
>
> (Crichton, 1961, p. 165)

Personnel work is an area of occupational life that many people enter early and remain with quite steadfastly. For others it is a stage in a more general management career, and for some it is one dimension of a multi-faceted role within general management. There can be no doubt that it is a part of the work of every manager, quite apart from those for whom it becomes a specialism. The specialists do not invariably become members of the IPD, although that membership is unchallenged as the appropriate professional qualification in the area. What then is the nature of the qualification to practise that IPD provides?

The development of the IPD qualification

Like many similar bodies, the Institute of Personnel and Development has followed a process of expanding its membership at the same time as making membership more difficult to attain. The twin objectives have always been to increase the influence and effectiveness of the Institute by extending membership to an increasing number of people active in the field, but also to make the membership an appropriate and near-exclusive qualification to practice. These are the two aspects of professionalisation: qualifying people to practise and achieving the benefit for members of restricting the opportunities to practise of those who are outside. Freidson provides a definition:

> Professionalisation might be defined as a process by which an organised occupation, usually but not always by virtue of making a claim to special esoteric competence and to concern for the quality of its work and its benefits to society, obtains the exclusive right to perform a particular kind of work, control, training for and access to it, and control the right of determining and evaluating the way the work is performed.
>
> (Freidson, 1973, p. 22)

After the initial expansion around the time of the First World War, membership languished during the inter-war years, with 739 members in 1939 being comparable with the number in 1920. The Second World War was a major stimulus to membership:

> The Second World War, however, brought an almost four-fold increase in membership to nearly 3000. By 1944 over three thousand factories employed personnel or welfare officers, and the total number so employed was almost 5000.
>
> (Clegg, 1970, p. 163)

There was further recognition when the Ministry of Labour published a career's pamphlet on personnel management and made special provision for the wartime training of personnel officers. In 1945 the Ministry established a personnel management Advisory Service, which subsequently became the advisory feature of ACAS. Continuing full employment during the post-war period prevented the membership decline that followed The First World War, and the membership of IPM increased inexorably.

Following the Ministry of Labour training initiative in the war years, IPM established its education and qualification process as a route to membership. Initially this was an optional extra, only one of several routes to membership, the most common of which was to join, following interview, with a couple of existing members on the basis of experience. By the 1970s there were moves to restrict entry in the way practised by some of the long-standing professions.

In 1977 Watson (p. 134) reported that only 14 of his 100 interviewees had entered the IPM by examination, although 48 were members. Twenty-one were student members and 31 were not members. Twenty years later only 18 per cent of our respondents were not IPM members and entry to IPM and now IPD is almost exclusively by 'examination', although examination is in inverted commas because of the various means whereby competence can now be assessed.

The early examination processes had what would now be regarded as too academic a tone, but we have to remember that the first British business schools were not set up until the late 1960s. Before that there were very few centres claiming any expertise in this area. UMIST had a Department of Industrial Administration in 1918 and introduced the first British degree in management in 1965. The London, Bradford and Manchester MBAs followed soon after as precursors of the current widespread provision of business and management education. The innovators of the IPM had to deal with the specialists that were available, so the study of personnel management became the very poor relation in departments of psychology, sociology and economics. The study of industrial relations became respectable much earlier than personnel management, despite the courses run in war time. Hugh Clegg was appointed Professor of Industrial Relations at Warwick in 1967 and George Bain to a similar post at UMIST in 1969, but it was nearly twenty years later that the first professor was appointed in personnel management, and then it was only in brackets! Keith Thurley was appointed at LSE to a chair in Industrial Relations (with a special interest in personnel management). It was the 1990s before the new label of HRM saw the widespread appointment of people to chairs in human resource management.

Prospective IPM members studied industrial psychology, industrial relations, industrial sociology, economics and statistics, together with the 'applied' subjects of training and development and employment and employee services.

By the 1980s the membership of IPM was expanding and the 'examinations only' route into membership was steadily becoming established as the norm. A small number of well-regarded university departments, such as LSE, UMIST and Warwick were allowed or encouraged to run courses of preparation that led to a university qualification, with the holders being granted complete exemption from IPM examination requirements. Alongside these courses there was a national education scheme that was delivered through a number of universities and colleges throughout the country, with the syllabus content, examination papers and examination marking being controlled centrally through an education committee and a small group of chief examiners. Students were mainly in full-time jobs, taking the qualification through part-time study, although some full-time courses were also provided.

This arrangement was a brilliant piece of political balancing. By having a small number of high profile departments involved in the Institute's qualification process, IPD ensured the active interest and participation of some of the best-known and influential academics, steadily altering the research agenda and gradually developing the magical requirement of prestige. These departments were willing and able to be involved because they were allowed significant degrees of academic freedom to determine their own interpretation of the IPD syllabus and to remain independent of the central examination system. At the same time other departments outside the magic circle ran courses for the IPD examinations and produced the numbers to increase the membership.

The qualification was in two stages. The first stage was sufficiently general for many holders of first degrees to be granted exemption from it. The key second stage was centred on the study of three core subjects: employee development, employee relations and employee resourcing, with a management project as an integrating feature. The older idea of basic disciplines was abandoned in favour of three applied subjects that were regarded as forming the essence of personnel management: anyone seeking to be a member of IPM needed to demonstrate understanding and competence in all three broad areas.

The nature of management education generally was changing, with basic disciplines having much less emphasis and more explicitly, management subjects being brought in. IPM was one of many influencing factors in that development.

Reverting to one of the research findings reported in the previous chapter, we can see that the generalised activities of personnel people are reflected accurately in the three applied subjects, even when the question is asked 10 years apart.

This marked a major change from the situation when the examination process began. Then IPM took what was available from the higher education system and the qualification was fitted in to existing academic disciplines. By the 1980s the emphasis was different. Academics who had developed their careers and their research under the industrial relations banner, began to re-invent themselves as specialists in employee relations or in employee resourcing. Posts were advertised with these titles and the academic agenda shifted towards that set by IPM. There developed a greater synergy between teaching and research in the area of employment on the one hand and the occupational interests and professionalisation of personnel managers on the other hand.

The significance of this synergy was considerable, because the range of subjects was so wide. The accountants had developed excellent working relationships in higher education rather earlier, but their interests did not stretch so widely as the large number of mini-specialisms that are under the personnel umbrella. There were contributions from the long-standing disciplines of economics, psychology, sociology and statistics, but also newer areas, like employment law, discrimination, international business and computer systems.

IPM achieved a position approaching hegemony in that part of the academic world in which it had an interest, and that influence spread more widely. As MBA courses developed, they needed a 'people' dimension and it was the 'personnel' academics that began to prescribe an MBA people component that was strongly influenced by their interface with IPM.

IPM becomes IPD

As IPM expanded its membership and the rigour of its entry process, there was a fledgling, rival body in the Institute of Training and Development. This began as the Institution of Training Officers in the aftermath of the Industrial Training Act of 1964. The boost to training that the Act provided increased considerably the number of training officers appointed by companies. Many were not members of IPD and could not obtain membership. Also it was a time when training was being regarded by some as a new specialism in its own right, breaking away from the amorphous personnel management, with its lingering connections to old-fashioned welfare, to say nothing of the muck and nettles associated with industrial relations.

The new body recruited members without the rigour of having to pass examinations, which were seen as an unsatisfactory method of assessment, quite apart from the fact that they might be difficult! Training and development remained a central feature of personnel management, so the existence of a rival body was not altogether welcome, although a number of people held membership of both institutes. There was a move in 1977 to merge the two, but this failed and the institutes continued their separate ways until the ITD achieved its greatest political coup in the 1990s by taking a salient position on NVQs.

After NVQs were launched in 1986 a Lead Body for Training and Development was set up quite separate from the Lead Body for Personnel Standards and without official IPM representation. By 1992 they had published their national standards, two of which were required by any NVQ assessor. The Training Standards Lead Body was dominated by members of the Institute of Training and Development, IPM was excluded and all NVQ assessors had to be qualified according to the TSLB standards before they could practise. This was a bitter blow for IPM, so a further attempt was made to merge the two bodies. This succeeded more easily than many people expected and the Institute of Personnel and Development came into existence in 1994. A part of the amalgamation was the development of a new educational and qualification process, acknowledging not only the new organisation, but also the impact of NVQs.

The Personnel Standards Lead Body and its legacy

As has already been indicated, the NVQ movement required the development of national standards for personnel work and many people in IPM were disappointed that the institute was not itself designated as the lead body, especially in view of the influence that ITD had had on the training standards. Lead bodies were designed to be employer-led – or employment-led – so that the work done and the training standards produced would reflect the reality of the work that members of the occupation undertake, without any distraction by academics. The Personnel Standards Lead Body (PSLB) was set up with David Sieff of Marks & Spencer to chair it and representation from IPM, although a large number of its members were members of PSLB in their capacity as representing the views of employers.

In view of the great, lingering debate about the difference between personnel management and human resource management, it is interesting that there was never a suggestion that the body should be the Human Resource Management Lead Body, apparently on the basis that it was to consider the specialist area rather than the more general aspects of human resource management.

PSLB set to work and commissioned consultants to carry out investigation and analysis on its behalf. The method was to produce an occupational map and then a functional map. The first was to identify the scope of the occupational area, its boundaries and its overall purpose. The second was to break the occupation down into functional areas, each with its own purpose. The key purpose of personnel management was defined by this process as being:

> . . . to enable management to enhance the individual and collective contribution of people to the short and long term success of the enterprise. This will be achieved by the management and provision of inter-related activities and initiatives in strategy and policy, operational processes and special services. These activities will support and modify the environment, climate and culture in which management operates.
>
> (PSLB, 1993, p. 18)

Apart from being a cumbersome and opaque statement, this clearly excludes the old-fashioned man-in-the-middle notion. Personnel is clearly there to '. . . enable management to enhance . . .'

The key functional areas or roles that were identified were:

- Strategy and organisation
- Resourcing

- Development
- Reward management
- Employee relations

Notwithstanding the extensive research conducted by the consultants, these – and the standards derived from them – were frequently reworded to get acceptable meanings. At one time the analysis of the survey data came to the interesting conclusion that employee relations was no part of personnel work at all!

The new qualification was to be based on assessment of the attainment of standards. The standards were:

> . . . the competencies required to perform the activities of the occupation at the levels of performance expected in employment.
>
> (Gibb, 1995, p.61)

Basic disciplines are way behind, and established bodies of knowledge nearly as far back. The starting point becomes what is required in actual working behaviour: learning begins with that definition.

For whatever reason the National Council for Vocational Qualifications had not called upon IPM to be the Lead Body, but the PSLB quickly found that it was absolutely dependent on IPM if the new standards were to have any take-up. At the same time, NCVQ were beginning to acknowledge the value of written examinations as a form of assessment. Discussions began in a joint working party with the objective of re-shaping the IPM qualification process so that it would be acceptable to NCVQ and still be workable within the IPM framework. That framework relied heavily on universities and colleges for delivery of the learning needed for its qualification and the recruitment of prospective members as students following the course. Although a founding principle of NVQs was that they should be available to all, a firm principle of IPM was that its qualification should be available only to those who showed intention to join the professional body, by paying a joining fee before their studies began. IPM did not shift from that position, nor did they abandon unseen, written examinations, but they did make available a competence-based route towards their qualification.

As NVQs struggled to gain some momentum and acceptance, there was some rationalisation of lead bodies, so PSLB was merged into a new Occupational Standards Council, containing the TDLB and the Trade Union Sector Lead Body as well as PSLB, so the edge was taken off some of the previous rivalries.

The IPD professional standards and qualification

Three significant events took place in the summer of 1994. The Occupational Standards Council was formed in May, the IPD came into existence at the beginning of July and the Personnel NVQs were launched at the end of July. In launching them the director of membership and education for IPD said:

> Graduate membership of the IPM required individuals to demonstrate a wide range of knowledge and understanding across the whole management and personnel management field, and it also required individuals to demonstrate their competence. The IPD has made it quite clear that its definition of a professional qualification is wider than that required in a single NVQ at level 4.
>
> (Whittaker, 1994, p. 29)

That uncompromising statement made it possible for IPD to continue its extraordinarily successful professional examination scheme, but IPD launching the new standards was not quite the same thing as them being accredited by NCVQ: that took nearly two more years:

> It has been a long and difficult gestation period, but the imminent birth of the full set of personnel and training NVQs is being anticipated with a mixture of pride and exhaustion by its creators.
>
> (Welch, 1996, p. 11)

So we now have a situation in which it is possible for people to acquire IPD membership by the well-established route, now called the professional qualification scheme, with centrally-set and marked examinations forming the core of the assessment. Alternatively, they can follow the NVQ route with a different form of assessment.

The basic structure of the professional qualification scheme is three fields with a different weighting: core management (33 per cent), core personnel and development (22 per cent) and specialist and generalist personnel and development (45 per cent). Candidates have to be successful in all three fields to attain full professional membership. The inclusion of core management, which is largely unaltered from its IPM precursor the professional management foundation programme, reflects the centrality of personnel work in all management areas. This theme is developed in core personnel and development, which locates personnel work firmly within the general management spectrum:

> It is now increasingly common for practitioners to move between functions and organisations through their working lives. As a consequence, it is important that all personnel and development practitioners are aware not only of their own area of specialist expertise, but also of the wider contribution which personnel and development can make to organisational success. A major theme underlying this module, and indeed the whole Professional Qualification Scheme, is the need for personnel and development specialists to gain support and commitment from other managers within the organisation. Being able to persuade colleagues of the merits of particular ideas, and their contribution to organisational and departmental goals, is a skill of the utmost importance.
>
> (IPD, 1996, p. 8)

181

The largest field is the oddly-named specialist and generalist personnel and development, where the prospective personnel practitioner has to complete four from a wide range of modules, most of which are in the familiar areas of resourcing, relations and development, to which reward has now been added:

Employee resourcing	Management development
Selection and assessment centres	Vocational education and training
Human resource planning	Managing learning processes
Career management	Managing training operations
Employee relations	Organisational consultancy
Employment law	Employee reward
International employee	Pensions
relations	Performance management
Health and safety	
Employee involvement and	*Others*:
communication	International personnel and
Employee counselling, support	development
and welfare	Strategic HRM/HRD
Employee development	Equality management

This programme is available by face-to-face as well as flexible learning methods at over 300 centres throughout the United Kingdom and the Republic of Ireland. Currently over 10 000 students are enrolled, compared with 8000 in 1995 (IPD, 1997).

The changing role requirements

Not all training of HR specialists takes place within the framework of the IPD national standards. There is also the need to focus training for individuals to fill gaps in their preparedness to take on new responsibilities.

At the opening of this chapter we reviewed the roles indicated from our research by using job titles as the role descriptor. We now pick up the theme that was running through our previous chapter on roles and styles to suggest the managerial roles that are important in view of the findings of our research. The standard point of reference is Mintzberg in his study of managerial work:

> . . . We use the concept of role, a term that has made its way from the theatre to management via the behavioural sciences. A role is defined as an organised set of behaviours belonging to an identifiable office or position.
>
> (Mintzberg, 1973, p. 55)

He got his place in the history books of management research by claiming that there were 10 roles of the manager:

Interpersonal roles
Figurehead, leader, liaison

Informational roles
Monitor, disseminator, spokesman

Decisional Roles
Entrepreneur, disturbance handler, resource allocator, negotiator.

Picking up on this approach, Quinn and his colleagues (1990) devised a competency framework to develop management skill and expertise, using a different set of roles:

Mentor, innovator, broker, producer, director, co-ordinator, monitor, facilitator and mentor.

In a similar vein, Torrington, Waite and Weightman (1992) developed a composite model to describe the work of personnel specialists working in the health service. This was used as a basis to determine individual training needs. For that particular situation the roles identified were:

Selector, paymaster, negotiator, performance monitor, welfare worker, human resource planner, trainer and communicator.

It is not our purpose here to produce yet another set of role models, but simply to suggest those aspects of role that are needed in the light of our findings. We present them under the headings of our principal themes: devolution, decentralisation, strategy, outsourcing and internal marketing.

Devolution

If the devolution of personnel activities to other managerial colleagues is to work, it needs to be undertaken thoroughly and constructively to avoid the risk of dumping jobs on people who feel unprepared and therefore resentful of the new chores. The requisite role aspects will include coach to help people acquire new skills and knowledge, counsellor to enable them to accept the new responsibilities and to feel confident in carrying them out, facilitator to provide continuing back-up, explanation and support, and designer to work out the nature of what is to be handed over and package it for transfer, bearing in mind that the appropriate package will vary according to its destination.

If all this is done thoroughly it will nurture a constructive working relationship with the person assuming the responsibility and ensure that only the right degree of devolution will take place.

Decentralisation

In suggesting role aspects for devolution, we assumed that the decision to devolve had been taken and was agreed. Although the same may be true of decentralisation, there seem to be a different range of roles that are involved. First of all there is the role of communicator to explain the rationale for the change, to listen, pick up feedback and shape the proposal. Similar to this is the role of negotiator, to find reconciliation between different positions and to confront problems squarely in search of solutions rather than smoothing them over in the hope that they will fade away. Third is the need to be a business person. There has to be a keen appreciation of the business imperatives that drive the decentralisation initiative, so that the business objectives are achieved. It is all to easy to find ways of dealing with the situation which satisfy people individually but lose sight of what it is all for.

Strategy

Here there are several interdependent roles in addition to the obvious one of strategic thinker, taking on board all the smart ideas of visioning and lateral thought. Another role is that of politician, understanding where the power lies and the reasons behind its manipulation. We have already suggested, in earlier chapters, that most people are uneasy with organisational politics, but working strategically requires political understanding or the strategic initiative is doomed. The networker is the person who has a wide range of contacts to provide information, ideas, suggestions and help of all kinds. Position in the hierarchy is essential to a good network, but so is expertise and social skilfulness. Networking is a reciprocal activity. You help someone else and they will help you; being 'a nice guy' is useful, but you have to have something to trade, and the best thing to trade is your expertise or your contacts. The final role in the strategy area is influencer. You have to be able to persuade people to your point of view, not all the time, but much of the time. There is no point in being a part of strategy if you have no impact; you have to sell people your ideas, so that they buy them. Nodding in agreement is not enough.

Outsourcing

Some of the methods of dealing with consultants and sub-contractors were considered in Chapter 7, but the roles involved are quite distinct from other aspects of HR work. There is first of all the need to be a contract negotiator, so that the right sub-contractor is chosen and then briefed very accurately. Making the right choice involves knowing and appreciating where the consultant's or sub-contractor's skills truly lie, and being sure that they really are what you need. Providing the brief is the process of being able to put yourself in the consultant's shoes and translating what you want into terms on which the consultant can quote realistically. 'Complete overhaul of the job evaluation system . . .' is such a loose brief that the quotation will probably be misleading, wrong and too expensive. Once the contract is agreed, there is a change of role to that of contract manager, keeping a close watch on what is being done, to make sure that what is done is what you want to have done and in line with what was offered. In addition, contract managers provide further information, feed in ideas, negotiate minor variations and so forth. None of these are necessarily familiar to HR specialists, so some rapid on-the-job learning will be needed in many instances.

Internal marketeer

In many ways the roles of the internal marketeer are the obverse of those involved in outsourcing. This time the contract negotiator will be negotiating to provide a service rather than to receive one, so there will be the process of analysing the perceived need and working out the best, and most attractive way of meeting that need. The business person will ensure that the cost structure is right and being met, although many organisations do not actually charge for these services, and the contract manager will monitor the quality of the service being provided. The basis of the marketeer role is that of seller; being proactive in seeking out opportunities. It involves construing HR work, not initially in terms of what the personnel people think should be done, but looking at operations and activities throughout the business to decide where there is a need or an interest in what personnel has to offer.

The training and development of personnel specialists

Those working in the personnel and HR area have a long and well-established tradition of education and training being provided through the system of higher education. The willingness of the professional body to collaborate with universities and colleges has led to the development of a number of degree and similar courses dealing with the subject area, quite apart from the IPD professional qualification, which is so widely recognised and esteemed. This can be achieved by either face-to-face or flexible learning followed by examination, or by the acquisition of NVQs. Where training and development is needed to round out a person's individual competence in their particular position, then the consideration of the various roles that personnel need to adopt can be used to identify specific ongoing, on-the-job training and development needs.

References

Clegg, H. A. (1970) *The System of Industrial Relations in Great Britain*, Oxford: Basil Blackwell.

Crichton, A. (1961) 'The IPM in 1950 and 1960', *Personnel Management*, December.

Freidson, E. (1973) *The Professions and their Prospects*, London: Sage.

Gibb, S. (1995) 'The lead body model of personnel management – a critique', *Human Resource Management Journal*, 5(5).

IPD (1996) *IPD Professional Standards*, London: Institute of Personnel and Development.

IPD (1997) *IPD Matters, Annual Report 1996–97*, London: Institute of Personnel and Development.

Mintzberg, H. (1973) *The Nature of Managerial Work*, New York: Harper & Row.

PSLB (1993) *Towards Standards for Personnel Work*, London: Personnel Standards Lead Body.

Quinn, R. E., Faerman, S. R., Thompson, M. P. and McGrath, M. R. (1990) *Becoming a Master Manager*, New York: John Wiley.

Torrington, D. P., Waite, D. and Weightman, J. B. (1992) 'A continuous development approach to training health service professionals', *Journal of European Industrial Training*, 16(3), 3–12.

Watson, T. J. (1977) *The Personnel Managers*, London: Routledge and Kegan Paul.

Welch, J. (1996) 'HR qualifications get the go-ahead at last', *People Management*, 20 May.

Whittaker, J. M. (1994) 'Personnel NVQs: a big step forward', *Personnel Management*, 26(8).

Woodruffe, C. (1992) 'What is meant by competency?' in R. Boam and P. Sparrow (eds) *Designing and Achieving Competency*, 16–30, London: McGraw-Hill.

11

Conclusions

We set out to report on the major trends and changes within the personnel/HR function over the last 10 years or so. We are not attempting to identify the prevalence of such changes and where they are more or less likely to occur, but rather to identify general nature of changes in mood and perspective and attempt to understand the reasons (explicit or implicit) for these, and their implications for the human resource function and the organisation. In this conclusion we first summarise the main findings that we have reported, and then go on to debate the meaning and implications of these, and attempt to integrate them.

Summary

There is a growing emphasis on both the devolution of operational personnel tasks and on the decentralisation of the personnel function. We recognised that both these trends are often interrelated both in the literature and reality, but since we argue that each may well have different implications for both the HR function and the organisation we have considered each separately. Our working definition of devolution is 'the transfer of activities from the personnel specialist to the non-specialist line manager', and our working definition of decentralisation is the 'transfer of personnel activities from one level of personnel specialist to another'. In terms of devolution we found senior personnel/HR specialists to be enthusiastic, and 26 of our 30 interviewees reported engaging in attempts to devolve activities. However, much of this was couched in terms of 'trying to', 'beginning to', and only a small amount of progress appeared to have been made. This reflected both an unwillingness on the part of some personnel specialists to let go and an unwillingness, or inability of the line to take on these activities. We found evidence of more progress being made if personnel budgets were also devolved to the line, if there was an organisational culture of people management, and if there was considerable support provided by the HR function – in terms of training, help-lines, toolkits, regular advice and coaching. Although our interviewees often mentioned devolution to the line as a better way to manage, they failed to convince us that there was an underlying philosophy which drove the process – to some extent it appeared that devolution was a solution to the pressure on numbers of staff within the HR function and the desire to get involved with strategy which was perceived as a much more attractive and valuable role. It was difficult to determine the extent to which the HR function was pushed towards devolution in a decentralised environment and the extent to which they proactively sought it. Although HR managers appeared enthusiastic, this was tinged with concerns of losing valued tasks, losing opportunities to maintain and develop valued skills, and losing control and authority when budgets are devolved. Senior level specialists were most affected by the last of these, but middle and lower level specialists were most affected by the first two, and it is these groups who are most vulnerable in a devolved environment. Not only are valued tasks lost, new roles need to be learned – that of consultant, facilitator, and coach – all of which are more demanding than many traditional personnel roles.

Decentralisation of the human resources function can more clearly be seen as a response to decentralising trend in organisations. The research we reported very clearly demonstrated how the creation of local HR units did not mean that the central HR unit was disbanded, but that each level of the HR function was, in theory, allocated different roles – broadly along the strategy (centre) and operations (local) divide. Different degrees of decentralisation were identified, along a continuum, and in the most complete form the local HR unit reports to the manager of the local department or business in which they are physically located rather than the central personnel unit. The difficulties experienced here were lack of clarity between the roles of the different personnel groups and some duplication. More serious was the fact that many line managers could not see the relevance of the central unit, and yet it was often by members of this unit that the HR strategy was produced. Vital business information did not appear to be fed up to the central units and central units did not appear to involve the local HR units or local line managers in developing HR strategy. As such it was seen as irrelevant and the central HR unit was isolated and marginalised, and the HR strategy was either tailored to meet local needs or ignored. At the same time, however, the local HR unit was becoming closer to the line, and was valued as such, but suffered conflicts of loyalty since their allegiance was primarily to the line manager rather than the personnel function.

As well as different types of decentralisation in HR, we also identified two different levels of decentralisation – from corporate level to business unit level and from business unit level to departmental level – each having a different impact. The situation described above has far reaching consequences in a context of decentralisation from business level to department level as it results in a lack of integration with employees in different departments being treated differently and exposes the organisation to legal challenge. In a context of decentralisation from corporate to business unit level the situation has different consequences as corporate level may not be the most appropriate level for

HR strategy development and a strong argument can be made that indeed it is more appropriate at business level.

We turn now to the theme of the HR strategy where we found HR/personnel specialists to be increasingly involved. We have discussed the reasons for this finding in the text, as most other research suggests a minimal involvement. The level of the organisation which we were researching (establishment level) no doubt had an impact as there is growing evidence of a strategic approach at this level. Also our definition of strategy included strategic thinking and was not confined to a strategy written down on a piece of paper. In fact we found little in terms of a fully formed vertically and horizontally integrated strategy – but what we did find was evidence of strategic thinking and activity clearly related to business strategy on an issue by issue basis, determined by the priorities of the business. Thus the strategy was piecemeal. There was very evident enthusiasm from the specialists we interviewed to be involved in strategy as opposed to operations, and most claimed the intention to do more of it and to do it better.

Strategic involvement, however, was not an example of specialists suddenly seeing the light and realising what their true role was in the organisation and then going for it. Strategic involvement can be better explained by business need, and senior managers providing the opportunity for personnel specialists to become more involved at this level, as this was to the advantage of the business. While a directorial role in the personnel/HR function was clearly shown to be an advantage in becoming involved in HR strategy this did not appear to be the determining factor. What appeared to be more powerful was the track record and credibility of the most senior personnel specialist. This was not just about their specific professional HR skill, but also about their political and networking skills and self confidence. Another influence was the mindset of the chief executive. Personnel specialists appeared to be increasingly involved in strategic issues in a partnership role with the line, rather than in an isolationist role, which may have been more characteristic in the past.

We found that the HR function was continuing to outsource significant amounts of work, particularly in the area of training, and we also draw a distinction between such outsourcing commissioned and managed by the personnel function, and that which was commissioned and managed by line managers. We found an increasing trend, particularly in organisations which were formally set up as an internal market, for line managers to threaten to buy their personnel services elsewhere. This did not appear to happen too often in reality, but the threat of this had an impact on the way some personnel specialists operated in relation to the line. Many threw themselves into the service provider role with the line manager customer as king. This often prevented them from using their professional expertise as they were afraid of offending the client by drawing their attention to HR problems in the client department thinking that this might lose them the HR contract for the forthcoming year. They also spent considerable time on related bureaucratic tasks and cross charging, and devising schemes and packages to get the line manager to buy more rather than less of their services. However, we did find that internal marketing skills and techniques were a very valuable asset to the HR specialist, when they were used in an environment not constructed as an internal market.

Discussion

It is fair to say that the roles of personnel/HR specialists were in a state of flux in our sample. To some extent the trends that we have identified in the personnel/HR function are in parallel with, and a response to, changes in society and changes in organisations. Thus decentralisation and devolution can be seen as allocating tasks to the lowest possible level of the organisation where the issue actually resides and as a method of empowering all employees – all of which are current themes in the organisational literature. The situation where 'everyone is their own personnel manager' is paralleled, for example, by the situation where everyone has to be their own accountant (where budgets are decentralised in organisations and where as individuals we are now responsible for assessing their own tax liabilities). It is also a reflection of the trend towards multi-skilling, flexible job descriptions and work intensification.

Strategic involvement can be seen as an expression of the current interest in strategy and of an opportunity arising from a recognition within organisations that in times of rapid change, competitive advantage is based on the quality of employees in the organisation and their ability to learn continuously. As such the organisation is looking to the personnel/HR function to contribute in the strategic arena as this is seen as critical to the needs of the organisation.

Similarly, outsourcing reflects a general trend to outsource, not only mundane activities not intrinsic to the core business, such as catering, security and site maintenance, but also professional functions – such as IT, marketing, and so on, as well as personnel and training activities. The trend towards internal marketing also reflects a general focus on the customer and the idea that every organisational member has internal customers whose needs should be met as comprehensively as external customers. In particular, this applies to 'staff' functions, and the internal market which has been set up very consciously in many public sector bodies has reinforced the idea of customer and supplier departments by allocating budgets and funds so that supplier departments have to function as profit centres – almost as mini businesses within the business.

As such what has been happening in the function is not unusual compared with other functions. It still seems that the personnel function does what it is allowed to do by the business – however, the opportunities do seem greater in the current environment, and there are some attractions in these as they appear to provide a means of tackling some of the perennial problems which the personnel function has historically experienced – that is: ambiguity, marginality, the ivory tower syndrome and being labelled as the organisational policemen. There are also, however, some pitfalls.

It could be argued that the personnel/HR function make the greatest contribution to the organisation when they can develop the most appropriate relationship with the line. From this research we found the idea of partnership the most attractive – again a reflection of a key theme in the world around us. Operating in a partnership role, where both specialists and line managers develop HR strategy together moves us away from the scenario where the HR function develops the strategy but everyone else avoids it, because it is not seen to have taken account of business need, or line managers' views. If personnel and the line can pull together rather than apart who knows what could be achieved? The partnership role sits well with strategic involvement, but is in direct conflict with the service role where the line manager is the customer agreeing to buy pre-specified services at an agreed price. This role seems to preclude a proactive professional role and the use of personnel expertise, and the expert loses an independent perspective. In the partnership role we have mutual obligations agreed by equals – they may each have different perspectives, but they cooperate to meet agreed goals. However, agreeing the nature of the goals is no mean feat.

Other relationships with the line are more concerned with relationships that are unequal – the supplier role, the policeman role, the monitor. As such, the relationship of the personnel specialist with the line more often than not reflects a power struggle. This is reflected, for example, in the devolution of operational tasks where the personnel function struggle to keep authority but are happy to hand over responsibility to the line; meanwhile, the line will only accept responsibility if they can also claim the authority.

We could also argue that the HR function could do with a bit of partnership within its own boundaries. There is a tendency in all of the changes we have documented to dismember the personnel function – almost to set one part against another in the quest for survival or enhancement. That devolution, for example, may benefit senior personnel specialists by ridding themselves of operational tasks with dubious value, enabling the function to shrink and save the organisation money. On the other hand, middle and lower level members of the departments may lose their jobs, lose valued tasks and be forced to retrain into roles which they don't necessarily seek. In the decentralised scenario either the centre was isolated from the business, and to some extent ignored, or if unit HR did report to the central unit then the local HR unit appeared to be by-passed by the department or business in which they were located. Specialist career paths for unit HR staff were limited by the centre, who seemed to have an elitist view of their role, whether or not they were isolated from the rest of the business. Also, HR staff are physically fragmented in a decentralised environment and as departmental HR units tended to be small groups, or one person alone, they were not in a strong position to challenge. Outsourcing attacks the middle level of professional staff rather than the top or the bottom as it is these roles that can be most easily outsourced when they have been redesigned as consultancy roles rather than 'hands-on roles'.

This infighting is particularly problematic at a time when the personnel/HR function have the opportunity of developing a range of new roles and relationships with the line. We have already referred to the need to develop consultancy and coaching skills, political, networking and business skills, negotiation and contract management skills, and marketing skills. We argue that these skills are most appropriately developed within the job rather than by a professional qualification, which may form the foundation for them. As such, a responsibility falls to the function to carry all members along, provide sufficient opportunities to develop and appropriate career paths to reward that development. In addition, the function needs to develop a strategic view of its role in the organisation *together with* the line and *together with* its own members. We suggest that this is an essential step if the personnel/HR function are to be in a position to develop the new opportunities which are presently more available to them.

Appendix 1

Characteristics of the sample

Main activities of the establishments in our sample

Organisation	Frequency	Valid per cent
Agriculture/forestry	1	0.5
Energy/water supply	4	1.9
Extraction/chemicals/pharmaceuticals	6	2.8
Metal goods/engineering/vehicles	18	8.4
Other manufacturing (e.g. consumer goods)	20	9.3
Construction	1	0.5
Wholesale/retail/distribution	12	5.6
Catering/hotels/repairs	8	3.7
Transport	7	3.3
Communication	5	2.3
Banking/finance/business service	23	10.7
Central/local government	44	20.6
Housing	8	3.7
Education	13	6.1
Health	13	6.1
Other services	31	14.5
Total	214	100.0

Size of establishments

Size	Number	Percentage
Less than 200	68	32
200–499	51	24
500–999	30	14
1000 and over	64	30
Total	213*	100*

* One recorded as missing.

Status of establishment

Status	Number	Percentage
Private	123	57
Trust	17	8
Public/trading	14	6
Public/non-trading	56	26
Other	4	2
Total	214	99*

* Due to rounding.

Ownership

Ownership	Number	Percentage
Mainly British	164	80
European	18	9
American	18	9
Japanese	2	1
Other	4	2
Total	206*	2†

* Data missing for eight establishments.
† Due to rounding.

Nature of establishment

Nature of establishment	Number	Percentage
Headquarters	77	37
Division of part of a larger organisation	97	46
Single establishment	37	18
Other	1	1
Total	212*	102†

* Two missing.
† Due to rounding.

Interview sample

Status of establishments in the interview sample

Status	Number	Percentage
Private	15	50
Trust/public trading/public non-trading	15	50
Total	30	100

Appendix 2

Summary of main research findings

The personnel role

Although the majority of the functions responding to our survey were titled 'Personnel' rather than 'Human Resources', the interview data suggests that a move towards 'Human Resources' continues and will continue.

The actual activities carried out by personnel specialists show only little change in their assessment of importance since our earlier studies, as shown in the table. However the level at which they are carried out and the methods of implementation have changed.

Ranking of importance of contribution to the business of a range of personnel activities:

Rank order NOW (1994/5)	Rank order PAST (1993/4)
1. Recruitment and selection	1. Employee relations
2. HR planning	2. Recruitment and selection
3. Employee relations/involvement	3. Training
4. Training	4. Manpower planning
5. Communications	5. Discipline/grievance
6. Management development	6. Changes in working organisation
7. Appraisal	7. Organisation and management development
8. Performance management	8. Redundancy/dismissal
9. Discipline/grievance	9. Appraisal
10. Redundancy/dismissal	10. Pay administration
11. Reward strategies and systems	11. Health, safety and welfare
12. Health, safety and welfare	12. Job evaluation
13. Quality initiatives	13. New technology
14. Career planning	14. Fringe benefits

Strategy

There has been much discussion about the need for personnel management to become more *strategic* in its functioning and this argument has typically been associated with a redesignation of the activity as human resource management. We found evidence of considerable strategic involvement, but very little evidence of an integrated HR strategy to be incorporated with the corporate

196

strategy. Rather there were a series of strategic HR initiatives to implement aspects of the corporate strategy, and sometimes developed with corporate strategy in an integrated way.

Decentralisation and devolution

There was a heavy emphasis on the devolution of some traditional personnel activities to line managers. The reasons behind this could rarely be described as strategic – although it may have been seen as a long-term change, there was often an absence of an HRM philosophy behind it. Devolution is progressing slowly and is accompanied by a lot of handholding. This trend continues alongside another of decentralisation, whereby personnel people are split up and re-located in divisions. This has not always been successful and some recentralisation has taken place.

Flexibility

The emphasis from our interview respondents was on numerical rather than functional (skills) flexibility. Although there was a significant level of flexibility in relation to the Atkinson model, the picture in each establishment was partial. There was rarely a long-term rationale for flexibility, and the pressures behind it were most often operational. Those few establishments pursuing functional flexibility tended to have a longer term, more strategic perspective. Respondents were often not familiar with academic models of flexibility (such as Atkinson) and for some flexibility was an employee benefit, or was required in order to demonstrate equal opportunities, rather than a strategic tool.

Organisational performance

Most organisations had some form of programme or initiative to improve quality. Respondents interviewed were very aware of possible initiative overload and many explained that having identified and implemented an approach they would add other priorities *into* this to meet organisational needs, rather than introducing new initiatives.

Individual performance

Appraisal continues to be a key tool in the management of individual performance, and most of the establishments visited were in the process of changing their appraisal system in either a major or minor way. The questionnaire showed that training and development were seen as much more important outcomes of the appraisal process than the determination of reward. Yet a high proportion of establishments had performance-related pay. The contradiction here is explained by separating appraisal and pay rises as much as possible, and by the use of implicit rather than explicit performance-related pay. However, a number were changing it to fit with a performance management process which was being introduced. Most establishments had some form of 'textbook' performance management system, although it was not always labelled as such.

Investors in People (IIP)

Investor in People was usually the only other initiative run alongside a quality approach. Although only 10 per cent of establishments had so far been accredited there was a much higher number that were in the process of gaining accreditation. All establishments who had implemented/were implementing IIP were convinced of its value (bar one respondent who had a reservation), and some explained how its value was not in being a stamp of approval, but the way that the business was run.

National Vocational Qualifications (NVQs)

National Vocational Qualifications were less popular with our respondents. Although a number of establishments were using them for some groups of employee, most identified problems in the bureaucracy, paperwork, the lack of challenge and new learning.

Career development

Career development was characterised by a lack of attention. Almost one-third of establishments carried out no career activities at all and the spread of different activities for those that did at least something was not great. Very often career development activity was reduced to the use of self-development plans.

Reward

Performance-related pay was widespread in our sample, being used by just over half the establishments. The interviews revealed that other establishments would be introducing it, and only two of our interview respondents had considered it and rejected it. The method whereby the level of performance pay was decided appeared often to be arbitrary. In less than half the cases it was decided on the basis of the formal performance appraisal system, which links with our findings above (Individual performance). Pay was most often assessed on the achievement of objectives which, depending on the way this is done, brings with it the danger of being subjective. The use of performance-related pay was almost universally unpopular with our interview respondents, who cited such problems as: difficulties with the objective-setting process, difficulties in making final assessments, forced distributions, insignificant differences in actual payments and contradictions with a teamwork philosophy. A number noted that it appeared to have value as an idea, but that it did not work in practice and did not motivate.

Employee relations and involvement

The influence of trade unions at the workplace is shown to be gradually fading where there is a tradition of union recognition and probably non-existent where there is no such tradition. Moves towards employee involvement are predominantly to meet management objective for the organisation; there appeared to be little emphasis on meeting other types of possible obligation.

Grievance, discipline and dismissal

There remained a strong involvement by the personnel function in disciplinary matters, and in comparison with our 1984 data this had increased over the past 10 years. And it is also noted that it is in these activates, more than any others which respondents were asked about, that the personnel specialist has the highest involvement. At a time when there is a great emphasis on 'empowering the line', this finding puts that general tendency into perspective. Central monitoring of these three activities – especially dismissal – is maintained to ensure consistency of treatment.

Appendix 3

Questionnaire

Questionnaire

Developments in the Personnel Function

Professor Derek Torrington
Dr Laura Hall
Miss Catherine Allen

UMIST
Manchester School of Management
Manchester Metropolitan University

DEVELOPMENTS IN THE PERSONNEL FUNCTION : ROLE AND ACTIVITY

This questionnaire is part of a study to establish the nature of personnel management as currently practised in this country, the nature of the changes over the past decade and the extent to which the PSLB standards match the present situation. It is being funded by the Economic and Social Research Council and being carried out in conjunction with the Institute of Personnel and Development. It follows a similar study by the same research team that was conducted in the early 1980s and published by IPM as **The Changing Nature of Personnel Management** in 1984.

The questionnaire is divided into 8 sections, though of course we will be making links between the sections when we analyse the data. The sections are as follows:

Section A	Organisational Background	Section E	Development
Section B	The Personnel Function	Section F	Involvement
Section C	Resourcing	Section G	Payment
Section D	Performance	Section H	About you and your job

The questions in each section usually require you to make a simple choice between alternatives, though a few require you to write in a short statement.

We hope you find the questions interesting, and we much appreciate the time and thought that you are able to give it.

NAME OF ESTABLISHMENT : _____
V1

ADDRESS OF ESTABLISHMENT: _____
V2

_____

_____

SECTION A : ORGANISATIONAL BACKGROUND

We need to ask for some information about the organisation for which you work, and then more specifically about the place where you work. This is for identification and statistical purposes only, and, as with all the questions we ask, it will be entirely confidential.

As we are trying to find out exactly what policies and practices are being used in the workplace, we want you to answer most of the questions from the perspective of the specific location where you work. We will at times ask you to respond to some questions about the wider organisation, but we will indicate where we wish you to do this.

I ABOUT THE ORGANISATION:

For background purposes, please tell us the following information about the organisation as a whole.

A1   What is the main activity of this organisation?   Please circle a number

Agriculture/Forestry	1	Transport	9
Energy/Water Supply	2	Communication	10
Extraction/Chemicals/Pharmaceuticals	3	Banking/Finance/Business Service	11
Metal Goods/Engineering/Vehicles	4	Central/Local Government	12
Other Manufacturing (eg. consumer goods)	5	Housing	13
Construction	6	Education	14
Wholesale/Retail/Distribution	7	Health	15
Catering/Hotels/Repairs	8	Other Services	16

V3

A2   What is the official status of the organisation? Please circle a number

private sector/plc/ltd company	1	public sector (trading)	5
self proprietorship/partnership	2	public sector (non-trading)**	6
trust/charity*	3	other (please specify) _____	
cooperative	4		

(*please include here NHS trusts)   (**please include here local central government and non-trust NHS)

V4

2

A3 **Has the official status of your organisation changed in the last 10 years in any of the following ways? Please circle a number**

emerged as a privatisation of a public corporation   1

transferred to trust status   2

transferred to grant-maintained status   3

none of these   4

V5

A4 **What is the ownership of this organisation? Please circle a number**

Mainly British owned   1

Mainly owned by an organisation based outside Britain

     - other European   2

     - American   3

     - Japanese   4

     - other   5

Don't know   6

V6

A5 **Please indicate which of the following comes closest to describing the way the organisation is run by circling a number on the scale, where 1 is a highly centralised structure, and 7 is highly decentralised.**

heavily centralised, corporate management makes the major long term decisions and formulates policies of the whole organisation including subsidiaries

decentralised, local management has much scope for making major strategic decisions as well as formulating policies

1   2   3   4   5   6   7

V7

3

II WHERE YOU WORK:

We are now shifting the focus to the workplace itself, and so we ask you to answer this next set of questions from the point of view of the specific place where you work.

A6   **What is the nature of this establishment? Please circle a number**

headquarters of a multi-location organisation	1
division or part of a multi-location organisation	2
single site establishment	3
other, please specify	_____

V8

A7   **Approximately what percentage of total costs at your establishment are employment costs (please include national insurance contributions, fringe benefits etc. in your estimate)? Please circle a number**

0 - 20 %	1
21 - 40 %	2
41 - 60 %	3
61 - 80 %	4
81-100%	5

V9

A8   **How many employees do you have?**   _____ employees

V10

4

204

A9	Please provide a breakdown of the number of employees according to the following categories*			
		Male	Female	Total
	Manual	_____	_____	_____
	Non - manual	_____	_____	_____
	Managerial	_____	_____	_____
	Full - time	_____	_____	_____
	Part - time	_____	_____	_____

V11-25

---

* This is a distinction which will be used throughout the questionnaire. We realise that these categories are not straightforward, so here are the sorts of people we would include in each category:

Manual	Please include in here all unskilled, semi-skilled and skilled manual workers
Non-manual	The sorts of people we include in this category are secretarial and clerical workers, as well as junior support staff and technical posts. Also nurses and physiotherapists
Managerial	This category includes all managerial posts, from line managers to senior managers, and also senior professional and technical posts

5

SECTION B : THE PERSONNEL FUNCTION - AN OVERVIEW

Having asked you some questions about the organisational structure, this section aims to locate the Personnel/Human Resource function within that structure. Where exactly do their responsibilities lie? For the purposes of these questions we make no distinction between HR and Personnel.

B1	**Is there a specialist Personnel/HR department where you work ? Please circle a number**
	YES 1
	NO 2
V26	

B2	**What is the department's title?** _____
V27	

B3	**How many people work in the department?** _____
V28	

B4	**Of these, how many people have professional and/or educational qualifications in personnel / personnel related matters?** _____
V29	

6

B5   What is the job title of the person who is responsible for this department?

V30   _____

B6   Does he/she have a decision-making place on the board *(where you work)* if applicable:

        Please circle a number

        YES, a decision making role   1

        YES, place on the board but not as a decision maker   2

        Other, please describe role   _____

        NO place on board   3

        Not applicable (no local board)   4

V31

7

207

B7 Which of the following most closely describes the nature of the personnel function's involvement at a *strategic* level in each of the areas listed below?

(1)   Develops strategy alone

(2)   Develops strategy with the line

(3)   Provides information to inform strategic decisions

(4)   Implements strategic decisions

(5)   No involvement at a strategic level

Please insert the appropriate number (1,2,3,4 or 5) for each of the following areas

Human Resource Planning   _____
Recruitment and Selection   _____
Redundancy and dismissal   _____
Work Design   _____
Performance Management   _____
Quality Initiatives   _____
Training   _____
Management Development   _____
Career Planning   _____
Communications   _____
Employee Relations/ Involvement   _____
Health and Safety   _____
Reward Strategies and Systems   _____

V32-44

8

B8 Which of the following most closely describes the nature of the personnel function's involvement *on a day to day basis* in each of the areas listed below?

(1) Makes decisions alone

(2) Makes decisions in conjunction with line

(3) Provide advice and information / consultancy

(4) Implements decisions made by others

(5) No involvement on a day to day basis

(6) Not applicable to this establishment

Please insert the appropriate number (1,2,3,4 or 5) for each of the following areas

Recruitment and Selection _____
Job Evaluation _____
Redundancy and Dismissal _____
Appraisals _____
Quality Initiatives _____
Training _____
Career Planning _____
Communications _____
Employee relations/Involvement _____
Health and Safety _____
Discipline and Grievance _____
Payment Administration _____
Fringe Benefits _____

V45-57

9

B9	In 1994 have you used an external consultant in any of the following areas at your place of work? Please circle as many numbers as appropriate	
	Human Resource Planning	1
	Recruitment and Selection	2
	Job Evaluation	3
	Work Design	4
	Redundancy and Dismissal	5
	Outplacement	6
	Performance Management	7
	Quality Initiatives	8
	Training	9
	Management Development	10
	Career Planning	11
	Communications	12
	Employee Relations/involvement	13
	Health and Safety	14
	Reward Strategies and Systems	15
	Other (please specify)	16
	None	17
V58-74		

If the place where you work is part of a larger organisation, please answer the following 2 questions.

B10	Is there a director or someone at the highest level of the organisation (in this country) with specific responsibility for Personnel and Personnel related matters? Please circle a number	
	YES	1
	NO	2
V75-6	If YES, what is his/her job title?	_____

B11	Does he/she have a decision making place on the board (or its equivalent)? Please circle a number	
	YES, decision making role	1
	YES, place on board but not as decision maker	2
	Other, please describe role	_____
	NO place on board	3
	Not applicable (no board)	4
V77		

10

SECTION C : RESOURCING

This section aims to find out who makes the decisions about employment strategy, and what criteria they use. It then moves on to ask some specific questions about recruitment and selection, as well as the employment contract.

I. HUMAN RESOURCE PLANNING

C1 Who makes the decisions to recruit for the various categories of jobs? In other words, who decides when there is a vacancy that is to be filled?
Please circle as many numbers as appropriate

	manual	non manual	managerial
Immediate manger	1	1	1
Level of authority above			
immediate manager	2	2	2
Personnel	3	3	3
Other (please specify)	____	____	____

V78-89

C2 In 1994 have you used any of the following ways of dealing with a vacancy as an alternative to recruiting a permanent employee? Please circle as many numbers as appropriate.

	manual	non manual	managerial
used temporary employees	1	1	1
reorganised the work tasks	2	2	2
used overtime	3	3	3
changed the hours	4	4	4
subcontracted the work	5	5	5

V90-104

11

C3 What data is available in your establishment or in the organisation as a whole, and how is it stored? Please circle *one* number for each item of information.

	stored on paper only	stored on computer only	stored on both	not available
personal information records	1	2	3	4
test results	1	2	3	4
training records	1	2	3	4
appraisal and development reviews	1	2	3	4
personal growth profiles	1	2	3	4
career development plans	1	2	3	4
strategic human resource plan	1	2	3	4
job grades / categories	1	2	3	4
person specifications	1	2	3	4
career structures	1	2	3	4

V105-114

II. CONTRACTS OF EMPLOYMENT

C4 Approximately what percentage of your employees, if any, have the following working arrangements? Please estimate if figures are not available.

Please differentiate for the following categories:

	% of manual employees	% of non-manual employees	% of managers
temporary contracts	_____	_____	_____
annualized hours	_____	_____	_____
flexible working hours	_____	_____	_____
homeworking	_____	_____	_____
job sharing	_____	_____	_____

V115-129

12

212

C5 To what extent has the use of the following changed in the last 3 years where you work? Please circle a number for each category

	decreased	increased	stayed the same	not applicable
shift work	1	2	3	N/A
overtime	1	2	3	N/A
short-time working	1	2	3	N/A
the use of subcontractors	1	2	3	N/A
the use of part-time employees	1	2	3	N/A

V130-134

III. RECRUITMENT

C6 Which of the following methods of recruitment have you used in 1994 for the various categories of job? Please circle as many numbers as appropriate

	manual	non manual	managerial
advertising in national newspapers	1	1	1
advertising in local newspapers	2	2	2
advertising in professional and trade journals	3	3	3
advertising on radio and television	4	4	4
job centres	5	5	5
announcements outside the establishment's premises	6	6	6
internal advertising	7	7	7
personal recommendation from existing staff	8	8	8
selection consultants	9	9	9
executive search	10	10	10
school visits	11	11	11
local authority careers service	12	12	12
further education/technical college visits	13	13	13
visits to universities	14	14	14
employment agencies	15	15	15
establishment list of job seekers	16	16	16
other (please specify)	_____	_____	_____

V135-185

13

C7 *Approximately* what percentage of all your vacancies did you fill in 1994 by recruitment from inside and outside your establishment for the various categories of job?

	inside	outside
	%	%
manual	_____	_____
non manual	_____	_____
management	_____	_____

V186-191

C8 Are there any jobs for which you have found it difficult to recruit in 1994? Please specify.

_____

_____

V192-196

IV   SELECTION METHODS

C9 If application forms are used in the selection process, how are they used? Please circle as many numbers as appropriate

Before the initial interview as a screening tool	1
As a guide to follow during the interview	2
Biodata is statistically analyzed	3
Data for personnel record	4
Other	_____

V197-201

C10 Do you regularly run assessment centres as part of the selection process? Please circle a number for each category of employee.

	manual	non-manual	managerial
YES	1	2	3
V202-4 NO	1	2	3

14

214

C11 Where tests are used in selection, which of the following comes closest to describing how are they *generally* used? Please circle one number for each category of employee.

	manual	non manual	managerial
before the initial interview as a screening tool	1	1	1
part of the selection process as a guide to suitability, but not as important as the interview in the selection decision	2	2	2
part of the selection process and a vital indication of a candidate's suitability for the job	3	3	3
not used	4	4	4

V205-207

C12 Who generally interviews candidates for the different categories of job? Please circle as many numbers as appropriate for each category of employee.

	manual	non manual	managers
Immediate manager	1	1	1
Level of authority above immediate manager	2	2	2
Personnel	3	3	3
Assessment Centre process	4	4	4
Other (please specify)	_____	_____	_____

V208-222

C13 Who generally makes the final selection decision for the different categories? Please circle as many numbers as appropriate

	manual	non manual	managers
Immediate manager	1	1	1
Level of authority above immediate manager	2	2	2
Personnel	3	3	3
Panel	4	4	4
Other (please specify)	_____	_____	_____

V223-237

15

215

V. RELEASING PEOPLE

C14 **Apart from normal turnover, has there been any action in the last three years to reduce the number of people employed or to change the composition of the workforce? Please circle any appropriate numbers.**

General reduction in the number employed to make us "leaner and fitter".

1	Overall reduction of less than 10%
2	Overall reduction of 11% to 20%
3	Overall reduction of 21% to 40%
4	Overall reduction of more than 40%

Selective "pruning" to move out people with skills and experience that are no longer relevant to the core business.

5	Among managers
6	Among non-manual employees
7	Among manual employees
8	No reductions or significant changes

V238, V239-242

C15 **What methods were used to bring about the changes referred to in C14? Please circle as many numbers as appropriate.**

	General Reduction	Selective Pruning
Transfer of people to other parts of the business	1	2
Halt on recruitment	1	2
Increased use of part-time staff	1	2
Increased use of consultants or sub-contractors	1	2
Increased use of temporary staff	1	2
Shedding of part-time or temporary staff / consultants	1	2
Early retirement	1	2
Voluntary redundancy	1	2
Enforced redundancy	1	2
Outplacement	1	2
Sale, or similar transfer, of part of the business to another employer	1	2
Not applicable	1	2

V243-254

16

SECTION D : PERFORMANCE

Having recruited the right people, it is still necessary to gain their optimum performance. There has been a lot of talk lately about quality and performance, but what exactly goes on in practice?

I. QUALITY INITIATIVES

D1   Have you implemented or discontinued using any of the following quality
initiatives/measures? Circle appropriate number(s)

	implemented	discontinued
just in time	1	2
right first time	1	2
quality circles	1	2
customer care	1	2
TQM	1	2
continuous improvement	1	2

V255-260

D2   Are you accredited with or are you working either any of the following quality
standards? Please circle appropriate number(s)

	accredited	working towards	not applicable
BS5750	1	2	3
ISO9000	1	2	3

V261-262

D3   If you have a quality steering committee or quality council, does a member of
personnel have a place on this? Please circle appropriate number

yes	1
no	2
not applicable	3

V263

17

217

D4   Does the personnel department carry out any of the following functions regarding the
implementation of quality initiatives? Please circle as many as appropriate

design and delivery of management development courses	1
training and coaching employees	2
producing standards and targets for quality performance	3
benchmarking reports from other organisations	4
designing communication events and publications to publicise quality	5
reviewing the process (eg. by attitude surveys)	6
none of these	7
other (please specify)	_____
no quality initiatives	8

V264-272

II. TEAM PERFORMANCE

*Some people think that the way to achieve optimum performance is to put people in teams. We want to
know if you do this where you work.*

D5   If some of your employees work in teams, which of the following comes closest to
describing the type of team which is most commonly formed? Please circle *one*
number for each category of employee

	manual	non manual	managerial
people within one department/ function permanently work in teams to produce a product or service or solve a problem	1	1	1
people from several departments/ functions permanently work in teams to produce a product or service or solve a problem	2	2	2
people form teams when the need arises to work on a particular project or problem	3	3	3
no team working (please skip to question D7)	4	4	4
other (please specify)	_____	_____	_____

V273-275

18

D6	Do the permanent teams perform any of the following tasks? Please circle as many as apply for the various categories of employee.		
		manual	non-manual	managerial
submit and act to a team budget	1	1	1
organise training needs	2	2	2
select new team members	3	3	3
plan production	4	4	4
schedule holidays and absence cover	5	5	5
deploy staff	6	6	6
solve quality problems	7	7	7

V276-296

III. PERFORMANCE MANAGEMENT AND INDIVIDUAL PERFORMANCE

Teams are all made up of individuals, so individual performance is still an important issue.

D7	How, if at all, is performance reviewed in your organisation for the various categories of jobs? Please circle *one* number for each category of employee		
	manual	non manual	managerial
a formal system of regular appraisals with reviews of past performance, setting of objectives and formal reviews of performance against these	1	1	1
informal, but regular reviews involving a chat about past performance and agreed action for the future	2	2	2
informal, ad hoc reviews taken especially when there is a performance problem	3	3	3
not reviewed (please skip to Question D10)	4	4	4

V297-299

19

D8 Who carries out/contributes to the performance review for each category? Please circle as many as appropriate.

	manual	non manual	managerial
Immediate manager	1	1	1
Level of authority above immediate manager	2	2	2
Member of personnel	3	3	3
Self-appraisal	4	4	4
Peer appraisal	5	5	5
Client/customer appraisal	6	6	6
Assessment centre	7	7	7
Other (please specify)	_____	_____	_____

V300-323

D9 For which of the following is your performance appraisal scheme used? Please circle as many as appropriate.

	manual	non manual	managerial
to assess past performance	1	1	1
to help improve current performance	2	2	2
to set performance objectives	3	3	3
to solve job problems	4	4	4
to identify training and development needs	5	5	5
to assess increases or new levels of salary	6	6	6
to identify future potential	7	7	7
to assist career planning decisions	8	8	8
to provide information for human resource planning	9	9	9
other, please specify	_____	_____	_____

V324-353

20

220

D10 **How is performance measured? Please circle as many numbers as apply**

meeting objectives	1
performance against job description	2
performance against job competencies	3
performance against performance indicators	4
behaviourally anchored rating scales	5
behavioural observation scales	6
not measured	7
other (please specify)	_____

V354-361

D11 **Is performance rewarded in the organisation by any of the following means? Please circle as many as apply**

monetary reward (eg. bonus or PRP)	1
articles in company newspapers	2
competitive awards	3
performance linked prizes	4
league tables	5
verbal or written recognition	6
other (please specify)	_____

V362-368

21

221

SECTION E : DEVELOPMENT

Having looked at the issue of performance, we now move on to address the issue of how employees are developed to produce their optimum performance. The section starts by asking you some questions about training.

I TRAINING

E1	How are training and development needs identified for the various categories of employee? Please circle appropriate number(s)		
		manual	non manual	managerial
self nomination	1	1	1
ad hoc manager identification	2	2	2
personnel department	3	3	3
performance appraisal	4	4	4
through career development	5	5	5
through succession planning	6	6	6
to promote an organisational strategy	7	7	7
member of senior management team	8	8	8
adhoc / not identified	9	9	9
assessment/development centres	10	10	10
other, please specify	___	___	___

V369-401

E2	*Approximately* what proportion of employees in the following categories received formal training		
	manual	non manual	managerial
in 1994?	--------%	--------%	--------%
in 1993?	--------%	--------%	--------%

V402-407

22

E3 In 1994, have you provided training through any of the following means for the various categories of employee? Please circle as many numbers as appropriate

	manual	non manual	managerial
training/personnel officer	1	1	1
line manager	2	2	2
training consultant (tailor made course)	3	3	3
training consultant (off the peg course)	4	4	4
professional body	5	5	5
technical college/university	6	6	6
distance learning courses	7	7	7
outward bound courses	8	8	8
commercial management college	9	9	9

V408-434

E4 Is the effectiveness of training monitored?

YES 1

NO 2

If so, how?

_____

_____

_____

V435 , 436 - 438

E5 In the last 3 years, have you provided training for line managers in any of the following areas? Please circle as many numbers as appropriate

health and safety	1
equal opportunities	2
counselling	3
interviewing and selection techniques	4
carrying out appraisals	5
absence control	6
handling disciplinary issues	7
unfair dismissal legislation	8
communication and consultation	9
career counselling	10
other (please specify)	_____

V439-449

23

E6 Have you achieved, or are you working towards, the Investors In People national
standard? Please circle appropriate number

achieved	1
working towards	2
not applicable	3

V450

II NVQs

E7 Is your establishment using NVQs, or in the process of introducing NVQs? Please
circle appropriate number

yes	1	
no	2	Please skip to question E10

V451

E8 If you answered yes, for which occupational groups are the NVQs being used, and to
what levels? Please circle any appropriate numbers

			levels		
manual	1	2	3	4	5
non-manual	1	2	3	4	5
managerial	1	2	3	4	5

V452-466

E9 Have you accepted national standards as they are or adapted them to your own
needs? Please circle a number for each category of employee

	accepted	adapted
manual	1	2
non-manual	1	2
managerial	1	2

V467-469

24

224

III CAREERS

Increasingly, development is not the smooth upwards path it used to be. Now, many people move between different jobs and even different organisations to make their careers.

E10 Does your company provide any of the following in order to assist people in their development? Please circle as many as appropriate for the various categories of employee.

	manual	non manual	managerial
formal mentoring scheme	1	1	1
self development plans	2	2	2
structured cross functional moves	3	3	3
formal career pathways (vertical moves only)	4	4	4
formal career pathways (vertical and horizontal moves)	5	5	5
career counselling	6	6	6
career workshops	7	7	7
self help workbooks	8	8	8
internal assessment centres	9	9	9
none	10	10	10
other (please specify)	_____	_____	_____

V470-502

E11 Do you have an equal opportunities policy? Please circle appropriate number

yes   1

no   2

V503

E12 If yes, what areas does it cover? Please circle as many numbers as apply

age	1
disability	2
gender	3
race and ethnic origin	4
religion	5
sexual orientation	6
other (please specify)	_____

V504-510

25

E13 **Have you carried out any of the following actions regarding equal opportunity**
Please circle as many as apply

our application forms have been specifically designed
to be sensitive to equal opportunities issues   1

we run equal opportunity awareness training   2

we encourage the use of career breaks   3

we have someone in the organisation who is specifically
concerned with promoting equal opportunities   4

we have schemes targeted to bring in / train minority groups   5

we are participating in opportunity 2000   6

none of these   7

other (please specify)   ———————

V511-518

26

SECTION F : INVOLVEMENT

We have recently witnessed a lively debate about various forms of employee participation in the decision making processes of business. This section looks at what employee involvement measures are actually being used in the workplace.

F1 Do you have any of the following methods of employee involvement? **Please indicate whether you have introduced any of them in the past 10 years, or whether you have discontinued using any. Please circle as many numbers as appropriate.**

	currently have this method	introduced in last 10 years	discontinued using in last 10 years
team briefing	1	1	1
quality circles	2	2	2
TQM	3	3	3
suggestion scheme	4	4	4
Joint Consultative Committee	5	5	5
Other (please specify)	_____	_____	_____
None (please skip to question F3)	6	6	6

V536-538

F2 Taking your most recent involvement initiative, could you indicate the reasons why the measure was introduced? (please indicate the reasons which apply by numbering them in order of importance 1 - 8 with 1 being the most important and 8 being the least)

to improve employee understanding of company policy _____
to gain acceptance of change _____
to enhance employee commitment _____
to enhance employee effectiveness _____
to give management more discretion _____
ethical "right to know" considerations _____
external pressures _____
other (please specify) _____

Does it cover all employees?
YES 1
NO 2
If not, who does it cover? _____

V539 - 546, 547, 548 - 550

27

F3 Do you recognise a Trade Union at your place of work?

YES 1
NO 2

If yes, how many? _____
V551+ 552

F4 What changes have there been, if any, with regard to Union Recognition? Please circle appropriate number.

moved to a single table agreement 1
recognised a new Trade Union 2
derecognised one or more unions 3
no real changes 4

V553

F5 Has the influence of unions at your workplace changed in the last 3 years?

increased 1
decreased 2
stayed the same 3
not applicable 4

V554

II. HEALTH AND SAFETY

F6 Is there someone in your establishment whose specific responsibility is Health and Safety? Please circle appropriate number

yes 1
no 2

V555

F7 Does this person come under the umbrella of the personnel function?
Please circle appropriate number

yes 1
no 2

V556

28

228

**F8   Which of the following does the personnel function undertake wholly or in part?
Please circle as many numbers as appropriate**

	wholly	in part	does not undertake
formulating policy statements on safety	1	2	3
formulating safety regulations	1	2	3
formulating safe systems of work	1	2	3
formulating accident reporting procedures	1	2	3
recording industrial accidents and notifiable diseases	1	2	3
formulating accident investigation procedures	1	2	3
advising management on health and safety legislation	1	2	3
designing, providing, recording health and safety training	1	2	3
compiling/analysing health and safety statistics	1	2	3
designing safety publicity, leaflets	1	2	3
liaising with occupational health and other bodies	1	2	3
liaising with Health and Safety Executive and its agents	1	2	3
monitoring health and safety policy/procedures	1	2	3
advising on provision of protective clothing	1	2	3

V557-570

F9   Do you have an occupational health department? Please circle appropriate number

yes   1
no   2

V571

III. DISCIPLINE AND GRIEVANCE

**F10   In what way is the personnel function involved in any of the following forms of disciplinary action?
Please circle a number for each disciplinary action.**

	acting independently of line management	acting in collaboration with line management	provides advice and information to line managers	acting in response to line managers' requests	not involved
verbal warnings	1	2	3	4	5
written warnings	1	2	3	4	5
dismissals	1	2	3	4	5
counselling	1	2	3	4	5
transfer/demotion	1	2	3	4	5
financial penalties	1	2	3	4	5
suspension	1	2	3	4	5

V572-578

29

SECTION G : PAYMENT

Having attracted employees to the organisation, developed them and hopefully attained the highest performance possible from them, the organisation has to give them some kind of reward, whether one calls this "reward", "compensation", "remuneration" or "pay".

G1 Which of the following payment arrangements do you use for the different categories of employees? Please circle as many numbers as appropriate

	manual	non manual	managerial
performance related pay	1	1	1
profit related pay	2	2	2
profit sharing	3	3	3
bonus scheme	4	4	4
skill based pay	5	5	5
competence based pay	6	6	6
payment by results	7	7	7
rate for the job	8	8	8

V579-602

G2 Which of the following comes closest to describing the pay structure(s) where you work. Please circle any appropriate numbers

	manual	non manual	managerial
broad banded structure with wide spread of jobs/pay in each band	1	1	1
narrow banded structure with small spread of jobs/pay in each band	2	2	2
individual job ranges, with separate pay range for each job	3	3	3
pay curve system	4	4	4
job family structure, with separate graded pay structures for each job family	5	5	5
incremental scale	6	6	6

V603-620

30

G3 Have you changed your payment arrangements in the last 12 months?
Please circle appropriate number

YES   1
NO   2

If YES, please indicate briefly what changes you have made and why have you made them.

_____

_____

_____

V621 , 622 - 625

G4 Approximately what percentage of your employees in the various categories are paid by an annual rate/ an hourly rate?

	manual %	non manual %	managerial %
annual salary	_____	_____	_____
hourly pay	_____	_____	_____

V626-631

G5 By what means are your employees paid? Please circle appropriate number(s)

	manual	non manual	managerial
bank transfer monthly	1	1	1
bank transfer weekly	2	2	2
cash monthly	3	3	3
cash weekly	4	4	4
cheque monthly	5	5	5
cheque weekly	6	6	6

V632-649

G6 Is there, or has there been in the last 3 years, a deliberate goal to move towards harmonisation of terms and conditions where you work? Please circle appropriate number

yes   1
no   2

If yes, how long has this process been underway? _____

V650-651

31

231

II. FRINGE BENEFITS

G7 Which of the following fringe benefits are available to the various categories of employees? Please circle any appropriate numbers

	manual	non manual	managerial
relocation expenses	1	1	1
subsidized meals	2	2	2
long-service awards	3	3	3
company car	4	4	4
medical facilities	5	5	5
subscription to professional bodies	6	6	6
employee discount on products	7	7	7
personal loans	8	8	8
petrol credit card	9	9	9
share option scheme	10	10	10
mortgage facilities	11	11	11
christmas bonus	12	12	12
company owned housing	13	13	13
transport to and from work	14	14	14
clothing allowance	15	15	15
subsidized holidays	16	16	16
share incentive scheme	17	17	17
contributory pension	18	18	18
non contributory pension	19	19	19
other	_____	_____	_____

V652-711

G8 Do you operate a Cafeteria Benefits System (i.e.where benefit packages have a high level of flexibility)? Please circle appropriate number.

YES   1
NO   2

V712

III. SICK PAY SCHEMES

G9   Have the 1994 changes to the Statutory Sick Pay Scheme caused you to make any alterations to your

     a)   sick pay scheme?

                yes   1

                no   2

     b)   absence control procedure?

                yes   1

                no   2

Please circle appropriate number

V713, 714

G10   Does your sick pay scheme differentiate between different occupational groups? (e.g.between salary and hourly-paid) Please circle appropriate number.

     yes   1

     no   2

V715

G11   Whose responsibility is the monitoring and control of absence?
Please circle the appropriate number(s) for each action

	monitoring	control
immediate manager	1	1
personnel	2	2
level above immediate manager	3	3
occupational health dept	4	4

V716-717

33

233

SECTION H : ABOUT YOU AND YOUR JOB

In the closing section we would like to ask you a few details about yourself and your role in the personnel function.

We have asked for your name because we may wish to come and interview you as part of the second stage of our research. Your name will be treated as confidential, as will all the other information we have asked for throughout the questionnaire.

NAME: _____

SEX: _____ V724

AGE GROUP: under 30 ____ V725
                       31 - 40   ____
                       41 - 50   ____
                       51-60   ____
                       over 60   ____

What is the title of your job?

_____ V726

What is the job title of the person to whom you report or to whom you are accountable?

_____ V727

How many people report to you?

   reporting directly to you   _____ V728

   reporting to your subordinates _____ V729

How long have you been in your present job?   _____ V730

How many years have you been working in personnel?   _____ V731

34

Have you worked in any other departments or managerial roles. If so, which?

_____

V732-733

Are you a member of the Institute of Personnel and Development (formerly the IPM) or any other professional body? Please give details.

_____

V734-736

_____

What educational qualifications, if any, have you obtained since leaving school?

_____

V737

_____

Approximately what percentage of your time is spent on the following matters?

Human resource planning	___ %	
Recruitment and Selection	___ %	
Job Evaluation	___ %	
Redundancy and Dismissal	___ %	
Appraisals	___ %	
Quality Initiatives	___ %	V738-750
Training	___ %	
Career Planning	___ %	
Employee Relations/Involvement	___ %	
Health and Safety	___ %	
Discipline and Grievance	___ %	
Payment Administration	___ %	
Fringe Benefits	___ %	

Do you know what the competencies are for a personnel professional, as set by the Personnel Standards
Lead Body?

yes ___   V751
no ___

35

If YES, do you think they resemble the competencies you use in your job?　　　V752

yes _____
no _____

If not, why?

_____

_____

_____　　　V753-755

In your opinion, what is the activity most central to the personnel function?

_____

V756-757

How would you rank the following activities (using numbers 1 - 13) in terms of their importance in the contribution made by the personnel function to organisational objectives in the last 3 years?

To what extent has this importance changed?

	ranking (1 - 14)	more important (1) less important (2) about the same (3)
Human Resource Planning	_____	_____
Recruitment and Selection	_____	_____
Redundancy and Dismissal	_____	_____
Discipline & Grievance	_____	_____
Appraisal	_____	_____
Performance Management	_____	_____
Quality Initiatives.	_____	_____
Training	_____	_____
Management Development	_____	_____
Career Planning	_____	_____
Communications	_____	_____
Employee Relations/Involvement	_____	_____
Health and Safety	_____	_____
Reward Strategies and Systems	_____	_____

V758-785

36

236

Appendix 4

Interview format

INTRODUCTION

Personnel management always seems to be on the move and is obviously changing a great deal at the moment. One of the things we are trying to do is to work out where it is right now rather than where it ought to be, or where it might be. What is the current practice among those people in the business who are **labelled** personnel, HR or something similar – the specialists in people management?

A STRATEGY AND THE PERSONNEL FUNCTION

First of all, there is a great emphasis on **strategy**.

1 What are the main strategic activities of the personnel function? (examples?)

2 Is there an integrated overall strategy being followed into which individual initiatives fit, or is it a question of taking a series of initiatives, responding to changing circumstances?

3 When there is some broad strategic initiative which has a personnel dimension, but which is not exclusively a personnel matter (such as business re-engineering of TQM), how would you describe the role personnel takes? Would your managerial colleagues agree with you?

4 Where would you say the emphasis lies here in people management matters, on a scale of 1 to 10?:

   (1) Personnel initiate the main changes in people management matters, determine the organisational culture and carry the main operational responsibility for implementing strategy.

   (10) Personnel 'keep the ship afloat' by finishing things off and sorting out problems of a routine nature.

(The question of balance between strategy and operations would then logically be the opening of Part B.)

B PERSONNEL'S OPERATIONAL ROLE. HOW DOES THE PERSONNEL FUNCTION OPERATE?

1 To what extent has there been a deliberate policy to devolve personnel issues to the line? What have the implications of this been? (e.g. involvement issues)

2 What do you regard as an effective way of getting the balance between personnel expertise and line empowerment? (examples?)

    (i)   To what extent does the personnel function take the initiative with the line to promote certain practices and activities compared with the extent to which personnel responds to line requests for help? (examples?)

    (ii) If they talk about personnel providing a service, ask if they think that this is consistent with professional standards and integrity within HR.

    (iii) Who holds the budget for personnel and training matters? What are the implications of this?

3 To what extent does the personnel function contract out its professional activities to external suppliers?

    (i)   Why was the decision made to contract out?

    (ii) What do you perceive to be the advantages/disadvantages of contracting out professional services?

4 How has the use of the computer impacted on the work and services of the function?

    (i)   What issues/problems are there with IT use?

    (ii) How do personnel staff react/cope with IT use?

C ISSUES IN THE EMPLOYMENT RELATIONSHIP

1 The **flexible firm,** and flexibility in the employment contract in general, have received a tremendous amount of publicity in the 1980s from both academics and consultants.

    (i)   Has this formed part of the policy of your firm?

    (ii) Is it a conscious effort, and if so what is the rationale behind it?

    (iii) What have been the implications in practice?

2 The idea of **performance management** has accelerated up the managerial agenda in recent years. What do you think the term means, and which policies/practices do you use to go about developing the performance of:

    (i)   your managers/professionals

(ii) your non-manual and manual workers

3 Teamwork (if applicable)
Either: What are the HR implications of having a **teamwork** structure?
Or: What role do you think HR plays in the successful installation and maintenance of teams?

4 Employee involvement:

What forms of **employee involvement** do you use? What is their impact?

Do you think you have a difference in the level of understanding and effective operation in the company because of a lack of communication?

If so, what efforts (if any) are you making to deal with this?

5 There has been a lot of mention among academics of the concept of 'the learning organisation'. What does this term mean, if anything, to your organisation?

Why do you think it is a helpful concept for your organisation?

D INTERNATIONAL

There has been a great deal of emphasis on **international** HRM, and I need to ask you what that means here. First of all, which category does this business fit into?

(a) Company with headquarters in UK and little or no overseas activity apart form direct export.

(b) Company with headquarters in UK and subsidiaries or joint ventures overseas.

(c) UK subsidiary of company with headquarters overseas.

(d) UK member of global business.

For (a) companies

1 What, if anything, does 'internationalisation of HRM' mean here?

2 What has been the effect here of European employment legislation and practice?

3 Do you ever recruit personnel from overseas?

For (b) companies

1 What aspects, if any, of HRM strategy and policy are centralised and determined for all subsidiaries by the UK headquarters?

2 What aspects of HRM strategy and policy are determined by subsidiaries within their own national boundaries?

3 What has been the effect here of European employment legislation and practice?

4 What type of mobility, if any, is there of personnel between the UK and overseas subsidiaries?

5 Would you say the culture of this company is British or international?

6 What make you say that?

For (c) companies

1 What aspects, if any, of HRM strategy and policy are centralised and determined for all subsidiaries by the overseas headquarters?

2 What aspects of HRM strategy and policy are determined by the UK subsidiary without reference to the overseas headquarters?

3 What has been the effect here of European employment legislation and practice?

4 What type of mobility, if any is there of personnel between the overseas headquarters, the UK company and other overseas subsidiaries?

5 Would you say that the culture of this company is British, _____ (nationality of HQ) or genuinely international?

6 What makes you say that?

For (d) companies

1 What aspects, if any, of HRM strategy and policy are centralised and determined uniformly for all group members?

2 What aspects of HRM strategy and policy are determined by your company without reference to other members of the group?

3 What has been the effect here of European employment legislation and practice?

4 What type of mobility, if any, is there of personnel between companies in the group?

5 Would you say that the culture of this company is British, _____ (other possible dominant nationality) or genuinely international?

6 What makes you say that?

This interview schedule was used as a framework and areas of interest were explored more deeply.

Appendix 5

Characteristics of research data in 1984

Sample composition by sector using the SIC groups taken from the CSO Standard Industrial Classification (Revised 1980), HMSO, 1979

Division	%	N
Agricultural, forestry and fishing	1	2
Energy and water supply industries	6	22
Extraction of minerals and ores other than fuels. Manufacture of metals, mineral products and chemicals	7	23
Metal goods, engineering and vehicle industries	19	65
Other manufacturing industries	11	38
Construction	1	5
Distribution, hotels and catering, repairs	8	29
Transport and communication	7	24
Banking, finance, insurance, business service and leasing	10	36
Other services	30	106
	100	350

Sample composition by establishment size

Number of employees	%	N
1–99	12	44
100–199	10	36
200–999	42	146
1000–4999	30	103
5000+	5	18
Missing	1	3
	100	350

Index

242